W9-BUQ-366

The Sporting News

BASEBALL

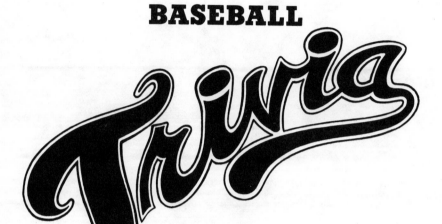

BOOK

Co-Editor-Writer
JOE HOPPEL

Co-Editor-Researcher
CRAIG CARTER

President-Chief Executive Officer
RICHARD WATERS

Editor
DICK KAEGEL

Director of Books and Periodicals
RON SMITH

Copyright © 1983 by The Sporting News Publishing Co. All rights reserved. Print-
ed in the U.S.A.

No part of this publication may be reproduced or transmitted in any form or by
any means, electronic or mechanical, including photocopy, recording or any
information storage and retrieval system now known or to be invented, without
permission in writing from the publisher, except by a reviewer who wishes to
quote brief passages in connection with a review written for inclusion in a maga-
zine, newspaper or broadcast.

Published in the United States by The Sporting News Publishing Co., 1212 North
Lindbergh Boulevard, St. Louis, Missouri 63132

ISBN: 0-89204-103-X
10 9 8 7 6 5 4

First Edition

TABLE OF
CONTENTS

The cover and inside illustrations were done by Staff Artist Bill Wilson.

Introduction

Baseball, perhaps more than any other sport, lends itself to a constant examination and re-examination of its past. Baseball fans, often contending that their game is the only team sport that has remained basically unchanged in the last 50 years (in terms of the athletes' physical strength and playing abilities), use statistics and reminiscences as yardsticks for measuring yesterday's hero against today's superstar. There seemingly is no end to the comparisons—or to the discussions about *that* play, or *that* player, or *that* game. Or *that* trivia.

The Sporting News Baseball Trivia Book presents a detailed look at major league baseball's glorious, unusual and heretofore little-known moments and the famous and not-so-famous persons who played roles in those events. The book is at once a reference source—the first two chapters contain item-by-item reviews of the game's great achievements—and a trivia "who's who." After recounting baseball's dramatic happenings, the book focuses on the game's characters, goats, lesser-known feats, oddities, coincidences, "firsts," "lasts" and numbers, with emphasis on those who—until now—have been little more than footnotes to baseball history. All entries reflect records and situations as they were through the 1982 season.

Atlanta's Hank Aaron receives congratulations from teammate Tom House (above) and is embraced by his mother (right) after hitting career homer No. 715 on April 8, 1974, breaking Babe Ruth's all-time record. House, a relief pitcher, caught the home run in the Atlanta bullpen and returned the ball to Aaron.

FIRST INNING:

Dramatic moments in hitting and baserunning, with supporting casts.

AARON'S 715th HOME RUN

On April 8, 1974, Hank Aaron of the Atlanta Braves became the major leagues' all-time home run king, hitting his 715th in a game against the Los Angeles Dodgers at Atlanta Stadium and surpassing Babe Ruth's total of 714.

Supporting Cast:

• **Al Downing.** Dodgers' pitcher off whom Aaron homered in the fourth inning and the losing pitcher in the Braves' 7-4 victory.

• **Darrell Evans.** Braves' third baseman who was on base when Aaron connected, having reached first on shortstop Bill Russell's error.

• **Joe Ferguson.** Downing's catcher.

• **Tom House.** Atlanta relief pitcher who caught Aaron's homer in the Braves' bullpen.

• **Ron Reed.** The Braves' starting and winning pitcher.

BOTTOMLEY'S 12 RUNS BATTED IN

St. Louis first baseman Jim Bottomley drove in a major league-record 12 runs on September 16, 1924, leading the Cardinals to a 17-3 triumph over Brooklyn at Ebbets Field. Bottomley went 6-for-6.

Supporting Cast:

● **Art Decatur.** Brooklyn pitcher off whom Bottomley collected six of his runs batted in. Decatur yielded a bases-loaded homer to Bottomley in the fourth inning and a two-run homer in the sixth.

● **Rube Ehrhardt.** Gave up a two-run single in the first inning.

● **Bonnie Hollingsworth.** Gave up a run-scoring double in the second.

● **Jim Roberts.** Gave up a run-scoring single in the ninth.

● **Tex Wilson.** Gave up a two-run single in the seventh. Wilson pitched in only one other major league game.

BROCK SURPASSES WILLS

Lou Brock of the St. Louis Cardinals broke Maury Wills' modern stolen-base record in 1974, getting his record-breaking 105th steal on September 10 against the Philadelphia Phillies at Busch Memorial Stadium. Brock finished with 118 steals.

Supporting Cast:

● **Bob Boone.** Phils' catcher when Brock broke Wills' record of 104 (set in 1962).

● **Ron Hunt.** Cardinals' batter when Brock made his seventh-inning steal.

● **Dick Ruthven.** Phils' pitcher when Brock stole second base.

CHAMBLISS' HOMER WINS PENNANT

Chris Chambliss of the New York Yankees hit a ninth-inning home run in Game 5 of the 1976 American League Championship Series, giving the Yanks a 7-6 victory over Kansas City and their first pennant in 12 years.

Supporting Cast:

● **George Brett.** Royals' third baseman whose three-run homer in the eighth inning off Grant Jackson tied the score, 6-6.

● **Mark Littell.** Relief pitcher off whom Chambliss homered.

● **Buck Martinez.** Littell's catcher.

● **Dick Tidrow.** Yankees' reliever who pitched the ninth inning and got the victory in the October 14 game at Yankee Stadium.

COBB FLEXES MUSCLES

Although he never hit more than 12 home runs in a season, Detroit's Ty Cobb had a three-homer game—and went 6-for-6 with five runs batted in—on May 5, 1925, against the St. Louis Browns at Sportsman's Park. Cobb's mark of 16 total bases—the Tiger star also singled twice and doubled—has been matched only by Lou Gehrig, Jimmie Foxx, Pat Seerey, Rocky Colavito and Fred Lynn in American League history.

Supporting Cast:

● **Joe Bush.** Permitted Cobb's first-inning homer and was the losing pitcher in the 14-8 game.

- **Milt Gaston.** Victim of Cobb's third homer, in the eighth inning.
- **Elam Vangilder.** Gave up a homer to Cobb in the second inning.

COLBERT'S DOUBLEHEADER SPREE

San Diego's Nate Colbert set a runs-batted-in record for a doubleheader on August 1, 1972, knocking in 13 runs as the Padres swept the Braves, 9-0 and 11-7, at Atlanta Stadium. Colbert slugged five home runs in the two games, tying the twin bill mark established by Stan Musial in 1954. The homers accounted for 12 of Colbert's RBIs, with the 13th coming in on a single.

Supporting Cast:

- **Jim Hardin.** Gave up a two-run homer to Colbert in the seventh inning of the nightcap.
- **Pat Jarvis.** Gave up a grand slam in the second inning of the nightcap.
- **Mike McQueen.** Gave up a bases-empty homer in the seventh inning of the opener.
- **Ron Schueler.** Gave up a three-run homer in the first inning of the opener.
- **Cecil Upshaw.** Gave up a two-run homer in the ninth inning of the second game, capping Colbert's three-homer, eight-RBI performance in the nightcap and giving the Padre slugger a doubleheader-record 22 total bases (five homers, two singles).

CRONIN'S PINCH-HOMER FEAT

Joe Cronin, player-manager for the Boston Red Sox, slugged pinch-hit homers in both games of a June 17, 1943, doubleheader against the Philadelphia Athletics at Fenway Park. Cronin's accomplishment has been equaled only once—by Hal Breeden of the Montreal Expos, on July 13, 1973, at Atlanta.

Supporting Cast:

- **Don Black.** A's pitcher off whom Cronin hit a three-run pinch homer in the eighth inning of the nightcap. Philadelphia won, 8-7.
- **Russ Christopher.** A's pitcher off whom Cronin hit a three-run pinch homer in the seventh inning of the opener. Boston won the first game, 5-4.
- **Lou Lucier.** Boston pitcher for whom Cronin batted in the opener.
- **Mike Ryba.** Boston pitcher for whom Cronin batted in the nightcap.

DiMAGGIO'S 56-GAME STREAK

Joe DiMaggio, New York Yankees' center fielder, compiled a major league-record 56-game batting streak in 1941. During the streak, DiMaggio batted .408 (91-for-223) with 15 home runs and 55 runs batted in. Immediately after being stopped, DiMaggio had a 16-game hitting streak—giving him hits in 72 of 73 games.

Supporting Cast:

● **Jim Bagby Jr.** Facing DiMaggio (hitless in two previous official at-bats) in the eighth inning of a July 17, 1941, game at Cleveland's Municipal Stadium, the Indians' Bagby induced the Yankee standout to hit into a double play—ending DiMaggio's streak.

● **Lou Boudreau.** Cleveland shortstop who started the streak-ending double play (Boudreau to Ray Mack to Oscar Grimes).

● **Ken Keltner.** Cleveland third baseman who made two fine fielding plays on DiMaggio earlier in the game.

● **Joe Krakauskas.** Cleveland pitcher who, on July 16, 1941, gave up the last hit to DiMaggio during the Yankee player's streak.

● **Al Smith.** Cleveland pitcher who started against the Yankees on July 17, 1941, and held DiMaggio hitless in two official at-bats (the ground balls to Keltner). He also walked DiMaggio. Smith was the losing pitcher as New York won, 4-3.

● **Edgar Smith.** Chicago White Sox's pitcher against whom DiMaggio started his streak on May 15, 1941, with a first-inning single.

FISK'S 1975 WORLD SERIES HOMER

Leading off the bottom of the 12th inning of Game 6 of the 1975 World Series against the Cincinnati Reds, Boston catcher Carlton Fisk homered high off the left-field foul pole to give the Red Sox a 7-6 victory and tie the Series at three games apiece.

Supporting Cast:

● **Bernie Carbo.** Boston pinch-hitter whose three-run homer in the eighth inning off Rawly Eastwick tied the score, 6-6. It was Carbo's second pinch homer of the Series, tying the record set by Los Angeles' Chuck Essegian in 1959.

● **Pat Darcy.** Cincinnati pitcher off whom Fisk homered in Game 6, played October 21 at Fenway Park.

● **Rick Wise.** Winning pitcher for Boston, having worked the top of the 12th.

HARTNETT'S HOMER IN GLOAMIN'

Manager Gabby Hartnett's two-out home run in the ninth inning—as darkness was descending over Wrigley Field on September 28, 1938—lifted the Chicago Cubs to a 6-5 victory over Pittsburgh and a half-game lead on the Pirates in the National League pennant race. Until Hartnett connected, the Pirates had led the N.L. since July 12. The Cubs kept the league lead, winning the pennant by two games.

Supporting Cast:

● **Mace Brown.** Pirates' pitcher off whom Hartnett homered on a two-strike pitch.

● **Billy Herman.** Cubs' player whose eighth-inning single tied the score, 5-5.

● **Tony Lazzeri.** Cubs' pinch-hitter whose eighth-inning double cut the Pirates' lead to 5-4.

● **Charlie Root.** Cubs' winning pitcher, having worked the top of the ninth.

Boston's Carlton Fisk applies a little body English to his 12th-inning drive to left field in Game 6 of the 1975 World Series against Cincinnati. The ball stayed fair, hitting high off the foul pole and giving the Red Sox a 7-6 victory.

Rickey Henderson of Oakland shows off the base he stole on August 27, 1982, in Milwaukee, giving him 119 steals for the season and a modern major league record. Looking on is Lou Brock, the man whose record Henderson shattered.

HENDERSON TOPS BROCK'S MARK

Rickey Henderson of the Oakland A's broke Lou Brock's modern stolen-base record in 1982, recording his record-breaking 119th steal on August 27 against the Milwaukee Brewers at County Stadium. Henderson finished with 130 steals.

Supporting Cast:

• **Wayne Gross.** A's batter when Henderson broke Brock's record of 118 (set in 1974) with a third-inning steal of second base.

• **Doc Medich.** Brewers' pitcher when Henderson stole second.

• **Ted Simmons.** Brewers' catcher when Henderson set the record.

JACKSON'S THREE-HOMER SERIES GAME

Reggie Jackson of the New York Yankees walloped three home runs in Game 6 of the 1977 World Series, becoming only the second player in Series history to accomplish the feat (Babe Ruth did it twice, in 1926 and 1928). Jackson's homers on October 18 at Yankee Stadium led the Yankees to a Series-clinching 8-4 victory over the Los Angeles Dodgers. Each homer was a first-pitch smash.

Supporting Cast:

• **Burt Hooton.** Dodgers' pitcher off whom Jackson hit a two-run homer into the right-field stands in the fourth inning.

• **Charlie Hough.** Pitcher off whom Jackson hit a leadoff homer into the center-field bleachers in the eighth inning.

• **Elias Sosa.** Pitcher off whom Jackson hit a two-run homer into the right-field stands in the fifth inning.

LAZZERI'S TWO GRAND SLAMS IN GAME

Playing against the Philadelphia Athletics on May 24, 1936, at Shibe Park, Tony Lazzeri of the New York Yankees became the first major leaguer to hit two bases-loaded homers in one game. The homers helped Lazzeri drive in an American League-record 11 runs in the Yankees' 25-2 victory. Lazzeri also tripled in five official at-bats.

Supporting Cast:

• **George Turbeville.** A's pitcher off whom Lazzeri hit a bases-loaded homer in the second inning.

• **Red Bullock.** A's pitcher off whom Lazzeri hit a bases-loaded homer in the fifth inning.

LYNN TEES OFF ON DETROIT

Fred Lynn of the Boston Red Sox enjoyed one of the best days in big-league history on June 18, 1975, hitting three home runs and driving in 10 runs as the Red Sox pounded Detroit, 15-1, at Tiger Stadium. Lynn, who knocked in eight runs with his homers, also had a two-run triple and infield single in going 5-for-6.

Supporting Cast:

● **Joe Coleman.** Detroit pitcher off whom Lynn hit a two-run homer in the first inning and a three-run homer in the second.

● **Tom Walker.** Detroit pitcher off whom Lynn hit a three-run homer in the ninth inning.

MARIS' 61st HOME RUN

Playing against the Boston Red Sox in the regular-season finale on October 1, 1961, at Yankee Stadium, Roger Maris of the New York Yankees hit his 61st homer of the year to surpass Babe Ruth's single-season record of 60 (set in 1927).

Supporting Cast:

● **Sal Durante.** A 19-year-old fan from Brooklyn, he grabbed Maris' home-run ball 15 rows up in the right-field stands. In exchange for the ball, Durante received $5,000 and two trips to the West Coast.

● **Russ Nixon.** Boston's catcher when Maris homered.

● **Bill Stafford.** With relief help from Hal Reniff and Luis Arroyo, he was the winning pitcher in the Yankees' 1-0 victory.

● **Tracy Stallard.** Boston pitcher off whom Maris homered.

● **Carl Yastrzemski.** Boston's left fielder (he went 1-for-4) who was still an active major leaguer in 1982.

MAZEROSKI'S HOMER WINS WORLD SERIES

Leading off the bottom of the ninth inning of Game 7 of the 1960 World Series, Bill Mazeroski homered over the left-field wall at Pittsburgh's Forbes Field to give the Pirates a 10-9 triumph over the New York Yankees and their first Series championship in 35 years.

Supporting Cast:

● **Yogi Berra.** Yankees' longtime catcher who was in left field when Mazeroski hit his climactic homer in the October 13 game.

● **John Blanchard.** Yankees' catcher when Mazeroski homered.

● **Joe DeMaestri.** Yankees' utility infielder who replaced Tony Kubek in the eighth inning when the New York shortstop was struck in the throat by a bad-hop grounder.

● **Harvey Haddix.** Pirates' winning pitcher who replaced reliever Bob Friend with two on and no one out in the Yankees' ninth.

● **Tony Kubek.** Struck in the throat by Bill Virdon's sharply hit, bad-hop grounder in the Pirates' eighth, he was unable to make a play on Virdon. Virdon was credited with a hit in one of the key plays of the Pirates' five-run inning that overcame a 7-4 New York lead.

● **Mickey Mantle.** His ninth-inning single scored Bobby Richardson, cutting Pittsburgh's lead to 9-8.

● **Gil McDougald.** He scored New York's tying run (9-9) in the ninth on a play in which Berra grounded out to first baseman Rocky Nelson.

Roger Maris (above) is greeted by Yogi Berra (8) after slugging his 61st home run of the 1961 season, then meets (left) with Sal Durante, a 19-year-old fan from Brooklyn who retrieved his smash into the right-field stands.

Only once has a World Series ended with a home run, and the ecstasy of that moment is apparent as Pittsburgh's Bill Mazeroski heads for home after connecting against New York's Ralph Terry in the ninth inning of Game 7 of the 1960 Series.

- **Hal Smith.** Having replaced Smoky Burgess as the Pirates' catcher in the top of the eighth, he hit a three-run homer in the bottom of the eighth off Jim Coates to give Pittsburgh a 9-7 lead.
- **Ralph Terry.** Yankees' pitcher off whom Mazeroski connected, making the Pittsburgh second baseman the only man in history to end a Series with a homer.

MONDAY'S HOMER

With the 1981 National League Championship Series tied at two games apiece and Game 5 deadlocked, 1-1, in the ninth inning, Rick Monday of Los Angeles hit a two-out, bases-empty home run at Olympic Stadium to give the Dodgers a 2-1 triumph over the Montreal Expos and the N.L. pennant.

Supporting Cast:

- **Ray Burris.** Expos' starting pitcher who left the October 19 game for a pinch-hitter in the eighth inning with the score tied, 1-1.
- **Steve Rogers.** Expos' pitcher who gave up the ninth-inning homer to Monday. Making only the third relief appearance of his big-league career, Rogers retired the first two batters he faced before Monday connected in the Monday afternoon game.
- **Fernando Valenzuela.** Dodgers' starting and winning pitcher who needed last-out relief help from Bob Welch.

MUSIAL'S FIVE-HOMER DOUBLEHEADER

Stan Musial of the St. Louis Cardinals established a doubleheader home-run record on May 2, 1954, at old Busch Stadium, hitting five homers as the Cards split with the New York Giants (St. Louis won the opener, 10-6, but lost the nightcap, 9-7).

Supporting Cast:

- **Johnny Antonelli.** Giants' pitcher off whom Musial hit a bases-empty homer in the third inning of the opener and a two-run homer in the fifth inning of the first game.
- **Jim Hearn.** Gave up a three-run homer to Musial in the eighth inning of the opener.
- **Hoyt Wilhelm.** Gave up a two-run homer to Musial in the fifth inning of the nightcap and a bases-empty homer in the seventh inning of the second game.

ROSE'S 44-GAME STREAK

Pete Rose of the Cincinnati Reds equaled Wee Willie Keeler's all-time National League batting-streak mark in 1978, hitting safely in 44 straight games.

Supporting Cast:

- **Gene Garber.** Braves' pitcher whose ninth-inning strikeout of Rose on August 1 at Atlanta Stadium ended Rose's streak. Rose had lined into a double play against Garber in the seventh inning.

After Babe Ruth hit three home runs in Game 4 of the 1926 World Series at St. Louis' Sportsman's Park, the auto agency across the street on Grand Avenue took note of the accomplishment. As the cracked glass in front of the Babe's image indicates, the dealership's showroom window was victimized by one of Ruth's drives.

Pete Rose acknowledges a standing ovation at Atlanta Stadium on July 31, 1978, after singling against the Braves and equaling the all-time National League batting-streak mark of 44 games. Ron Plaza, Cincinnati first-base coach, takes note of the "Pete" being flashed on a message board.

- **Larry McWilliams.** Braves' rookie pitcher who helped to stop Rose's streak August 1, retiring him on a liner in the third inning and a grounder in the fifth after walking him in the first.
- **Phil Niekro.** Braves' pitcher who allowed a sixth-inning single to Rose on July 31, enabling Rose to tie Keeler's mark (set in 1897).
- **Dave Roberts.** Chicago Cubs' pitcher off whom Rose started his streak June 14 with two hits.

RUTH'S THREE-HOMER SERIES GAMES

Babe Ruth put on a power display unprecedented in World Series history in 1926, then matched the feat in 1928. Ruth, New York Yankees' superstar, belted three home runs in Game 4 of each classic—and both performances came at Sportsman's Park against the St. Louis Cardinals.

Supporting Cast:
- **Grover Cleveland Alexander.** Cardinals' pitcher who gave up a bases-empty homer to Ruth in the eighth inning on October 9, 1928.
- **Hi Bell.** Cardinals' pitcher who gave up a two-run homer to Ruth in the sixth inning on October 6, 1926.
- **Flint Rhem.** Cardinals' pitcher off whom Ruth hit bases-empty homers in the first and third innings on October 6, 1926.
- **Willie Sherdel.** Cardinals' pitcher off whom Ruth hit a leadoff homer in the fourth inning on October 9, 1928, and a bases-empty homer in the seventh inning of the same game.

21

RUTH'S CALLED SHOT

Batting in the fifth inning of Game 3 of the 1932 World Series, New York's Babe Ruth—taunted by Cub fans at Wrigley Field—homered to deep center field after seemingly calling his shot. While many on hand at the October 1 game claimed Ruth pointed to the spot where he then hit the ball, others said the Yankee slugger made a gesture that really was never adequately explained.

Supporting Cast:

● **Lou Gehrig.** Yankees' first baseman who followed Ruth's fifth-inning shot with another homer, his second of the game.

● **George Pipgras.** The winning pitcher in the Yankees' 7-5 victory.

● **Charlie Root.** Cubs' pitcher who gave up the noted homer, a drive that broke a 4-4 tie. Root also yielded a three-run homer to Ruth in the first inning.

● **Joe Sewell.** Yankees' third baseman who preceded Ruth to the plate in the fifth. He grounded out to shortstop Billy Jurges.

RUTH'S 60th HOME RUN

Babe Ruth struck his 60th homer of the 1927 season on September 30, breaking the major league record of 59 he had achieved six years earlier.

Supporting Cast:

● **Walter Johnson.** Washington Senators' pitching great who—as a pinch-hitter in the ninth inning—made his last appearance as a big-league player in Ruth's 60th-homer game.

● **Mark Koenig.** New York Yankees' shortstop who was on third base with a triple when Ruth homered at Yankee Stadium.

● **Muddy Ruel.** Senators' catcher when Ruth connected.

● **Tom Zachary.** Senators' pitcher off whom Ruth homered in the eighth inning. The drive broke a 2-2 tie, sending the Yankees to a 4-2 triumph in the next-to-last game of the regular season.

SLAUGHTER'S MAD DASH

With Game 7 of the 1946 World Series tied with two out in the bottom of the eighth inning, St. Louis' Enos Slaughter raced home from first base on Harry Walker's hit to left-center field to give the Cardinals a 4-3 victory over the Boston Red Sox and the world championship.

Supporting Cast:

● **Harry Brecheen.** Cardinals' reliever who was the winning pitcher in the October 15 game at Sportsman's Park. He worked two innings.

● **Leon Culberson.** Boston center fielder who fielded Walker's hit and made the throw to the relay man. Culberson had entered the game in the top of the eighth as a pinch-runner.

● **Dom DiMaggio.** Boston center fielder whose two-run double in the eighth tied the score, 3-3. DiMaggio twisted his ankle rounding first and was re-

Emerging from a cloud of dust in Game 7 of the 1946 World Series is St. Louis' Enos Slaughter, who raced home from first base with the Series-winning run on a hit by Harry Walker. Boston catcher Roy Partee, up the third-base line, takes the late throw from shortstop Johnny Pesky as umpire Al Barlick focuses on Slaughter's slide.

placed by Culberson.

● **Bob Klinger.** Boston reliever and losing pitcher off whom Walker got the game-winning hit.

● **Johnny Pesky.** Boston shortstop who hesitated in relaying Culberson's throw to the plate, helping Slaughter to score from first.

● **Harry Walker.** Cardinals' left fielder who made it to second base on his decisive hit and was credited with a double (not a single, as often reported).

THOMSON'S SHOT HEARD 'ROUND THE WORLD

Batting with one out in the bottom of the ninth inning of the third game of the 1951 National League playoffs, Bobby Thomson hit a three-run homer to give the New York Giants a 5-4 victory over the Brooklyn Dodgers and the N.L. pennant.

Supporting Cast:

● **Ralph Branca.** Dodgers' pitcher off whom Thomson homered in the October 3 game at the Polo Grounds, capping a four-run inning.

● **Al Dark.** Giants' shortstop who opened the bottom of the ninth with an infield single.

● **Clint Hartung.** Giants' reserve outfielder who ran for Don Mueller in the ninth when Mueller fractured his ankle sliding into third base.

● **Monte Irvin.** Only New York player to be retired in the ninth. He popped out.

Bobby Thomson (above) was riding high after his pennant-winning home run for the New York Giants in 1951, while Giants Manager Leo Durocher and second baseman Eddie Stanky (wearing jacket) wrestled with their team's stunning success in the National League playoff against Brooklyn.

- **Larry Jansen.** Giants' winning pitcher, having worked the ninth inning.
- **Whitey Lockman.** Giants' first baseman whose ninth-inning double scored Dark and sent Mueller to third.
- **Willie Mays.** A 20-year-old rookie, he was on deck when Thomson homered.
- **Don Mueller.** Giants' right fielder who followed Dark's hit with a single.
- **Don Newcombe.** Brooklyn's starting pitcher who took a 4-1 lead into the ninth but left after Lockman's double cut the lead to 4-2. With Hartung on third and Lockman at second, Brooklyn Manager Charlie Dressen brought in Branca to pitch to Thomson.
- **Al (Rube) Walker.** Branca's catcher when Thomson homered.

WILLIAMS' ALL-STAR SHOW

Ted Williams of the Boston Red Sox went 4-for-4 in the 1946 All-Star Game at Fenway Park, hitting two home runs and driving in five runs as the American League routed the National League, 12-0.

Supporting Cast:

- **Ewell Blackwell.** National League pitcher off whom Williams got a scratch single in the seventh inning of the July 9 game.
- **Kirby Higbe.** National League pitcher off whom Williams hit a leadoff homer in the fourth and a run-scoring single in the fifth.
- **Rip Sewell.** National League pitcher whose blooper pitch was hit for a three-run homer by Williams in the eighth inning.

WILLIAMS REACHES .400

"I don't care to be known as a .400 hitter with a lousy average of .39955," said Boston's Ted Williams, commenting on his playing status for a season-ending doubleheader against the Philadelphia Athletics on September 28, 1941. "If I'm going to be a .400 hitter," added the eager-to-play Williams, "I want to have more than my toenails on the line." Williams went 4-for-5 in the first game, boosting his average to .4039. Giving no thought to resting on his laurels, Williams went 2-for-3 in the second game to finish at .4057 (.406 in the record books).

Supporting Cast:

- **Fred Caligiuri.** A's pitcher off whom Williams singled and doubled in his first two at-bats in the nightcap. Caligiuri beat the Red Sox, 7-1, in a game called after eight innings because of darkness; it was one of only two victories he had in the majors. Caligiuri outpitched Boston's Lefty Grove, who took the loss while making his last major league appearance.
- **Dick Fowler.** A's pitcher off whom Williams singled and homered in his first two at-bats in the opener at Shibe Park.
- **Porter Vaughan.** A's pitcher off whom Williams singled in his third and fourth at-bats in the opener, which Boston won, 12-11.

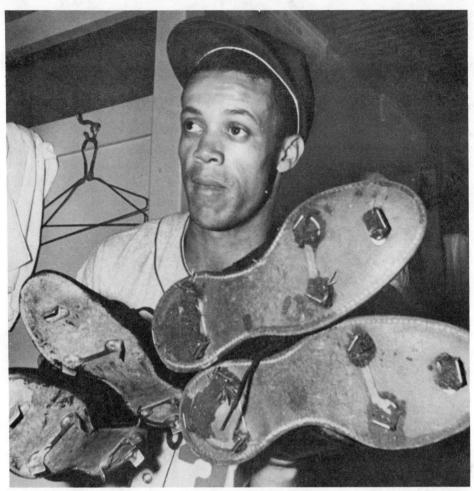

Maury Wills of the Los Angeles Dodgers gave his shoes quite a workout in 1962 when he broke Ty Cobb's modern stolen-base record of 96. Wills finished the season with 104 steals, getting his last theft of the year against San Francisco in the N.L. playoffs.

WILLS BEATS COBB

Maury Wills of the Los Angeles Dodgers shattered Ty Cobb's modern stolen-base record in 1962, getting his record-breaking 97th steal on September 23 against the St. Louis Cardinals at old Busch Stadium. Wills finished with 104 steals.

Supporting Cast:

● **Jim Gilliam.** Dodgers' batter when Wills broke Cobb's record of 96 (set in 1915).

● **Larry Jackson.** Cardinals' pitcher when Wills stole second base in the seventh inning.

● **Carl Sawatski.** Cardinals' catcher when Wills stole.

SECOND INNING:

Dramatic moments in pitching and fielding, with supporting casts.

AGEE FOILS ORIOLES

Tommie Agee's defensive heroics in Game 3 of the 1969 World Series at Shea Stadium saved the Mets as many as five runs and led New York to a 5-0 triumph over the Baltimore Orioles, giving the Mets a two-games-to-one lead in the Series. Agee, New York's center fielder, also hit a leadoff homer in the first inning off Baltimore's Jim Palmer.

Supporting Cast:

● **Paul Blair.** Orioles' center fielder who came to bat with two out and the bases loaded in the seventh inning and Baltimore trailing, 4-0. Blair drove the ball to right-center field, where Agee, sliding on his stomach, made a one-handed catch.

● **Elrod Hendricks.** With Boog Powell (single) on first base and Frank Robinson (single) on third and New York ahead 3-0 in the fourth, Hendricks hit a smash to deep left-center, where Agee made a backhanded, fingertip catch at the base of the wall.

● **Gary Gentry.** Mets' pitcher off whom Baltimore's Elrod Hendricks hit his long drive with two out and two on in the fourth inning of the October 14 game.

One of the Game 3 defensive gems turned in by Mets center fielder Tommie Agee in the 1969 World Series came with two out in the seventh inning and the bases loaded when Baltimore's Paul Blair drove a line drive to right-center field and Agee made a diving, one-handed catch.

- **Nolan Ryan.** Mets' pitcher off whom Blair hit his drive in the seventh. Ryan had just replaced Gentry, who had walked Mark Belanger, pinch-hitter Dave May and Don Buford after two Orioles had been retired.

ALEXANDER RESCUES CARDINALS

Having pitched a complete-game victory the day before, 39-year-old Grover Cleveland Alexander was summoned from the bullpen with two out and the bases loaded in the seventh inning and saved the St. Louis Cardinals' 3-2 victory over the New York Yankees in Game 7 of the 1926 World Series.

Supporting Cast:

- **Earle Combs.** Yankee center fielder whose leadoff single in the seventh started the Yanks' threat in the October 10 game at Yankee Stadium.

- **Lou Gehrig.** Yankee first baseman whose walk in the seventh filled the bases.

- **Jesse Haines.** Cardinals' starting and winning pitcher (6⅔ innings) who gave way to Alexander (2⅓ innings).

- **Waite Hoyt.** New York's starting and losing pitcher.

- **Mark Koenig.** Yankee shortstop who sacrificed Combs to second in the seventh.

- **Tony Lazzeri.** Yankee rookie second baseman who struck out against Alexander with the bases loaded in the seventh.

- **Bob Meusel.** Yankee left fielder whose seventh-inning grounder forced Babe Ruth at second base and sent Combs to third.

Brooklyn's lone World Series championship came in 1955, thanks largely to the defensive heroics of left fielder Sandy Amoros. With two Yankees on base in the sixth inning of Game 7 and the Dodgers leading 2-0, Amoros raced to the left-field corner to snare Yogi Berra's fly ball and then doubled a runner off first.

- **Bob O'Farrell.** Cardinals' catcher.
- **Babe Ruth.** Yankee right fielder who drew an intentional walk in the seventh.

AMOROS' GAME-SAVING CATCH

With Brooklyn leading 2-0 in the sixth inning of Game 7 of the 1955 World Series and the Yankees having the potential tying runs on base, Dodgers' left fielder Sandy Amoros squelched New York's rally by making a sensational catch and then doubling up a Yankee baserunner. The Dodgers' lead stood up, giving Brooklyn its only Series championship.

Supporting Cast:

- **Yogi Berra.** Yankee catcher who, with runners on first and second and no one out in the sixth inning, lofted a drive down the left-field line. Amoros raced into the corner and made a glove-hand catch, turning the grab into a double play.
- **Jim Gilliam.** The man Amoros replaced in left field at the start of the Yankees' sixth in the October 4 game at Yankee Stadium.
- **Billy Martin.** Yankee second baseman who started New York's sixth with a walk.
- **Gil McDougald.** Yankee third baseman who was doubled off first base after Amoros' catch. He had reached base on a bunt single.
- **Johnny Podres.** Brooklyn pitcher off whom Berra hit the drive to Amoros. Podres finished with an eight-hit shutout.

● **Pee Wee Reese.** Brooklyn shortstop whose relay throw to first baseman Gil Hodges after Amoros' catch doubled up McDougald.

● **Don Zimmer.** Brooklyn second baseman whose removal from the game in the top of the sixth for pinch-hitter George Shuba led to the move of Gilliam to second base and the insertion of Amoros into left field.

ARMBRISTER MAKES PRESENCE FELT

In his only official at-bat in World Series competition, coming October 14, 1975, at Riverfront Stadium against the Boston Red Sox, Cincinnati's Ed Armbrister was the focal point of a controversial no-interference ruling on his sacrifice-bunt attempt. The 10th-inning play in Game 3 helped the Reds to a 6-5 victory and a two-games-to-one lead in the Series, which they won in seven games.

Supporting Cast:

● **Larry Barnett.** Home-plate umpire who rejected the Red Sox's claim of interference on the play.

● **Rawly Eastwick.** Reds' reliever and winning pitcher for whom Armbrister batted in the 10th with the score tied, 5-5.

● **Carlton Fisk.** Boston catcher who collided with Armbrister while attempting to get to Armbrister's bunt in front of the plate, then threw wildly into center field (leaving Cincinnati with runners on second and third base). The play was ruled an error on Fisk.

● **Cesar Geronimo.** Reds' center fielder who led off the 10th with a single preceding Armbrister's attempted bunt.

● **Joe Morgan.** Reds' second baseman who, after an intentional walk to Pete Rose and a strikeout by pinch-hitter Merv Rettenmund in the 10th, drove in Geronimo with a fly over the head of Fred Lynn, Boston's drawn-in center fielder.

● **Jim Willoughby.** Red Sox's reliever and losing pitcher who gave way to Roger Moret after the Armbrister incident.

BEVENS LOSES SERIES NO-HIT BID

One out away from becoming the first man in history to pitch a World Series no-hitter, Floyd (Bill) Bevens of the New York Yankees lost his bid—and the game—on a two-run double in Game 4 of the 1947 World Series as the Brooklyn Dodgers beat the Yanks, 3-2.

Supporting Cast:

● **Hugh Casey.** Dodgers' reliever and winning pitcher. He pitched two-thirds of an inning.

● **Carl Furillo.** After catcher Bruce Edwards flied out to open the Dodgers' ninth in the October 3 game at Ebbets Field, center fielder Furillo drew a walk off Bevens (trying to protect a 2-1 lead).

● **Al Gionfriddo.** After third baseman Spider Jorgensen fouled out for the second out of the Dodgers' ninth, Gionfriddo went in to run for Furillo. With Pete Reiser at the plate, Gionfriddo stole second on a 2-1 pitch.

PINELLI STIRNWEISS HENRICH McQUINN McGOWAN

PITLER

MIKSIS

GIONFRIDDO

BEVENS

BERRA

LAVAGETTO

GOETZ

The flight of Cookie Lavagetto's ninth-inning double, the positioning of the Yankees' defense and movement of Brooklyn baserunners is diagrammed (above) during Game 4 of the 1947 World Series played at Ebbets Field. Lavagetto, whose hit gave Brooklyn a 3-2 victory and broke up Bill Bevens' no-hit bid, is escorted (left) from the field by police and happy teammates.

● **Cookie Lavagetto.** Dodgers' pinch-hitter whose ninth-inning double off the right-field wall scored Gionfriddo and Eddie Miksis, giving Brooklyn its only hit and a Series-squaring 3-2 victory.

● **Eddie Miksis.** He ran for Reiser in the Dodgers' ninth.

● **Pete Reiser.** A pinch-hitter for Casey in the Dodgers' ninth, he was walked intentionally after the count reached 3-1.

● **Eddie Stanky.** Dodgers' second baseman for whom Lavagetto pinch-hit in the ninth.

CARLTON STRIKES OUT 19, LOSES

Steve Carlton of the St. Louis Cardinals set a modern major league record on September 15, 1969, for most strikeouts in a nine-inning game, getting 19 against the New York Mets. Carlton, though, was a 4-3 loser to the Mets in a game played at Busch Memorial Stadium.

Supporting Cast:

● **Tim McCarver.** Carlton's catcher.

● **Tug McGraw.** Mets' reliever and winning pitcher who worked the final three innings.

● **Amos Otis.** Mets' rookie left fielder who was Carlton's chief victim, striking out four times. Otis, the last batter in the Mets' ninth, was Carlton's record-breaking 19th strikeout victim (Tom Seaver in 1970 and Nolan Ryan in 1974 have matched the nine-inning total of 19).

● **Ron Swoboda.** Mets' right fielder who accounted for Carlton's downfall with two-run homers in the fourth and eighth innings.

DRYSDALE'S SCORELESS STREAK

Don Drysdale of the Los Angeles Dodgers held opponents scoreless for 58 consecutive innings in 1968, breaking the major league mark of 55⅔ set by Washington's Walter Johnson in 1913. Included in Drysdale's streak, which started in the first inning on May 14 and lasted through the fourth inning on June 8, were six shutouts.

Supporting Cast:

● **Howie Bedell.** Philadelphia Phillies' pinch-hitter whose sacrifice fly in the fifth inning of a June 8 game at Dodger Stadium ended Drysdale's streak.

● **Chicago Cubs.** Team against whom Drysdale began his streak May 14 with a 1-0 victory.

● **Clay Dalrymple.** Phillies' catcher who got a key fifth-inning single June 8.

● **Houston Astros.** Shut out by Drysdale, 1-0, on May 18, and by a 5-0 score on May 26.

● **Larry Jackson.** Phillies' pitcher for whom Bedell pinch-hit June 8.

● **Pittsburgh Pirates.** Shut out by Drysdale, 5-0, on June 4.

● **St. Louis Cardinals.** Shut out by Drysdale, 2-0, on May 22.

● **San Francisco Giants.** Shut out by Drysdale, 3-0, on May 31.

● **Tony Taylor.** Phillies' third baseman who singled in the fifth inning June 8,

Detroit first baseman Norm Cash comes up empty on a ninth-inning swing against Cardinals ace Bob Gibson during Game 1 action in the 1968 World Series. Cash was Gibson's record-breaking 16th strikeout victim en route to a game total of 17.

moved into scoring position on Dalrymple's hit and scored the streak-ending run on Bedell's sacrifice fly. Drysdale nevertheless won the game, 5-3.

GIBSON STRIKES OUT 17 TIGERS

Bob Gibson of St. Louis struck out a World Series-record 17 batters in Game 1 of the 1968 classic, pitching the Cardinals to a 4-0 victory over the Detroit Tigers at Busch Memorial Stadium. Eleven Tigers struck out swinging in the October 2 game; five were called out on strikes and one bunted foul for a third strike.

Supporting Cast:

● **Norm Cash.** With one out in the ninth inning, the Tigers' first baseman became Gibson's record-breaking 16th strikeout victim as the St. Louis pitcher surpassed Sandy Koufax's Series mark of 15 (set in 1963).

● **Willie Horton.** Tigers' left fielder, the game's final batter, was called out on strikes, giving Gibson 17 strikeouts.

● **Al Kaline.** After Tigers' shortstop Mickey Stanley singled to open the ninth, Kaline became Gibson's record-equaling 15th strikeout victim.

● **Tim McCarver.** Gibson's catcher.

● **Denny McLain.** Tigers' loser in the heralded pitching matchup. McLain was coming off a 31-victory season (he was the majors' first 30-game winner in 34 years), while Gibson posted a National League-record 1.12 earned-run average in 1968 and pitched 13 shutouts.

GIONFRIDDO'S CATCH

With two Yankees on base and the Dodgers ahead 8-5 in the sixth inning of Game 6 of the 1947 World Series, Brooklyn left fielder Al Gionfriddo denied New York a score-tying home run with an outstanding catch in front of the bullpen at Yankee Stadium. The Dodgers went on to win, 8-6, to even the Series at three games apiece, but the Yankees won the Series the next day.

Supporting Cast:

● **Yogi Berra.** Yankees' right fielder whose two-out single in the sixth inning put runners at first and second base.

● **Joe DiMaggio.** Yankees' center fielder whose two-out, sixth-inning drive with two runners on base was caught by Gionfriddo just as it appeared the ball might drop over the fence. Gionfriddo made a twisting, glove-hand catch near the 415-foot mark.

● **Joe Hatten.** Dodgers' pitcher off whom DiMaggio hit his sixth-inning drive in the October 5 game.

● **Eddie Miksis.** Dodgers' left fielder who was replaced defensively by Gionfriddo as the Yankees prepared to come to bat in the bottom of the sixth. Miksis had entered the game in the fifth inning as a pinch-hitter for left fielder Gene Hermanski, then went in to play left field.

● **George Stirnweiss.** Yankees' second baseman who walked in the sixth and advanced to second on Berra's single.

HADDIX PITCHES 12 PERFECT INNINGS

Harvey Haddix of the Pittsburgh Pirates pitched 12 perfect innings against Milwaukee on May 26, 1959, at County Stadium, only to end up a 1-0, one-hit loser to the Braves in 13 innings.

Supporting Cast:

● **Hank Aaron.** Braves' right fielder who drew an intentional walk from Haddix in the 13th inning of the 0-0 game.

● **Joe Adcock.** Braves' first baseman who, with one out and Felix Mantilla on second base and Aaron on first, hit a 13th-inning pitch from Haddix over the fence in right-center field. Aaron, figuring the ball had dropped at the fence and that Mantilla's run had ended the game, touched second base and headed for the dugout. Adcock circled the bases, but he was credited with a double—not a home run—because he was ruled out before reaching third base for having passed Aaron. Nevertheless, Adcock's hit made Milwaukee a 1-0 winner.

● **Lew Burdette.** Braves' winning pitcher who went the distance and permitted 12 hits (all singles).

● **Smoky Burgess.** Haddix's catcher.

● **Don Hoak.** Pittsburgh third baseman whose throwing error opening the Braves' 13th ended Haddix's perfection at 36 straight batters.

● **Felix Mantilla.** Braves' second baseman was the first baserunner against Haddix, reaching first on Hoak's misplay. Mantilla had entered the game in the 11th inning, after Del Rice pinch-hit for second baseman Johnny O'Brien in the Braves' 10th.

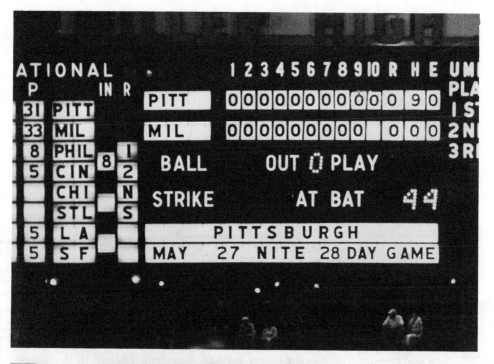

The scoreboard (above) tells the story as Pittsburgh's Harvey Haddix enters the 10th inning of his 1959 gem against Milwaukee in perfect form, while Al Gionfriddo's catch (left) of a long drive by Joe DiMaggio told the story in Game 6 of the 1947 World Series. Gionfriddo's play kept the Yankees from tying the score and Brooklyn went on to win, 8-6.

• **Eddie Mathews.** Braves' third baseman who sacrificed Mantilla to second in the 13th.

HUBBELL'S ALL-STAR FEAT

Carl Hubbell of the New York Giants turned in one of the most memorable pitching performances in baseball history on July 10, 1934, at the Polo Grounds, striking out five straight American League All-Stars in the major leagues' second All-Star Game. Despite Hubbell's performance, the National League, ahead 4-0 after three innings, lost, 9-7.

Supporting Cast:

• **Babe Ruth.** After Charlie Gehringer (Detroit Tigers) and Heinie Manush (Washington Senators) singled and walked, respectively, to open the A.L.'s first, the Yankees' Ruth became Hubbell's first strikeout victim.

• **Lou Gehrig.** Yankees' first baseman who was Hubbell's second consecutive strikeout victim in the first inning.

• **Jimmie Foxx.** Philadelphia Athletics' slugger who was Hubbell's third straight strikeout victim in the first inning.

• **Al Simmons.** Chicago White Sox's outfielder who led off the second inning for the A.L. and became Hubbell's fourth straight strikeout victim.

• **Joe Cronin.** The second batter for the American League in the second inning, the Washington Senators' shortstop became Hubbell's fifth straight strikeout victim.

• **Bill Dickey.** New York Yankees' catcher who, after Cronin struck out in the second inning, ended Hubbell's strikeout streak with a single.

• **Lefty Gomez.** Yankees' pitcher who struck out after Dickey's hit, giving Hubbell six strikeouts in the first two innings (Hubbell did not record a strikeout in the third, his last inning of work).

• **Mel Harder.** Cleveland Indians' pitcher who hurled one-hit, shutout ball over the last five innings for the A.L. and was credited with the victory.

• **Van Lingle Mungo.** Brooklyn Dodgers' pitcher who was the National League's loser. He gave up four runs and four hits in the fifth inning.

JOSS PERFECT

Addie Joss of Cleveland was at his best on October 2, 1908—and it was out of necessity. Ed Walsh of the Chicago White Sox, Joss' pitching opponent that day in Cleveland, hurled one of the best games of his career. But Joss was even better, pitching a perfect game and winning, 1-0.

Supporting Cast:

• **John Anderson.** White Sox's pinch-hitter whose groundout completed Joss' perfect game. The at-bat was Anderson's last in a 14-year major league career.

• **Nig Clarke.** Joss' catcher.

• **Ossee Schreckengost.** White Sox's catcher who broke a finger in this game—a game that proved Schreckengost's last in an 11-year big-league career.

Yankee pitcher Don Larsen receives a big hug from catcher Yogi Berra after striking out Brooklyn's Dale Mitchell to complete his perfect game in the 1956 World Series.

● **Ed Walsh.** White Sox's losing pitcher who struck out 15 batters, allowed only four hits and walked one. Joss had three strikeouts.

LARSEN'S PERFECT GAME

On October 8, 1956, at Yankee Stadium, Don Larsen accomplished the unprecedented feat of hurling a no-hit game in the World Series. Larsen pitched a perfect game as the Yankees defeated the Brooklyn Dodgers, 2-0, in Game 5.

Supporting Cast:

● **Hank Bauer.** Yankee right fielder whose sixth-inning single scored Andy Carey with New York's second run. Carey had singled and advanced to second on Larsen's sacrifice.

● **Yogi Berra.** Larsen's catcher.

● **Roy Campanella.** Brooklyn catcher who, as the second batter in the ninth, grounded out to second baseman Billy Martin.

● **Carl Furillo.** Leading off the ninth, Brooklyn right fielder flied out to Bauer.

● **Sal Maglie.** Dodgers' losing pitcher who allowed only five hits, walked two batters and struck out five.

● **Mickey Mantle.** Yankee center fielder whose fourth-inning home run staked Larsen to a 1-0 lead.

● **Dale Mitchell.** Pinch-hitting for Maglie, he was the last out in Larsen's perfect game. The sequence of pitches: Ball one, outside; strike one, called; strike two, swinging; foul ball to the left, into the crowd; strike three called.

The strikeout was the seventh of the game for Larsen.

● **Pee Wee Reese.** Brooklyn shortstop who was the only Dodger to reach ball three against Larsen. The second batter of the game, Reese was called out on strikes on a 3-2 pitch.

MALONEY, WILSON NO-HITTERS

Jim Maloney of Cincinnati and Don Wilson of Houston pitched back-to-back no-hitters in a 1969 Reds-Astros series, marking only the second time such a performance had occurred in major league history. Maloney beat the Astros, 10-0, on April 30 at Crosley Field, striking out 13 and walking five. Wilson foiled the Reds, 4-0, on May 1, walking six and striking out 13.

Supporting Cast:

● **Wade Blasingame.** Astros' starting and losing pitcher in Maloney's no-hitter.

● **Darrel Chaney.** Reds' shortstop who helped to preserve Maloney's no-hitter with a somersaulting catch of Johnny Edwards' sixth-inning looper into short left field.

● **Bobby Tolan.** Reds' right fielder whose three hits and four RBIs backed Maloney.

● **Denis Menke.** Astros' shortstop who had two hits and two runs batted in May 1 in support of Wilson. Third baseman Doug Rader hit a bases-empty home run, and Wilson contributed a sacrifice fly.

● **Jim Merritt.** Reds' starting and losing pitcher in Wilson's no-hitter.

MARTIN TO THE RESCUE

Trailing 4-2 with two out and the bases loaded in their half of the seventh inning, the Brooklyn Dodgers saw their hopes rise in Game 7 of the 1952 World Series when a popup near the mound seemed on the brink of going unattended. With two Dodgers having crossed the plate and another runner rounding third base, Yankee second baseman Billy Martin dashed in and grabbed the ball about knee-high. The score stood up, and the Yankees had their fourth straight World Series championship.

Supporting Cast:

● **Joe Collins.** Yankee first baseman who apparently would make the play on the seventh-inning popup, but he lost sight of the ball.

● **Billy Cox.** Brooklyn third baseman whose single helped the Dodgers fill the bases in the seventh.

● **Carl Furillo.** Brooklyn right fielder who led off the Dodgers' seventh with a walk.

● **Bob Kuzava.** Yankee relief pitcher who stood transfixed when the seventh-inning popup was hit.

● **Pee Wee Reese.** Brooklyn shortstop whose seventh-inning walk loaded the bases.

● **Jackie Robinson.** Brooklyn second baseman who, on a 3-2 pitch, hit the popup that Martin snared in the October 7 game at Ebbets Field.

Second baseman Billy Martin saved the day for the Yankees when he made a running, knee-high catch of a bases-loaded, infield pop with two out in the seventh inning of Game 7 of the 1952 World Series.

One of the more remarkable catches in baseball history occurred during the opening game of the 1954 World Series when New York Giants center fielder Willie Mays, his back to the plate, made an over-the-shoulder grab of a 460-foot drive off the bat of Cleveland's Vic Wertz.

MAYS' REMARKABLE CATCH

With the opening game of the 1954 World Series between the Cleveland Indians and New York Giants tied, 2-2, in the eighth inning and two Indians on base, Giants' center fielder Willie Mays made an over-the-shoulder catch of a 460-foot smash while running with his back to the plate. Saved by Mays' remarkable play, the Giants went on to beat the Indians, 5-2, in 10 innings on the way to a Series sweep.

Supporting Cast:

● **Larry Doby.** Cleveland center fielder who led off the Indians' eighth with a walk. He moved to second on a single and tagged up and went to third after Mays' catch (but was left on base).

● **Marv Grissom.** Giants' reliever and winning pitcher who worked 2⅔ innings.

● **Don Liddle.** Giants' relief pitcher who faced only one batter in the September 29 game at the Polo Grounds—Vic Wertz, who came to the plate with two runners on and no one out in the Indians' eighth.

● **Dusty Rhodes.** Giants' pinch-hitter who batted for left fielder Monte Irvin in the 10th inning and hit a game-winning three-run homer off Cleveland starter and loser Bob Lemon.

● **Al Rosen.** Cleveland third baseman whose eighth-inning single, following Doby's walk, brought on Liddle in relief of Giants' starter Sal Maglie.

● **Vic Wertz.** Cleveland first baseman who singled twice, doubled and tripled in the game . . . and hit the eighth-inning drive that Mays hauled in.

McLAIN NOTCHES 30th

Denny McLain of Detroit became the major leagues' first 30-game winner in 34 years on September 14, 1968, when the Tigers scored two runs in the bottom of the ninth inning and edged the Oakland A's, 5-4. McLain struck out 10 batters and walked one, allowing six hits. Not since Dizzy Dean won 30 games for the St. Louis Cardinals in 1934 had a big-league pitcher reached the select figure.

Supporting Cast:

● **Bill Freehan.** McLain's catcher in the game at Tiger Stadium.

● **Willie Horton.** Detroit left fielder whose one-out hit over left fielder Jim Gosger's head scored Mickey Stanley with the winning run in the ninth inning, boosting McLain's record to 30-5 (he finished at 31-6).

● **Reggie Jackson.** A's right fielder who hit a two-run home run and a bases-empty homer off McLain.

● **Al Kaline.** Pinch-hitting for McLain in the ninth with the Tigers trailing 4-3, he drew a leadoff walk.

● **Jim Northrup.** With one out in the Tigers' ninth and runners on first and third, the Detroit right fielder grounded to A's first baseman Danny Cater. Cater made a poor throw to the plate, allowing Kaline to score from third and Stanley to move from first to third.

● **Diego Segui.** A's losing pitcher who worked the final 4⅓ innings.

Willie Horton's one-out, game-winning hit prompted this burst of excitement from Tiger teammates Al Kaline (left) and Denny McLain, who received credit for his 30th victory of the 1968 season.

● **Mickey Stanley.** Detroit center fielder whose one-out single in the ninth sent Kaline to third.

OAKLAND'S FOUR-PITCHER NO-HITTER

Trying to tune up his pitching staff for the 1975 American League Championship Series, Oakland Manager Alvin Dark used four pitchers in the A's regular-season finale on September 28—and the foursome responded with a no-hitter. Vida Blue, the A's starter and winner in a 5-0 victory over California at the Oakland Coliseum, held the Angels hitless for five innings. Blue walked two and struck out two.

Supporting Cast:

● **Glenn Abbott.** A's second pitcher who retired the Angels in order in the sixth inning.

● **Paul Lindblad.** A's third pitcher who retired the Angels in order in the seventh inning.

● **Rollie Fingers.** A's fourth pitcher who retired the Angels in order in the eighth and ninth innings, completing the unprecedented four-man no-hitter.

● **Reggie Jackson.** A's right fielder who hit two homers in the game and drove in three runs.

● **Dal Maxvill.** A's shortstop who, playing his last major league game, threw out the game's final batter.

● **Joe Pactwa.** Angels' pitcher who was appearing in his fourth and last major league game. Working in relief, he pitched the eighth inning (giving up a hit and a walk, but no runs).

● **Mickey Rivers.** Pinch-hitting for Angels' third baseman Dave Chalk, he grounded to Maxvill for the game's final out.

● **Gary Ross.** Angels' starting and losing pitcher who was making his only big-league appearance of the season.

PERRY, WASHBURN NO-HITTERS

Gaylord Perry of San Francisco and Ray Washburn of St. Louis pitched consecutive no-hitters in a 1968 Giants-Cardinals series at Candlestick Park, the first such occurrence in big-league history. Perry stopped the Cardinals, 1-0, on the night of September 17, striking out nine and walking two. Washburn defeated the Giants, 2-0, the next afternoon, walking five and striking out eight.

Supporting Cast:

● **Bob Gibson.** Cardinals' losing pitcher in Perry's no-hitter. He yielded only four hits and struck out 10 batters in going the distance.

● **Ron Hunt.** Giants' second baseman whose first-inning home run accounted for the only run in Perry's no-hitter and enabled San Francisco to beat St. Louis in the Cardinals' first game since clinching the National League pennant two days earlier.

● **Bob Bolin.** Giants' starting and losing pitcher in Washburn's no-hitter.

• **Mike Shannon.** Cardinals' third baseman who broke up a 0-0 game on September 18 with a run-scoring double off Bolin in the seventh inning.

RUDI'S CATCH

With the A's leading the Reds, 2-0, with one Cincinnati runner on base and no one out in the ninth inning of Game 2 of the 1972 World Series, Oakland left fielder Joe Rudi raced to the fence for a long drive and made a leaping, backhanded catch against the wall. The A's, who got a bases-empty homer from Rudi in the third inning, went on to win, 2-1, for a two-games-to-none lead in the Series, which they won in seven games.

Supporting Cast:

• **Rollie Fingers.** A's relief pitcher who ended the Reds' ninth-inning threat, getting the only batter he faced, pinch-hitter Julian Javier (batting for reliever Tom Hall), to foul out to first baseman Mike Hegan.

• **Jim (Catfish) Hunter.** A's starting and winning pitcher who lost his shutout with two out in the ninth in the October 15 game at Riverfront Stadium.

• **Hal McRae.** Cincinnati pinch-hitter who batted for shortstop Darrel Chaney in the ninth and singled across the Reds' only run.

• **Denis Menke.** Cincinnati third baseman who hit the long smash on which Rudi made an outstanding catch in the ninth.

• **Tony Perez.** Cincinnati first baseman who led off the Reds' ninth with a single preceding Menke's at-bat. Perez later went to second on right fielder Cesar Geronimo's low liner to first (Hegan knocked down the ball and retired Geronimo at the bag) and scored on McRae's hit.

RYAN'S FIFTH NO-HITTER

Nolan Ryan pitched a major league-record fifth no-hitter on September 26, 1981, hurling the Houston Astros to a 5-0 victory over the Los Angeles Dodgers at the Astrodome. Ryan, who had shared the record for no-hit games with Sandy Koufax of the Los Angeles Dodgers, pitched no-hitters for the California Angels in 1973 (two), 1974 and 1975. Koufax's no-hitters came in 1962, 1963, 1964 and 1965 (perfect game).

Supporting Cast:

• **Alan Ashby.** He caught Ryan's fifth no-hitter and contributed a two-run single in the third inning.

• **Dusty Baker.** Dodgers' left fielder who was the last out against Ryan, grounding to third baseman Art Howe.

• **Ken Landreaux.** The second batter in Ryan's 1-2-3 ninth inning, the Dodgers' center fielder grounded out to first baseman Denny Walling.

• **Ted Power.** Dodgers' starting and losing pitcher.

• **Terry Puhl.** Houston right fielder who had to make a tough running catch near the wall in right-center field on a seventh-inning drive hit by Dodgers' catcher Mike Scioscia.

• **Reggie Smith.** Pinch-hitting for Dodgers' second baseman Davey Lopes, he struck out leading off the ninth.

Oakland left fielder Joe Rudi makes a leaping, backhanded catch against the wall to rob Cincinnati's Denis Menke and short-circuit a ninth-inning Reds' rally in Game 2 of the 1972 World Series.

A young Tom Seaver holds the Cy Young Award he was presented before an April 22, 1970, game against San Diego. Seaver celebrated the occasion by striking out a record 10 straight Padres en route to a record-tying game total of 19.

SEAVER STRIKES OUT 10 STRAIGHT

Tom Seaver of the New York Mets set a major league record for consecutive strikeouts in one game on April 22, 1970, fanning 10 straight San Diego batters in the Mets' 2-1 triumph over the Padres. Seaver, presented with his 1969 Cy Young Award before the game at Shea Stadium, finished with a two-hitter and 19 strikeouts, with the strikeout total equaling the modern big-league mark for a nine-inning game set a year earlier by St. Louis' Steve Carlton against the Mets.

Supporting Cast:

● **Mike Corkins.** San Diego's starting and losing pitcher.

● **Clarence Gaston.** San Diego center fielder who, as the Padres' second batter in the ninth inning, became Seaver's record-breaking ninth consecutive strikeout victim (the previous modern record of eight had been reached seven times through 1982).

● **Jerry Grote.** Seaver's catcher.

● **Al Ferrara.** San Diego left fielder who followed Gaston to the plate in the ninth and became Seaver's 10th straight strikeout victim, ending the game. Ferrara had accounted for the Padres' run with a second-inning homer.

● **Van Kelly.** San Diego third baseman who struck out leading off the ninth, enabling Seaver to tie the modern record of eight consecutive strikeouts.

SHORE 'PERFECT'

Coming on in relief when Boston's starting pitcher was ejected after issuing a walk to the game's first batter, Ernie Shore was on the mound for the Red Sox as 27 consecutive Washington players were retired in the first game of a June 23, 1917, doubleheader at Fenway Park. While Shore's feat is listed as a perfect game in most record books (with an asterisk alongside the entry), some baseball "purists" debate the point because of the leadoff walk. Shore won, 4-0, striking out two batters.

Supporting Cast:

● **Sam Agnew.** Boston catcher who entered the game with Shore when the Red Sox's starting battery departed after the game-opening walk. Agnew had a 3-for-3 day at the plate.

● **Doc Ayers.** Washington's losing pitcher.

● **Mike Menosky.** Washington pinch-hitter who made the final out against Shore.

● **Ray Morgan.** Washington second baseman who led off the game with a walk, then was thrown out trying to steal by Agnew (with reliever Shore pitching).

● **Brick Owens.** Home-plate umpire whose ejection of Boston's starting pitcher set the stage for Shore's masterpiece.

● **Babe Ruth.** Boston's starting pitcher who was thrown out of the game for disputing Owens' ball-and-strike calls on Morgan.

● **Pinch Thomas.** Boston's starting catcher who left the game with the banished Ruth after the walk to Morgan.

SWOBODA'S SERIES CATCH

With Baltimore runners on first and third base and the New York Mets leading, 1-0, in the ninth inning of Game 4 of the 1969 World Series, Mets right fielder Ron Swoboda made a diving, one-handed catch of a one-out liner. While a run scored on the play, Swoboda's catch prevented further damage and the Mets went on to win, 2-1, in 10 innings.

Supporting Cast:

● **Rod Gaspar.** Pinch-running for Mets' catcher Jerry Grote (who had doubled) in the 10th inning, he scored the winning run on Baltimore reliever Pete Richert's throwing error.

● **Brooks Robinson.** Baltimore third baseman who hit the ninth-inning liner on which Swoboda turned a "sure" rally-extending hit into a sacrifice fly.

● **Frank Robinson.** Baltimore right fielder who scored on Brooks Robinson's sacrifice fly after singling with one out in the ninth and advancing to third on first baseman Boog Powell's single.

● **Tom Seaver.** Mets' pitcher who went the distance in the October 15 game at Shea Stadium. Allowing only six hits he positioned the Mets for the Series clincher the next day.

TONEY, VAUGHN: NO HITS THROUGH NINE

When Fred Toney of the Cincinnati Reds and Jim Vaughn of the Chicago Cubs hooked up in a May 2, 1917, game in Chicago, the words "pitching duel" didn't begin to tell the story. After nine innings, it was a 0-0 game— and neither team had a hit. Cincinnati managed two hits and an unearned run in the 10th inning, though, and won, 1-0, as Toney finished with his no-hitter intact.

Supporting Cast:

● **Emil Huhn.** Toney's catcher.

● **Larry Kopf.** Cincinnati shortstop who got the first hit off Vaughn, a one-out single in the 10th inning.

● **Al Orth.** Home-plate umpire in the Toney-Vaughn double no-hitter.

● **Jim Thorpe.** Cincinnati right fielder and football great whose infield single in the 10th inning scored Kopf with the winning run.

● **Cy Williams.** Cubs' center fielder whose error on Cincinnati first baseman Hal Chase's 10th-inning fly ball enabled Kopf to move from first base to third.

● **Art Wilson.** Vaughn's catcher.

VANDER MEER'S CONSECUTIVE NO-HITTERS

Johnny Vander Meer is the only major leaguer in history to have pitched two straight no-hitters, accomplishing the feat in 1938 as he led the Cincinnati Reds to a 3-0 triumph over the Boston Bees on June 11 and a 6-0 victory over the Brooklyn Dodgers on June 15.

Facing Brooklyn in the first night game in Ebbets Field history, Johnny Vander Meer of the Cincinnati Reds delivers a pitch en route to his second straight no-hitter of the 1938 season.

Supporting Cast:

● **Max Butcher.** Brooklyn's losing pitcher in Vander Meer's second no-hitter.

● **Leo Durocher.** Brooklyn shortstop who was the last out in the June 15 game, which was the first night game in Ebbets Field history. Durocher flied to Cincinnati center fielder Harry Craft.

● **Debs Garms.** Boston third baseman who got the first hit off Vander Meer following his two no-hitters. Garms' one-out single in the fourth inning of a June 19 game ended Vander Meer's hitless streak at 21⅔ innings.

● **Hank Leiber.** New York Giants' center fielder who got the last hit off Vander Meer before his two no-hitters. Leiber had a two-out single in the ninth inning of a June 5 game.

● **Ernie Lombardi.** Vander Meer's catcher in both no-hit games.

● **Danny MacFayden.** Boston's losing pitcher in Vander Meer's first no-hitter.

● **Ray Mueller.** Pinch-hitting for Boston first baseman Elbie Fletcher, he made the last out in the June 11 game at Crosley Field by grounding to Cincinnati third baseman Lew Riggs.

Cleveland second baseman Bill Wambsganss (top, left) wheels around and tags out Brooklyn's Otto Miller, completing an unassisted triple play in Game 5 of the 1920 World Series. Pete Kilduff, doubled off second base, is shown reaching third base as Indians third baseman Larry Gardner watches Wambsganss.

WAMBSGANSS' TRIPLE PLAY

The only triple play in World Series history was made in Game 5 of the 1920 classic—and it was an unassisted play by Cleveland second baseman Bill Wambsganss.

Supporting Cast:

● **Jim Bagby Sr.** Cleveland hurler who was the winning pitcher in the 8-1 game, going the distance and allowing 13 hits. In the fourth inning, Bagby became the first pitcher in Series history to hit a home run.

● **Burleigh Grimes.** Brooklyn starting and losing pitcher who gave up the first bases-loaded homer in Series history (to Cleveland right fielder Elmer Smith in the first inning) and the first Series homer by a pitcher (Bagby's drive).

● **Pete Kilduff.** Brooklyn second baseman who led off the fifth with a single.

● **Otto Miller.** Brooklyn catcher who followed Kilduff's fifth-inning single in the October 10 game with another single.

● **Clarence Mitchell.** Batting third in Brooklyn's fifth, the relief pitcher lined to Wambsganss at second for one out. Wambsganss then stepped on second base, doubling off Kilduff, and wheeled around to tag Miller (who had broken for second) to complete the triple play.

THIRD INNING:

Goats, victims and futile performances.

JACK BILLINGHAM

The Cincinnati pitcher who gave up Hank Aaron's 714th career home run on April 4, 1974, in Cincinnati. The Atlanta Brave slugger's homer tied Babe Ruth's lifetime mark.

Supporting Cast:

● **Ralph Garr.** Braves' baserunner on second when Aaron homered.

● **Mike Lum.** Braves' baserunner on first when Aaron homered.

RALPH BRANCA

The losing pitcher in the first playoff game in major league history. Pitching for the Brooklyn Dodgers against the St. Louis Cardinals on October 1, 1946, Branca was the Dodgers' starter and loser in a 4-2 defeat.

Branca was the losing pitcher in three of the first five N.L. playoff games. Besides losing Game 1 in 1946 when the Dodgers dropped two straight games in the best-of-three playoff, Branca was charged with defeats in Games 1 and 3 of the 1951 playoff against the New York Giants.

Branca, whose 0-1 pitch to Bobby Thomson in the ninth inning of Game 3 of the '51 playoff ended in a pennant-winning home run (New York won, 5-4), had given up a two-run homer to Thomson in Game 1 (which the Dodgers lost, 3-1).

BOB BUHL

The Milwaukee Braves-Chicago Cubs pitcher who went 0-for-the-season as a batter in 1962. Going hitless in 70 at-bats, Buhl, who was traded to Chicago during the season, established the big-league mark for most at-bats in a season without getting a hit.

WILLIE DAVIS

The Los Angeles Dodgers' center fielder who made three errors in the fifth inning of Game 2 of the 1966 World Series, helping Baltimore to a 6-0 triumph (and the Orioles went on to sweep the Series). Davis lost two fly balls in the sun, with errors being charged on both plays, and threw wildly to third base after the second misplay.

Supporting Cast:

● **Paul Blair.** His fly ball to deep center field dropped at Davis' feet.

● **Andy Etchebarren.** His lazy fly to center glanced off Davis' glove for error No. 2. Davis grabbed the ball and made a bad throw to third for error No. 3, with Boog Powell and Blair scoring on the play. Etchebarren was doubled home by Luis Aparicio, capping the three-run inning.

● **Boog Powell.** He led off the Orioles' fifth with a single against Sandy Koufax (who was in a 0-0 duel with Baltimore's Jim Palmer at the time).

AL DOWNING

The Los Angeles Dodgers' lefthander who gave up Hank Aaron's 715th career homer on April 8, 1974, during a game in Atlanta. With the Braves' slugger needing one more homer to break his tie with Babe Ruth for the all-time record, Downing, the Dodgers' starting pitcher, avoided notoriety in the first inning by walking Aaron on four pitches. In the fourth, however, Downing became a footnote to baseball history when Aaron hit a 1-0 pitch over the fence in left-center. The two-run drive tied the score, 3-3, and the Braves went on to win, 7-4.

DON DRYSDALE

The Brooklyn and Los Angeles Dodgers' pitcher from 1956 through 1969 who gave up more home runs (17) to Hank Aaron, the career leader with 755, than any other hurler.

JACK FISHER

The Baltimore Orioles' pitcher who gave up a bases-empty home run to Boston's Ted Williams in the Red Sox slugger's final at-bat in the major leagues on September 28, 1960, at Fenway Park. Williams hit a 1-1 pitch into

Game 2 of the 1966 World Series was just one of those days for center fielder Willie Davis (3) and the rest of the Los Angeles Dodgers. Davis, who had committed three errors an inning earlier, couldn't get together with right fielder Ron Fairly on this sixth-inning smash off the bat of Baltimore's Frank Robinson and the ball dropped in for a triple. The Dodgers made six errors in the game and lost, 6-0.

After crashing into catcher Ray Fosse and scoring the winning run in the 12th inning of the 1970 All-Star Game, Pete Rose (left) surveys the damage he has done. National League teammate Dick Dietz hugs Rose, and Leo Durocher, an N.L. coach, applauds the play.

the seats in right-center field in the eighth inning.

Roger Maris hit his 60th homer of the 1961 season against Fisher, connecting in the Yankees-Orioles game of September 26.

CURT FLOOD

The Cardinals' center fielder who misjudged a seventh-inning drive during Game 7 of the 1968 World Series, helping to send the Detroit Tigers to the Series title. With St. Louis' Bob Gibson and Detroit's Mickey Lolich locked in a 0-0 duel and two Tigers on base, Flood broke in on the ball, realized he had misjudged it and ran back. The ball sailed past Flood, and both runners scored. Detroit went on to win the game, 4-1, and the Series, four games to three.

Supporting Cast:

• **Norm Cash.** He singled with two out in the Tigers' seventh.

• **Bill Freehan.** His run-scoring double capped the Tigers' three-run seventh.

• **Willie Horton.** He followed Cash's seventh-inning single with another single.

• **Jim Northrup.** Hitting the drive that Flood misplayed, Northrup was credited with a triple and two runs batted in.

RAY FOSSE

The catcher and representative of the Cleveland Indians in the 1970 All-Star Game who was bowled over at the plate in the '70 classic on a 12th-inning play that enabled the National League to defeat the American League, 5-4.

Supporting Cast:

• **Jim Hickman.** Chicago Cubs' player who delivered the game-winning single in the 12th.

• **Amos Otis.** The Kansas City Royals' center fielder who fielded Hickman's single and made the throw to the plate.

• **Pete Rose.** Racing for home on Hickman's hit, the Cincinnati Reds' star barreled into Fosse just as the ball arrived and scored the winning run.

FRED GLADDING

A relief pitcher who appeared in 450 big-league games from 1961 through 1973 and managed only one hit in the majors. Playing for the Houston Astros in 1969, Gladding singled off Ron Taylor of the New York Mets in the first game of a July 30 doubleheader. Gladding's lone hit in 63 major league at-bats came in an 11-run inning in which Houston's Denis Menke and Jim Wynn hit bases-loaded home runs.

TOMMY GLAVIANO

The St. Louis Cardinals' third baseman who made errors on three consecutive plays in the ninth inning of a May 18, 1950 game, giving Brooklyn four

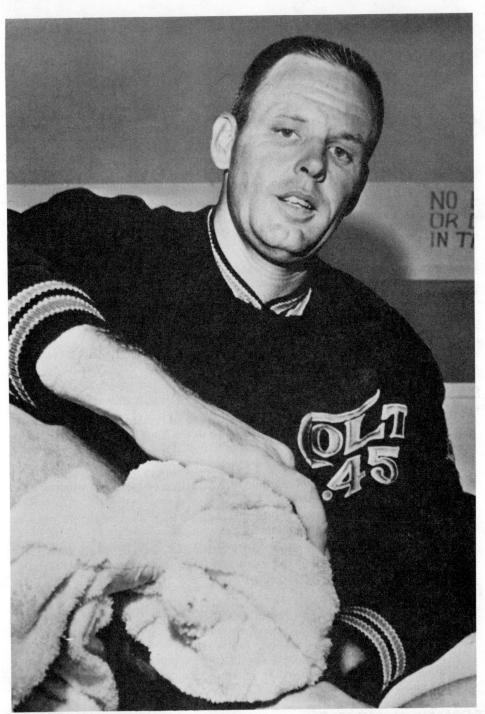

Not only did Houston's Ken Johnson lose a nine-inning, complete-game no-hitter on April 23, 1964, but the Colts' pitcher had to nurse a sore shin after being struck by a line drive during the game against the Cincinnati Reds.

runs and a 9-8 victory. The Dodgers, who had trailed, 8-0, scored four runs in the bottom of the eighth, then closed within 8-5 with a run in the ninth and had the bases loaded with one out when Glaviano experienced his nightmare.

Supporting Cast:

● **Roy Campanella.** He hit a bases-loaded grounder to Glaviano, who made a wide throw to second on a force-play attempt. The error allowed a run to score, cut the Cardinals' lead to 8-6 and kept the bases loaded.

● **Eddie Miksis.** He grounded to Glaviano, whose wide throw to the plate allowed another run to score (making it 8-7 with the bases still loaded).

● **Pee Wee Reese.** His grounder went through Glaviano's legs, enabling the tying and winning runs to score.

BABE HERMAN

An extra-base hit with the bases loaded means two or three runs batted in. Usually. But Herman of the Brooklyn Dodgers hit a bases-full double against the Boston Braves on August 15, 1926, and came away with one RBI . . . and was victimized as part of a double play. With Hank DeBerry on third base, Dazzy Vance on second and Chick Fewster on first, Herman hit a George Mogridge pitch off the right-field wall. DeBerry scored, but Vance—seemingly in no hurry—got caught between third and the plate. Vance retreated to third, and Fewster slowed up between second and third so Vance wouldn't be forced to run home. Herman, meanwhile, was running with his head down—and he passed Fewster. With Herman joining Vance on third, Fewster sped up and soon there were three Dodgers at the bag. Herman was out for passing Fewster on the bases, and Fewster was out because Vance, as the lead runner who wasn't forced to advance home, had rights to third base.

KEN JOHNSON

Pitching for the Houston Colts against the Cincinnati Reds on April 23, 1964, he became the only man in major league history to lose a nine-inning, complete-game no-hitter.

Supporting Cast:

● **Joe Nuxhall.** He pitched a five-hitter in the Reds' 1-0 victory.

● **Pete Rose.** He reached second in the Reds' ninth when Johnson fielded his bunt attempt and threw wildly to first. Rose moved to third on a groundout and scored on second baseman Nellie Fox's error.

FRED LINDSTROM

The New York Giants' third baseman who watched a bad-hop grounder bounce over his head for the game-winning hit in the 12th inning of Game 7 of the 1924 World Series against the Washington Senators.

Supporting Cast:

● **Earl McNeely.** His ground ball bounded over Lindstrom, giving the Senators a 4-3 victory and the Series title.

● **Muddy Ruel.** Given life when Giants' catcher Hank Gowdy misplayed his pop foul in the 12th, Ruel then doubled and later scored on McNeely's single.

MARK LITTELL

The Kansas City Royals' relief pitcher who gave up Chris Chambliss' pennant-winning homer in 1976. In 60 regular-season games during the season, Littell had allowed only one home run—to Detroit's Pedro Garcia—in 104 innings. But in the ninth inning of Game 5 of the '76 American League Championship Series, Chambliss hit Littell's first pitch to give the New York Yankees a 7-6 victory and the A.L. pennant.

MARK LITTELL

Pitching for the St. Louis Cardinals against the Philadelphia Phillies on August 10, 1981, Littell surrendered Pete Rose's 3,631st career hit, a single, making Rose the National League's all-time hit leader.

ERNIE LOMBARDI

The Cincinnati Reds' catcher famous for his 1939 World Series "snooze." Amid the New York Yankees' Series-clinching, three-run outburst in the 10th inning of Game 4, Lombardi failed to hold right fielder Ival Goodman's throw to the plate when Yankee baserunner Charlie Keller crashed into the Reds' catcher. Lombardi fell down and the ball rolled away, enabling Joe DiMaggio (whose single had been misplayed by Goodman) to circle the bases as Lombardi lay stunned. New York won, 7-4, to sweep the Series.

Knocked out of the play seconds earlier by baserunner Charlie Keller, Cincinnati catcher Ernie Lombardi is sprawled on the ground as Joe DiMaggio of the Yankees scores in the 10th inning of Game 4 of the 1939 World Series.

Johnny Lewis (left) of the Mets rounds third base on June 14, 1965, after leading off the 11th inning with a home run against Cincinnati's Jim Maloney, who had pitched no-hit ball through 10 innings but ended up a 1-0 loser. Coach Don Heffner is about to congratulate Lewis, while Reds third baseman Deron Johnson looks the other way.

JIM MALONEY

The Cincinnati Reds' pitcher who had a no-hitter through 10 innings against the New York Mets on June 14, 1965, but ended up with a two-hitter—and a 1-0 loss in 11 innings.

Supporting Cast:

● **Larry Bearnarth.** Mets' reliever and winning pitcher who worked the last three innings after replacing starter Frank Lary.

● **Johnny Lewis.** He led off the Mets' 11th with a home run. Roy McMillan singled later in the inning.

TIM McCARVER

The Philadelphia Phillies' catcher who, playing against Pittsburgh in the first game of a July 4, 1976, doubleheader, hit a bases-loaded drive over the right-field wall—but was denied a grand slam on the United States' Bicentennial. After hitting his second-inning smash, McCarver passed teammate Garry Maddox on the basepaths and was declared out. Maddox had held up at first base, thinking the ball might be caught.

MICKEY McDERMOTT

The Boston Red Sox pitcher who gave up home runs to Bob Nieman of the St. Louis Browns in his first two big-league at-bats on September 14, 1951. Nieman is the only player ever to accomplish the feat.

FRED MERKLE

The New York Giants' first baseman whose 1908 baserunning boner might have cost his team a pennant. With the pennant-contending Chicago Cubs and Giants tied, 1-1, with two out in the bottom of the ninth inning of a September 23 game, Merkle failed to touch second base when a Giant teammate delivered an apparent game-winning hit. The Cubs retrieved the ball and touched second base, forcing Merkle and negating the run. New York fans, thinking their team had scored on the play, swarmed the field, which led to a halting of the tie game. The game was made up October 8—when other National League clubs had finished their seasons and the Cubs and Giants were tied for first place with 98-55 records—and Chicago prevailed, 4-2, to win the N.L. pennant.

Supporting Cast:

● **Al Bridwell.** With two out in the ninth and Moose McCormick on third base and Merkle on first for the Giants, Bridwell hit safely into center field. Merkle, after seeing McCormick cross the plate, headed for the clubhouse instead of touching second base. The alert Cubs then made the run-nullifying force play on Merkle (a play that also deprived Bridwell of a hit).

● **Johnny Evers.** Cubs' second baseman who tagged second, forcing out Merkle.

● **Hank O'Day.** The home-plate umpire who made the ruling on Merkle and, because of the fans' rush onto the field, called the game a 1-1 tie.

● **Jack Pfiester.** Cubs' pitcher when the Merkle incident occurred.

JOHN MILJUS

The only pitcher in World Series history to end a classic with a wild pitch. With the score tied, 3-3, in the ninth inning of Game 4 of the 1927 Series, Pittsburgh's Miljus threw a wild pitch while facing Tony Lazzeri of the New York Yankees with the bases loaded. Miljus' errant pitch scored Earle Combs, enabling the Yanks to beat the Pirates, 4-3, and win the Series in four straight games.

STAN MUSIAL

The focal point—and victim—of a June 30, 1959, play in which two baseballs were in use at the same time. In the fourth inning, a 3-1 pitch from Bob Anderson of the Chicago Cubs got past catcher Sammy Taylor and St. Louis' Musial—hearing umpire Vic Delmore's ball-four call—headed for first base. Certain that the ball had struck Musial's bat, Taylor and Anderson ignored the loose ball and began arguing with Delmore. Musial, seeing the ball at the screen, took off for second base. Cubs' third baseman Al Dark ran in to retrieve the ball, grabbing it from a batboy. Dark then made a low throw to second base, where shortstop Ernie Banks scooped up the ball. Meanwhile, Delmore "automatically" reached into his pocket and gave Taylor a new ball. Anderson, seeing Musial en route to second, grabbed the ball and threw wildly toward second (with the ball going into center field). Musial, aware of only the ball thrown into center, ran toward third but was tagged out by

A third strike on Tommy Henrich of the Yankees eludes Dodger catcher Mickey Owen with two out in the ninth inning of Game 4 of the 1941 World Series, setting the stage for a four-run inning and a 7-4 New York triumph.

Banks, who had the first ball. After considerable confusion and debate, the umpires ruled Musial out because he was tagged with the original ball in play.

MICKEY OWEN

The Brooklyn Dodgers' catcher whose passed ball cost his team a victory in the 1941 World Series. With two out and no Yankees on base and the Dodgers leading, 4-3, in the ninth inning of Game 4, a third strike on New York's Tommy Henrich got past Owen. The Dodgers, instead of wrapping up a victory that would have tied the Series at two games apiece, saw the Yankees break loose for four runs in the inning and win, 7-4. New York clinched the Series the next day.

Supporting Cast:

● **Hugh Casey.** Brooklyn relief pitcher whose strikeout of Henrich in the ninth inning was in vain.

● **Joe DiMaggio.** After Henrich reached base in the ninth, DiMaggio singled. Charlie Keller then doubled home Henrich and DiMaggio.

● **Joe Gordon.** With Keller on second base and Bill Dickey on first (with a walk) in the ninth. Gordon doubled home both runners to cap the four-run rally.

● **Johnny Murphy.** Yankees' reliever and winning pitcher who worked the final two innings.

BABE RUTH

The New York Yankee slugger whose ninth-inning basestealing attempt ended the 1926 World Series. With the Classic tied at three games apiece and the St. Louis Cardinals leading New York, 3-2, in Game 7 with two out in the Yankees' ninth, Ruth was thrown out attempting to steal second base after drawing his 11th walk of the Series.

Supporting Cast:

• **Bob Meusel.** Yankees' cleanup hitter who was at bat when Ruth was thrown out to end the Series.

• **Bob O'Farrell.** Cardinals' catcher whose throw to second baseman Rogers Hornsby caught Ruth in the ninth. Ruth, who stole second in Game 6, twice had 17 steals in a season during his career.

AL SMITH

Some misplays and misadventures are enough to leave a player crying in his beer. A fifth-inning home run by Charlie Neal of the Los Angeles Dodgers in Game 2 of the 1959 World Series is a good example. Al Smith, Chicago White Sox's left fielder, watched as Neal's drive sailed over the wall. A fan, also following the flight of the ball, accidentally knocked a cup of beer off the ledge of the wall, sending the brew splashing onto Smith's head. The Dodgers went on to win the game, 4-3—the first of three consecutive Los Angeles triumphs on the way to a four-games-to-two Series victory.

FRED SNODGRASS

The New York Giants' center fielder who made an error in the 10th inning of the eighth and final game of the 1912 World Series, helping the Boston Red Sox to victory. But Snodgrass wasn't alone when it came to misdeeds as the Red Sox overcame a New York run in the top of the 10th with two runs of their own in the bottom of the inning (Boston won the game, 3-2, and the Series, four games to three, with one tie).

Supporting Cast:

• **Clyde Engle.** After the Giants had broken a 1-1 tie on Fred Merkle's run-scoring single, Engle led off Boston's 10th by hitting a fly ball to center that Snodgrass dropped for a two-base error.

• **Tris Speaker.** After Snodgrass' misplay on the routine fly, an out (Snodgrass made a great catch on Harry Hooper's drive) and then a walk, Speaker lofted a pop foul between first baseman Merkle and catcher Chief Meyers. The foul dropped between the players and Speaker, given another life, singled home Engle with the tying run.

• **Steve Yerkes.** After walking and advancing to third on Speaker's hit, Yerkes scored the winning run for Boston on Larry Gardner's long fly.

TRACY STALLARD

The Boston Red Sox' pitcher who yielded Roger Maris' 61st home run of the 1961 season. Stallard allowed the Yankees only one run and five hits in

White Sox left fielder Al Smith received an unexpected shower during Game 2 of the 1959 World Series when a fan, intent on following the flight of a home run by the Dodgers' Charlie Neal, tipped a cup of beer onto his head.

Mickey Mantle displays the home-run ball he hit an estimated 565 feet on April 17, 1953. The battered ball had caromed off the side of the football scoreboard at Washington's Griffith Stadium and landed in the backyard across the street.

seven innings, giving up one walk and striking out five batters in the October 1 game in New York. Stallard got Maris to fly to left fielder Carl Yastrzemski in the first inning, was touched for the homer on a 2-0 pitch in the fourth and struck out Maris on a 3-2 pitch in the sixth. (In the eighth against reliever Chet Nichols, Maris popped to second baseman Chuck Schilling.) Maris' homer accounted for the only run of the game.

CHUCK STOBBS

The Washington Senators' pitcher who surrendered a home run in 1953 to New York's Mickey Mantle that traveled an estimated 565 feet (as figured by Yankees' publicist Red Patterson). Mantle's homer, hit April 17 at Griffith Stadium, came when the Yankees' switch-hitter was batting righthanded against lefthander Stobbs. The ball caromed off the side of the football scoreboard in left field (the scoreboard was 460 feet from the plate) and landed in the backyard across the street at 434 Oakdale St. Later in the game, Mantle reached base on a bunt single.

RALPH TERRY

The New York Yankees' pitcher who surrendered Bill Mazeroski's ninth-inning, World Series-deciding home run in 1960. Called on in relief in the eighth inning of Game 7 after Hal Smith hit a three-run homer that gave Pittsburgh a 9-7 lead, Terry ended the Pirates' five-run inning by getting Don Hoak to fly to left field. Terry wasn't as fortunate in the next inning, though. After the Yankees tied the score with two runs in the ninth, Terry gave up Mazeroski's leadoff smash on a 1-0 pitch, ending one of the strangest Series in history. The Pirates became world champions despite being outscored, 55-27, and outhit, 91-60. The Yankees scored 16-3, 10-0 and 12-0 victories, while Pittsburgh won 6-4, 3-2, 5-2 and 10-9.

LEON WAGNER

As a rookie outfielder for the San Francisco Giants, he was the victim of a ruse on July 1, 1958, at Chicago's Wrigley Field. Tony Taylor of the Chicago Cubs hit a smash to left field that bounced into the Cubs' bullpen, and Chicago players jumped up and peered intently under the bench. Wagner scrambled around, looking for the ball; actually, it lay 45 feet down the line in a rain gutter. By the time Wagner realized he had been duped, Taylor had circled the bases for an inside-the-park home run.

RUBE WALBERG

The New York Giants, Philadelphia Athletics and Boston Red Sox pitcher (1923 through 1937) who gave up more home runs (17) to Babe Ruth than any other hurler.

DAVE WICKERSHAM

Entering an October 1, 1964, game (his final start of the year), the Detroit pitcher had compiled a 19-12 record in what proved his only real shot at a

20-victory year. But Wickersham was victimized in his bid for No. 20 . . . by himself. With the Tigers and New York Yankees locked in a 1-1 game in the seventh inning, the Yanks' Phil Linz was called safe on a close play at first base as the tie-breaking run scored. Wickersham, trying to get umpire Bill Valentine's attention, put his hand on the umpire, which meant an automatic ejection. Detroit went on to win, 4-2, with Mickey Lolich getting the victory. Wickersham never won more than 12 games in any other season, finishing his big-league career with a 68-57 record.

HACK WILSON

The Cubs' center fielder who lost a seventh-inning drive in the sun in Game 4 of the 1929 World Series between Chicago and the Philadelphia Athletics. The misplay turned into a key three-run, inside-the-park home run as the A's, down 8-0 entering the inning, erupted for 10 runs and seized a three-games-to-one lead in the Series when it seemed certain the Cubs had deadlocked the classic. Philadelphia wrapped up the Series in five games.

Supporting Cast:

● **Sheriff Blake.** Cubs' losing pitcher who faced two batters in the seventh inning, giving up singles to Al Simmons and Jimmie Foxx.

● **Jimmie Dykes.** His two-run double off Pat Malone broke an 8-8 tie and capped the A's 10-run seventh.

● **Jimmie Foxx.** Foxx's single in the seventh scored Mickey Cochrane, tying the score, 8-8.

● **Mule Haas.** A's player whose smash was mishandled by Wilson and brought Philadelphia within 8-7.

● **Art Nehf.** Cubs' pitcher who was the victim of Haas' inside-the-park homer.

● **Eddie Rommel.** A's reliever and winning pitcher who worked the top of the seventh and allowed two hits, a walk and one run in his lone appearance of the Series.

● **Charlie Root.** Cubs' pitcher who took an 8-0 lead into the seventh. He retired only one batter in the inning and was charged with six runs.

● **Al Simmons.** He led off the A's seventh with a homer and singled later in the inning (eventually scoring the winning run).

TOM ZACHARY

While noted for having permitted Babe Ruth's 60th home run of the 1927 season, the pitcher has another link to Ruth. Only Zachary gave up home runs to Ruth in 1927 while pitching for two clubs, yielding No. 22 to the Yankees' Ruth on June 16 while a member of the St. Louis Browns and No. 60 on September 30 while with the Washington Senators.

HEINIE ZIMMERMAN

The New York Giants' third baseman who chased Eddie Collins of the Chicago White Sox across the plate on a rundown play in the fourth inning of Game 6 of the 1917 World Series. The play accounted for the first run in a

As Giants catcher Bill Rariden (left) checks the action elsewhere on the field in the fourth inning of Game 6 of the 1917 World Series, third baseman Heinie Zimmerman chases Eddie Collins of the White Sox across the plate during a rundown play.

three-run inning that sparked the White Sox to a 4-2 triumph and the Series title (four games to two).

Supporting Cast:

● **Happy Felsch.** With Collins and Joe Jackson on third and first base (after errors by Zimmerman and right fielder Dave Robertson) in a 0-0 game in the fourth inning, Chicago's Felsch grounded to pitcher Rube Benton. Seeing Collins break from third, Benton threw to Zimmerman. Zimmerman ran Collins toward the plate, but Collins darted past catcher Bill Rariden to make it a Zimmerman-Collins race to home. Collins won, helped on the play because Rariden, Benton and first baseman Walter Holke left the plate unattended.

● **Chick Gandil.** His two-run single followed the rundown play, giving White Sox pitcher Red Faber all the runs he needed.

A young Hank Aaron gets a lift from his teammates after hitting an 11th-inning home run that defeated the second-place Cardinals and clinched the 1957 pennant for the Milwaukee Braves.

FOURTH INNING:

Other offensive and defensive feats; "only" achievements.

HANK AARON

His two-run, 11th-inning home run off Billy Muffett of the second-place St. Louis Cardinals on September 23, 1957, clinched the National League pennant for the Milwaukee Braves. The Braves' 4-2 triumph gave Milwaukee a six-game lead over the Cards with five games left for both clubs.

BABE ADAMS

The only rookie pitcher to win three games in a World Series. Adams hurled three complete-game victories for Pittsburgh in the 1909 Series, defeating the Detroit Tigers 4-1, 8-4 and 8-0 as the Pirates won the classic in seven games. Adams had compiled a 12-3 record in 1909, his first full season in the majors, after appearing in one game for the St. Louis Cardinals in 1906 and four games for the Pirates in 1907.

JOE ADCOCK

The first of three men (excluding exhibition-game players) to reach the distant center-field bleachers at New York's Polo Grounds with a home-run

The flight of Milwaukee first baseman Joe Adcock's long Polo Grounds homer, an estimated 475-foot shot into the center-field bleachers in 1953, is diagrammed above.

drive after the bleachers were remodeled (and the distance to the fence lengthened) in 1923. Adcock, playing for the Milwaukee Braves, hit a homer off the New York Giants' Jim Hearn on April 29, 1953, that carried an estimated 475 feet.

Lou Brock of the Chicago Cubs and Hank Aaron of the Braves became the second and third players to reach the bleachers—and they did it on consecutive days. Brock connected against Al Jackson of the New York Mets on June 17, 1962, and Aaron hit his shot off Jay Hook of the Mets on June 18, 1962.

JESSE BARNES

Winning pitcher in the fastest nine-inning game in big-league history. Pitching for the New York Giants against the Philadelphia Phillies in the first game of a September 28, 1919, doubleheader, Barnes beat the Phils, 6-1, in a 51-minute game.

JULIO BECQUER

Washington's leading base stealer in 1957 when the Senators established a major league club record for fewest steals, 13, in a season. Becquer had three steals.

JOHNNY BENCH

The only player in major league history with at least three career home runs in the All-Star Game, League Championship Series and World Series. Through 1982, Bench (who came up with the Cincinnati Reds in 1967) had three homers in All-Star competition, five in Championship Series play and five in the World Series.

YOGI BERRA

The only player to hit a bases-loaded home run in a World Series game that his team lost. Berra's second-inning grand slam in Game 2 of the 1956 Series staked the New York Yankees to a 6-0 lead over Brooklyn, but the Dodgers rebounded for a 13-8 victory.

VIDA BLUE

Only pitcher in modern major league history to strike out 300 or more batters in a season without leading the league. Pitching for the Oakland A's, Blue struck out 301 American League hitters in 1971—but Detroit's Mickey Lolich fanned 308.

VIDA BLUE

The only American League pitcher to win an All-Star Game in the 20-year span from 1963 through 1982. Blue, representing the Oakland A's, was the starting and winning pitcher in the 1971 classic at Tiger Stadium in Detroit as the A.L. won, 6-4. Blue got the victory despite yielding three runs—all earned—in three innings of work.

Blue also is the only major league pitcher to win an All-Star Game for each league. Blue, representing San Francisco, pitched a scoreless seventh inning in the 1981 classic in Cleveland's Municipal Stadium and received credit for the win when the Nationals rallied for two eighth-inning runs and a 5-4 victory.

No other pitcher has ever earned a decision for both the A.L. and N.L.

DAVE BOSWELL, DEAN CHANCE, JIM KAAT

Pitching for the Minnesota Twins in 1967, each recorded 200 or more strikeouts—the first time a major league team had three pitchers attain that figure in the same season. Chance struck out 220 batters, Kaat fanned 211 and Boswell was at 204.

Only one other big league threesome has reached the 200 strikeouts-per-man milestone. Pitching for the Houston Astros in 1969, Don Wilson had 235 strikeouts, Larry Dierker 232 and Tom Griffin 200.

LOU BOUDREAU

The only modern major leaguer to manage a team the entire year during which he won a batting championship. Boudreau, who managed the Cleveland Indians to a fifth-place tie with the Philadelphia Athletics in 1944, posted an American League-leading .327 batting average that season.

Rogers Hornsby led the National League in hitting with .403 and .387 averages in 1925 and 1928, years in which he replaced Branch Rickey and Jack Slattery as manager of the St. Louis Cardinals and Boston Braves, respectively. Hornsby managed the Cardinals for 115 games in 1925 and guided the Braves for 122 games in 1928.

CLETE, KEN BOYER

The only brothers to hit home runs in the same World Series—and they did it in the same game. Ken, St. Louis Cardinals' third baseman, homered against the New York Yankees in the seventh inning of Game 7 of the 1964 Series; Clete, New York third baseman, homered in the ninth inning. Ken also hit a grand slam in Game 4.

LOU BROCK

One of only three players to collect 3,000 or more hits and not attain a lifetime batting average of .300. Brock, who came up to the majors at the end of the 1961 season and played through 1979, had 3,023 hits for the Chicago Cubs and St. Louis Cardinals and a career average of .293.

Al Kaline (Detroit, 1953-74) had 3,007 hits and a .297 average, while Boston's Carl Yastrzemski (who came up with the Red Sox in 1961) had 3,318 hits and a .286 mark through 1982.

When St. Louis' Lou Brock got his 3,000th hit on August 13, 1979, Hall of Famer Stan Musial, a former Cardinal and also a member of the elite club, was there to present the ball.

LLOYD BROWN

The only pitcher to surrender two of Lou Gehrig's major league-record 23 career grand slams. Brown gave up bases-loaded home runs to the New York Yankees' slugger while pitching for the Washington Senators on August 31, 1931, and for the Cleveland Indians on May 13, 1934.

JOHN BUZHARDT

The Philadelphia pitcher who beat the Milwaukee Braves, 7-4, in the second game of an August 20, 1961, doubleheader, ending the Phillies' 23-game losing streak (a modern major league record). Buzhardt also was the last Philadelphia pitcher to win before the streak, defeating the San Francisco Giants, 4-3, in the second game of a July 28, 1961, doubleheader.

LEON CADORE, JOE OESCHGER

Pitchers who went the distance on May 1, 1920, when Brooklyn and Boston played to a 26-inning, 1-1 tie in a game called because of darkness. En route to sharing the major league record for most innings pitched in one game, Brooklyn's Cadore and Boston's Oeschger matched zeroes over the last 20 innings. Cadore gave up 15 hits overall, walking five and striking out eight; Oeschger yielded only nine hits, walking three and fanning four.

JOHNNY CALLISON

Philadelphia Phillies' right fielder whose three-run homer off Dick Radatz of the Boston Red Sox in the ninth inning of the 1964 All-Star Game enabled the National League to defeat the American League, 7-4, at New York's Shea Stadium.

HAL CHASE

The only lefthanded-throwing, righthanded-hitting player to win a major league batting title. Playing for the Cincinnati Reds in 1916, Chase hit a National League-leading .339.

TOM CHENEY

Washington Senators' pitcher who on September 12, 1962, established a big-league strikeout record by fanning 21 batters in a 16-inning game. Cheney, who beat the Baltimore Orioles, 2-1, on a homer by Bud Zipfel (the last of 10 that Zipfel hit in the majors), had 12 strikeouts after nine innings. Only one Baltimore starter, left fielder Boog Powell, did not strike out in the game.

CHUCK CHURN

Working in relief of Sandy Koufax, Churn was the winning pitcher on September 11, 1959, when Los Angeles handed Pittsburgh reliever Roy Face his only loss in an 18-1 season. The Dodgers beat the Pirates, 5-4.

A big reception of National Leaguers was there to greet Philadelphia's Johnny Callison after his three-run, ninth-inning home run broke up the 1964
All-Star Game at New York's Shea Stadium.

TONY CLONINGER

The only player in National League history to hit two bases-loaded home
runs in one game—and he was a pitcher. In a July 3, 1966, game in San
Francisco, Atlanta's Cloninger hit first- and fourth-inning grand slams off
the Giants' Bob Priddy and Ray Sadecki and added a run-scoring single in
the eighth. Cloninger's nine runs batted in and seven-hit pitching led the
Braves to a 17-3 triumph.

MICKEY COCHRANE, FRANKIE FRISCH

The managers in the last World Series in which both clubs had their field
leaders in the lineup. Frisch, St. Louis Cardinals' manager and second baseman in the 1934 Series, batted .194 against Detroit in the classic (which the
Cards won in seven games). Cochrane, Tigers' manager and catcher, hit
.214.

DICK COFFMAN

Pitching for the St. Louis Browns on August 23, 1931, he ended Lefty Grove's
winning streak at 16 games (which had tied the American League record
for one season) by shutting out the Philadelphia Athletics, 1-0. Coffman
pitched a three-hitter as Grove's record went to 25-3 (the A's pitcher finished at 31-4).

EDDIE COLLINS

Despite getting 3,309 hits in a major league career that started in 1906 and ended in 1930, Collins (who played for the Philadelphia Athletics and Chicago White Sox) failed to win a batting championship in the majors. Collins' lifetime average was .333.

Lou Brock is the only other big leaguer to amass 3,000 hits and not capture a hitting title. Brock, a .293 career hitter with the Chicago Cubs and St. Louis Cardinals, totaled 3,023 hits from 1961 through 1979.

MORT COOPER

The only pitcher in major league history to lose two straight All-Star Games. Representing the St. Louis Cardinals, Cooper started the 1942 and 1943 games for the National League and was the loser in 3-1 and 5-3 decisions.

GAVVY CRAVATH

The major leagues' modern career home run king until displaced by Babe Ruth. Cravath, whose 11-season big-league career took him to Boston, Chicago and Washington in the American League and Philadelphia in the National and ended in 1920, had 119 lifetime homers (with a high of 24 in 1915). While playing for the Phillies, Cravath won five N.L. homer championships outright and shared another title.

Ruth, playing for the New York Yankees, hit his 120th career homer on June 10, 1921, connecting off Cleveland's Jim Bagby Sr.

BABE DAHLGREN

The player who moved into the New York Yankees' lineup at first base on May 2, 1939, in Detroit, ending Lou Gehrig's consecutive-game streak at 2,130. Gehrig played the last game of his streak—and of his career—on April 30, 1939. (The Yankees were not scheduled on May 1, 1939.)

ALVIN DARK

Only man to manage both the American League and National League in the All-Star Game. Dark managed the N.L. All-Stars to a 5-3 victory in the 1963 game at Cleveland's Municipal Stadium and directed the A.L. squad in 1975 when the Nationals scored a 6-3 triumph at Milwaukee's County Stadium.

DIZZY DEAN

With the National League pennant race having gone down to the final day of the 1934 season, Dean proceeded to win his 30th game of the year for the St. Louis Cardinals by defeating the Cincinnati Reds, 9-0, at Sportsman's Park. The Cardinals entered the last day one game ahead of the second-place New York Giants, who played Brooklyn in their season finale. While having little trouble overall with the Reds, Dean nevertheless got into a no-out, bases-loaded jam in the ninth inning. Word came that the Dodgers had beaten the Giants, 8-5, in 10 innings, ensuring the pennant for St. Louis.

The brothers Dean, Paul (left) and Dizzy, are pictured in a 1934 photo as members of the St. Louis Cardinals.

Dean then finished with a flourish, striking out Clyde Manion and Ted Petoskey and getting Sparky Adams to foul out.

DIZZY, PAUL DEAN

The pitching brothers who established the major league record for fewest total hits, three, allowed by one team in a doubleheader. Pitching for the St. Louis Cardinals in the opening game of a September 21, 1934, twin bill, Dizzy Dean hurled a three-hitter as the Cards walloped Brooklyn, 13-0. In the nightcap, Paul Dean tossed a no-hitter as St. Louis beat the Dodgers, 3-0.

The Deans' record was tied on May 27, 1945, when Dave (Boo) Ferriss and Emmett O'Neill pitched one-hit and two-hit games, respectively, for the Boston Red Sox in a doubleheader against the Chicago White Sox.

In the two other doubleheaders in which one team allowed only three hits, the record-tying performances involved more than two pitchers. On June 21, 1964, Jim Bunning of the Philadelphia Phillies threw a perfect game against the New York Mets, then Rick Wise (notching his first big-league victory) and Johnny Klippstein combined on a three-hitter. On June 8, 1969, Cleveland's Sam McDowell pitched a two-hitter against California before four Indian pitchers (Mike Paul, Gary Kroll, Jack Hamilton and Stan Williams) combined for a one-hitter—in a 3-2 loss to the Angels.

BUCKY DENT

New York shortstop whose three-run, seventh-inning homer off Boston's Mike Torrez overcame a 2-0 deficit and sparked the Yankees to a 5-4 triumph over the Red Sox in the one-game playoff for the 1978 American League East Division championship.

DOM, JOE DiMAGGIO

The only brothers with major league batting streaks of 30 or more games. Joe, playing for the New York Yankees, had his record 56-game streak in 1941. Dom, as a member of the Boston Red Sox, hit in 34 straight games in 1949.

JOE, VINCE DiMAGGIO

The only brothers in big-league history to hit homers in the All-Star Game. Joe, of the New York Yankees, hit one for the American League in 1939, while Vince, representing the Pittsburgh Pirates, hit his for the National League in 1943.

JIGGS DONAHUE

Chicago White Sox's first baseman who singled in the seventh inning for the only hit off Ed Reulbach of the Chicago Cubs in Game 2 of the 1906 World Series. Reulbach and the Cubs prevailed, 7-1.

WILD BILL DONOVAN

First of only two pitchers who have lost final World Series games in consecutive years. Pitching for the Detroit Tigers, Donovan lost the 1908 finale to the Chicago Cubs and the last game in 1909 to the Pittsburgh Pirates.

Christy Mathewson of the New York Giants was the losing pitcher in the decisive games of the 1912 and 1913 Series against the Boston Red Sox and Philadelphia Athletics.

DON DRYSDALE

The only pitcher to start two All-Star Games in one season (from 1959 through 1962, the major leagues had two All-Star Games per year). Drysdale, Los Angeles Dodgers' hurler, had no decision in the National League's 5-4 first-game victory in 1959 at Forbes Field in Pittsburgh but was the loser in the American League's 5-3 second-game triumph in '59 at the Los Angeles Memorial Coliseum.

HOWARD EHMKE

Having pitched only 55 innings during the regular season, the 35-year-old Ehmke was a surprise starter in Game 1 of the 1929 World Series for the Philadelphia Athletics. Connie Mack had six pitchers on his staff with 11 or more victories—including 24-game winner George Earnshaw and 20-game winner Lefty Grove—but the A's manager opted for Ehmke, who had posted a 7-2 record, in the opener. Ehmke struck out a then-Series record of 13 Chicago Cubs as the A's won, 3-1. He allowed eight hits, yielding the Cubs' lone run in the ninth inning.

KID ELBERFELD

The New York Highlanders' player who on August 1, 1903, collected all of his team's hits when Rube Waddell of the Philadelphia Athletics pitched a four-hitter. Sparked by Elberfeld's four singles, the Highlanders beat the A's, 3-2.

Billy Williams is the only other player in major league history to get all of his club's hits when the opposing pitcher allowed as many as four hits. Steve Blass of the Pittsburgh Pirates pitched a four-hit, 9-2 triumph over Chicago on September 5, 1969, and the Cubs' Williams hit two home runs and two doubles. Blass had four hits himself, including a homer.

DOCK ELLIS

The only National League pitcher to lose an All-Star Game in the 20-year period from 1963 through 1982. Ellis, representing the Pittsburgh Pirates, was the N.L.'s starter and loser at Detroit's Tiger Stadium in 1971 as the American League won, 6-4. Ellis, who gave up four runs in three innings, permitted two-run homers to Reggie Jackson and Frank Robinson in the third inning.

CHUCK ESSEGIAN

One of two players to slug two pinch-hit homers in a World Series. Batting for Los Angeles pitcher Johnny Podres in the seventh inning of Game 2 of the 1959 World Series, Essegian homered with the bases empty against Bob Shaw of the Chicago White Sox. In the ninth inning of Game 6, Essegian batted for Dodgers' right fielder Duke Snider and hit a bases-empty homer off Ray Moore.

Bernie Carbo of the Boston Red Sox, batting for pitcher Reggie Cleveland, hit a solo homer off Cincinnati's Clay Carroll in the seventh inning of Game 3 of the 1975 World Series. Pinch-hitting for pitcher Roger Moret in the eighth inning of Game 6, Carbo slammed a three-run homer off the Reds' Rawly Eastwick that tied the score, 6-6 (Boston went on to win, 7-6, in 12 innings).

BOB, KEN FORSCH

The only brothers to pitch big-league no-hitters. Bob pitched a no-hitter for the St. Louis Cardinals on April 16, 1978, beating the Philadelphia Phillies, 5-0; Ken threw a no-hitter for the Houston Astros in 1979, stopping the Atlanta Braves, 6-0.

Ken's gem, which came in the Astros' second game of the '79 season, was the earliest calendar-date (April 7) no-hitter in major league history.

DICK FOWLER

The only pitcher in modern big-league history to record a no-hitter for his only victory of the season. Fowler, who went 1-2 in 1945, held the St. Louis

Philadelphia A's pitcher Dick Fowler's only win of the 1945 season was a memorable one while Hal Griggs (right), a journeyman pitcher for Washington, had his memorable moment in 1957.

Browns hitless on September 9 as the Philadelphia Athletics notched a 1-0 triumph.

JIMMIE FOXX

Lone major leaguer to have hit 50 or more home runs in a season for two teams. Foxx slugged 58 homers for the Philadelphia Athletics in 1932 and 50 for the Boston Red Sox in 1938.

Willie Mays hit 51 homers for New York in 1955 and 52 for San Francisco in 1965, but it was for the same franchise, the Giants.

FRED FRANKHOUSE

Brooklyn Dodgers' pitcher who defeated Carl Hubbell and the New York Giants, 10-3, in the first game of a May 31, 1937, doubleheader, ending Hubbell's major league-record 24-game winning streak (over two seasons) by a pitcher.

Bill Lee of the Chicago Cubs had dealt Hubbell his last previous loss, stopping the Giants, 1-0, on July 13, 1936.

MILT GASTON

One of two American League pitchers who gave up as many as four home runs to Babe Ruth of the New York Yankees during Ruth's 60-homer season of 1927. Pitching for the St. Louis Browns, Gaston yielded Ruth's seventh, 32nd, 33rd and 50th homers of the year.

Rube Walberg, Philadelphia A's pitcher, surrendered Ruth's second, sixth, 14th and 44th homers of 1927.

FLOYD GIEBELL

He won only three games in the major leagues, but one of them clinched the American League pennant for the Detroit Tigers in 1940. Leading second-place Cleveland by two games entering a season-ending, three-game series against the Indians, Detroit decided to use Giebell—up from Buffalo—opposite Bob Feller in the first-game pitching matchup. Tigers' Manager Del Baker, figuring Feller (a 27-game winner) would be tough, thought it would be wise to hold out his aces—headed by Schoolboy Rowe—for use later in the series. Giebell, a 30-year-old who had beaten the Philadelphia A's eight days earlier after going 15-17 in the International League, outdueled Feller by pitching a six-hitter in a 2-0 triumph at Municipal Stadium on September 27. Feller permitted only three hits, but one was a two-run homer to Rudy York. Giebell's victory not only wrapped up the A.L. flag for Detroit—it was his last triumph in the majors.

LEFTY GOMEZ

The American League's starting pitcher in five of the first six All-Star Games. Gomez, of the New York Yankees, compiled a 3-1 All-Star record from 1933 through 1938 (failing to get a decision in 1934 and not appearing in 1936).

Another Lefty—Boston's Grove—started (and lost) for the A.L. in '36.

HANK GREENBERG

Detroit left fielder whose ninth-inning, bases-loaded home run in the opening game of a scheduled season-ending doubleheader at St. Louis clinched the 1945 American League pennant for the Tigers. Greenberg's homer off Nelson Potter overcame a 3-2 deficit, giving Detroit a 6-3 triumph over the Browns. The Tigers started the day with an 87-65 record and a one-game lead over Washington (87-67 and finished with its schedule). The second game was rained out after Detroit batted in the first inning.

HAL GRIGGS

Washington Senators' pitcher who had a cumulative 6-26 record in the big leagues, but who stopped Ted Williams' reaching-base streak in 1957. Boston's Williams, having reached first base in his previous 16 trips to the plate (a major league record), grounded out against Griggs on September 24.

RON HANSEN

Only man to play in the last games of both the original and second Washington franchises in the American League. Hansen played shortstop for the Baltimore Orioles on October 2, 1960, at Washington in the original Senators' last game before their relocation in Minnesota, and he was at third base for the visiting New York Yankees on September 30, 1971, when the second Senators played their last game before moving to Texas.

Sandy Koufax (above) mugs for the camera after pitching a perfect game against the Chicago Cubs on September 9, 1965. The four balls with zeroes signify the four career no-hitters Koufax compiled. Lou Johnson (right) was Dodger hero No. 2, collecting the only hit of the 1965 game and scoring the only run after drawing a walk.

CARROLL HARDY

A .225 hitter in 433 big-league games, Hardy pinch-hit for Roger Maris and Ted Williams during his career. As a rookie in 1958, Hardy pinch-hit for Maris (then a second-year player) and hit a three-run homer off Billy Pierce in the 11th inning, giving the Cleveland Indians a 7-4 victory over the Chicago White Sox on May 18. On September 20, 1960, Hardy pinch-hit for Williams, who was unable to complete a first-inning at-bat after fouling a ball off his ankle, and lined into a double play against Baltimore's Hector (Skinny) Brown.

BOB HENDLEY

The losing pitcher in the only nine-inning complete game in major league history in which there was only one hit. Pitching for the Chicago Cubs at Los Angeles on September 9, 1965, Hendley allowed only a looping, opposite-field double by Lou Johnson in the seventh inning . . . but the Dodgers' Sandy Koufax pitched a perfect game as Los Angeles won, 1-0. The Dodgers scored in the fifth inning, getting an unearned run when Johnson walked, moved to second on a sacrifice, stole third and continued home on catcher Chris Krug's high throw.

ROGERS HORNSBY

The lone player to bat .400 and slug 40 home runs in the same season. Hornsby hit .401 with 42 homers for the 1922 St. Louis Cardinals.

ROGERS HORNSBY, TED WILLIAMS

The only two-time winners of major league baseball's Triple Crown. Hornsby won the Triple Crown for the St. Louis Cardinals in 1922 (.401 average, 42 home runs and 152 runs batted in) and again in 1925 (.403, 39 homers and 143 RBIs). Williams captured the honor for the Boston Red Sox in 1942 (.356, 36 homers and 137 RBIs) and again in 1947 (.343, 32 homers and 114 RBIs).

RALPH HOUK

The only man to have World Series champions in his first two seasons as a major league manager. Houk led the 1961 and 1962 New York Yankees to Series triumphs over the Cincinnati Reds and San Francisco Giants.

REX HUDSON

The only man who pitched in just one major league game and surrendered a home run to Hank Aaron. Pitching against the Atlanta Braves on July 27, 1974, the Los Angeles Dodgers' Hudson gave up Aaron's 726th lifetime homer.

HANK HULVEY

The only man who pitched in just one big-league game and gave up a home run to Babe Ruth. Pitching against the New York Yankees on September 5,

Larry Jaster, an 11-5 pitcher for the Cardinals in 1966, gets a handshake from Dick Hughes after shutting out the Los Angeles Dodgers for the fifth time in the '66 season.

1923, the Philadelphia Athletics' Hulvey permitted Ruth's 230th career homer.

JOE JACKSON

One of two players to hit .400 in a modern major league season without winning a batting championship that year. Cleveland's Jackson batted .408 in 1911, but Detroit's Ty Cobb had an American League-leading mark of .420.

Cobb compiled a .401 average for the Tigers in 1922, but George Sisler of the St. Louis Browns led the A.L. with .420.

LARRY JASTER

St. Louis Cardinals' pitcher who faced the National League champion Los Angeles Dodgers five times in 1966—and shut them out all five times, allowing only 24 hits (all singles) in 45 innings. Between the first and second shutouts, Jaster was optioned to Tulsa for six weeks. He finished the '66 season with an 11-5 record and 3.26 earned-run average for the Cardinals.

JULIAN JAVIER

St. Louis Cardinals' second baseman whose two-out double in the eighth inning of Game 2 of the 1967 World Series was the only hit off Boston's Jim Lonborg. The Red Sox won, 5-0.

WALTER JOHNSON

One of two pitchers in big-league history with 300 or more career victories and 3,000 or more strikeouts. Johnson, who pitched for the Washington Senators from 1907 through 1927, won 416 games and struck out 3,508 batters.

Gaylord Perry, who made his major league debut in 1962, had 307 victories and 3,452 strikeouts through 1982.

AL KALINE

The only major leaguer to hit 300 career home runs and not have 30 or more in one year. Kaline, who played for the Detroit Tigers from 1953 through 1974 and hit 399 homers, had a season high of 29 homers (achieved in both 1962 and 1966).

WILLIE KEELER

The only player to collect 200 or more singles in one season. Keeler singled 202 times for Baltimore of the National League in 1898.

DICKIE KERR

Chicago White Sox's pitcher who stood out in the 1919 World Series despite the fact eight of his teammates were later implicated in the Series-fixing "Black Sox" scandal. Kerr pitched a three-hit, 3-0 triumph over Cincinnati in Game 3 and went the distance in a 10-inning, 5-4 victory over the Reds in Game 6. Along with a 2-0 Series record, Kerr had a 1.42 earned-run average for his 19 innings of work.

HARMON KILLEBREW

One of only two players to hit 40 or more home runs while batting less than .250 in the same season—and he did it twice. Killebrew, playing for the Washington Senators in 1959, had 42 homers and a .242 average. In 1962, Killebrew hit 48 homers and batted .243 for the Minnesota Twins.

Gorman Thomas of the Milwaukee Brewers walloped 45 homers while batting only .244 in 1979.

RALPH KINER

The only player to hit All-Star Game home runs in three consecutive years. Representing the Pittsburgh Pirates, Kiner hit homers for the National League in 1949, 1950 and 1951.

RALPH KINER, JOHNNY MIZE

Major league baseball's only instance where the same two players shared a home-run championship twice. The Pittsburgh Pirates' Kiner and the New York Giants' Mize tied for the National League homer titles in 1947 and 1948 with totals of 51 and 40.

DENNIS KINNEY

The lone pitcher in major league history to give up two pinch-hit, bases-loaded home runs in one season. Pitching for the American League's Cleveland Indians on May 6, 1978, Kinney yielded a pinch grand slam to Merv Rettenmund of the California Angels; on June 27, 1978, while a member of the National League's San Diego Padres, Kinney permitted a pinch grand slam to Jack Clark of the San Francisco Giants.

Hank Borowy is the only other pitcher to yield pinch grand slams in both leagues—but his misfortunes were more than three years apart. Pitching for the New York Yankees on July 15, 1945, Borowy gave up a pinch grand slam to Zeb Eaton of the A.L.'s Detroit Tigers; on September 11, 1948, while a member of the N.L.'s Chicago Cubs, Borowy surrendered a pinch grand slam to Ralph Kiner of the Pittsburgh Pirates.

CHUCK KLEIN

Playing for the Philadelphia Phillies in 1932, Klein shared the National League homer lead and topped the N.L. in stolen bases. Klein hit 38 homers, tying Mel Ott of the New York Giants, and had 20 steals.

Ty Cobb of the Detroit Tigers is the only other major leaguer to lead his league in homers and stolen bases in the same season. Cobb had American League-leading figures of nine home runs and 76 steals in 1909.

CHUCK KLEIN

His 1930 hit total of 250 ranks as the highest non-leading figure in major league history. Klein, of the Philadelphia Phillies, was second in the National League in 1930 to the New York Giants' Bill Terry, who had an N.L. record-tying 254 hits.

DAROLD KNOWLES

The only man to pitch in every game of a seven-game World Series. Knowles, Oakland A's relief ace, accomplished the feat in 1973.

Relievers Dan Quisenberry of Kansas City and Mike Marshall of Los Angeles are the only other pitchers to appear in every game of a World Series, with the Royals' Quisenberry pitching in all six games in 1980 and the Dodgers' Marshall pitching in all five games in 1974.

RON LeFLORE

The only player in major league history to lead the National and American

A's pitcher Darold Knowles, shown receiving congratulations from Manager Dick Williams after finishing the opener of the 1973 World Series, was just getting started. Knowles pitched in all seven games of the '73 classic.

leagues in stolen bases. LeFlore topped the American League with 68 steals while playing for the Detroit Tigers in 1978, and headed the National League with 97 steals while playing for the Montreal Expos in 1980.

DALE LONG

Pittsburgh Pirates' first baseman who hit home runs in a record eight straight games in 1956. Long homered May 19, May 20 (both ends of a doubleheader), May 22, May 23, May 25, May 26 and May 28, connecting off Jim Davis of the Chicago Cubs, Ray Crone and Warren Spahn of the Milwaukee Braves, Herman Wehmeier and Lindy McDaniel of the St. Louis Cardinals, Curt Simmons and Ben Flowers of the Philadelphia Phillies and Carl Erskine of the Brooklyn Dodgers.

Don Newcombe of the Dodgers stopped Long's homer streak on May 29, 1956, holding Long hitless in four at-bats.

HECTOR MAESTRI

One of only three players to play for the American League's original Washington Senators franchise in its last season, 1960, and the expansion Senators franchise in its first season, 1961. Maestri, a pitcher, appeared in only two major league games in his career—one with each Washington franchise.

Rudy Hernandez and Hal Woodeshick, both pitchers, also played for both the '60 and '61 Senators.

MICKEY MANTLE

One of two major leaguers to hit 50 or more home runs in a season and fail to lead the league in that category. Mantle slammed 54 homers for the New York Yankees in 1961, but teammate Roger Maris captured American League honors with his record-setting 61.

Jimmie Foxx of the Boston Red Sox hit 50 in 1938, but finished second in the A.L. to Detroit's Hank Greenberg, who hit 58.

ROGER MARIS

The only major leaguer to bat less than .300 and hit 50 or more home runs in the same season. Maris batted .269 in 1961 when he slugged 61 homers for the New York Yankees.

JIM MASON

The only player to hit a home run in his only World Series at-bat. Playing shortstop for the New York Yankees in Game 3 of the 1976 World Series, Mason homered off Pat Zachry of the Cincinnati Reds in the seventh inning.

CHRISTY MATHEWSON

Pitching for the New York Giants, he shut out the Philadelphia Athletics three times in a six-day span during the 1905 World Series. Mathewson gave up four, four and six hits, struck out 18 batters and walked only one in winning 3-0, 9-0 and 2-0.

The Giants' other victory in their four-games-to-one triumph also was a shutout, with Iron Man Joe McGinnity winning Game 4, 1-0. The A's lone victory was a shutout, too, as Chief Bender won Game 2, 3-0.

Waite Hoyt of the New York Yankees is the only other man to pitch three complete games in a World Series without allowing an earned run, giving up two unearned runs in the 1921 classic. Hoyt beat the Giants, 3-0, in Game 2 and was a 3-1 victor in Game 5 before losing, 1-0, in Game 8.

WILLIE MAYS

The only player to collect three hits in each of two All-Star Games played in the same year. San Francisco's Mays went 3-for-4 for the National League in both the July 11, 1960, All-Star Game at Municipal Stadium in Kansas City, and the July 13, 1960, classic at Yankee Stadium.

Nellie Fox is the only other player to get two or more hits in each of two All-Star Games played in the same season. Fox, of the Chicago White Sox, singled twice in both of the 1959 classics.

JOE McGINNITY

Pitcher who in 1903 proved "Iron Man" was an apt nickname, setting a modern National League record of 434 innings pitched in one season and

Baltimore pitcher Dave McNally gets a big greeting after connecting for his grand slam in Game 3 of the 1970 World Series against Cincinnati.

hurling three complete doubleheaders. McGinnity was 6-0 in the twin bills as the New York Giants defeated Boston, 4-1 and 5-2 (on August 1); Brooklyn, 6-1 and 4-3 (on August 8), and Philadelphia, 4-1 and 9-2 (on August 31).

Pitching for Baltimore of the American League in 1901, McGinnity completed doubleheaders against Milwaukee on September 3 (winning, 10-0, and losing, 6-1) and Philadelphia on September 12 (winning, 4-3, and losing, 5-4).

McGinnity's feat of pitching two complete games in one day five times is unequaled.

BILL McKECHNIE

The only man to manage three different franchises in the World Series. McKechnie managed the Pittsburgh Pirates in the 1925 Series, the St. Louis Cardinals in the 1928 classic and the Cincinnati Reds in 1939 and 1940. The '25 Pirates and '40 Reds were world champions.

DAVE McNALLY

The only pitcher to hit a bases-loaded home run in the World Series. Baltimore's McNally walloped his grand slam against Cincinnati's Wayne Granger in the sixth inning of Game 3 of the 1970 Series, helping the Orioles to a 9-3 victory on the way to a four-games-to-one Series triumph.

MINNIE MINOSO

Nine months past his 53rd birthday, Minoso became the oldest batter to get a hit in a major league game. Minoso, the Chicago White Sox's starting designated hitter in the first game of a September 12, 1976, doubleheader against the California Angels, singled in his first at-bat off Sid Monge. It was Minoso's only hit in eight at-bats that year.

Nick Altrock had just turned 53 when he collected a hit for the Washington Senators in 1929.

JOHNNY MIZE

The lone player in major league history to hit 50 home runs while striking out fewer than 50 times in the same season. Playing for the New York Giants in 1947, Mize walloped 51 homers and struck out only 42 times.

STAN MUSIAL

St. Louis Cardinals' left fielder whose first-pitch home run in the 12th inning off Frank Sullivan of the Boston Red Sox lifted the National League to a 6-5 triumph over the American League in the 1955 All-Star Game at Milwaukee's County Stadium.

STAN MUSIAL

The only player to hit 400 or more home runs in the major leagues without slugging 40 or more in one season. Musial, who hit 475 homers for the St. Louis Cardinals in a big-league career that started in 1941 and ended in 1963, had a season high of 39 in 1948.

ERNIE NEVERS

Pro Football Hall of Famer who gave up two of Babe Ruth's 60 home runs in 1927. Pitching for the St. Louis Browns, Nevers surrendered Ruth's eighth homer of the year on May 11 and the Yankee slugger's 41st of the season on August 27.

BOBO NEWSOM

One of two pitchers in major league history with more than 200 victories and a sub-.500 winning percentage. Newsom, whose big-league career started in 1929 and ended in 1953, won 211 games and lost 222 (.487).

Jack Powell, who pitched in the majors from 1897 to 1912, compiled a 247-254 record (.493).

SATCHEL PAIGE

A big-league rookie at age 42, Cleveland's Paige pitched his first complete game in the majors—a 5-0 shutout of the White Sox—before a sellout crowd of 51,013 at Chicago's Comiskey Park on August 13, 1948. Paige, who permit-

Ernie Nevers earned his greatest fame as a pro football Hall of Famer, but he also pitched in the major leagues and allowed two of Babe Ruth's 60 homers during the 1927 season.

Satchel Paige, a 42-year-old rookie with Cleveland in 1948, watches on-field action while seated next to coach Muddy Ruel in late July.

ted five hits, was making his 12th appearance and second start since being signed by the Indians five weeks earlier.

Paige helped attract a record crowd for a major league night game, 78,382 fans, to Cleveland's Municipal Stadium on August 20, 1948—and pitched his second straight shutout, a three-hit, 1-0 triumph over Chicago.

MILT PAPPAS

One of only two pitchers in major league history to win 200 or more games without achieving a 20-victory season. Pappas won 209 games in his career, with a season high of 17 (reached while pitching for the Chicago Cubs in 1971 and 1972).

Jack Quinn won 212 games in the majors, reaching a high of 18 (with the New York Yankees in 1910 and 1920 and with the Philadelphia Athletics in 1928). Quinn had a 26-victory year in the Federal League in 1914, but The Sporting News does not consider the Federal League a major league.

TONY PEREZ

Cincinnati Reds' third baseman whose 15th-inning home run off Jim (Catfish) Hunter of the Kansas City A's gave the National League a 2-1 victory over the American League in the 1967 All-Star Game at Anaheim Stadium.

Third basemen accounted for all of the scoring in the '67 classic (the longest All-Star Game in history), with Dick Allen of the Philadelphia Phillies also homering for the N.L. and Brooks Robinson of the Baltimore Orioles homering for the A.L.

JOHNNY PESKY

The only player to lead his league in hits in the first three seasons in which he appeared in the majors. Playing for the Boston Red Sox as a rookie in 1942, Pesky led the American League with 205 hits. After spending the next three years in military service, Pesky topped the A.L. in hits in 1946 with 208 and in 1947 with 207.

Tony Oliva of Minnesota led the A.L. in hits in his first three full seasons, 1964 through 1966, after getting a total of seven hits in brief appearances with the Twins in 1962 and 1963.

FRITZ PETERSON

The only man in All-Star Game history to have pitched in the classic and not recorded an out. Pitching for the American League and representing the New York Yankees, Peterson faced one batter, Willie McCovey (who singled), in the ninth inning of the 1970 game at Riverfront Stadium in Cincinnati and then was replaced by Mel Stottlemyre.

TOM PHOEBUS

The most recent of nine pitchers who have tossed shutouts in their first two

Jack Reed's one moment in the sun came in 1962 when the backup outfielder lifted the Yankees past Detroit with a 22nd-inning home run.

major league games. Making his big-league debut on September 15, 1966, Phoebus stopped the California Angels, 2-0, on four hits. On September 20, Phoebus defeated the Kansas City Athletics, 4-0, on a five-hitter.

Others breaking in with two shutouts: Al Spalding (Chicago, N.L., 1876), Monte Ward (Providence, N.L., 1878), Jim Hughes (Baltimore, N.L., 1898), Joe Doyle (New York, A.L., 1906), Johnny Marcum (Philadelphia, A.L., 1933), Dave (Boo) Ferriss (Boston, A.L., 1945), Al Worthington (New York, N.L., 1953) and Karl Spooner (Brooklyn, N.L., 1954).

WALLY PIPP

New York Yankees' first baseman who reportedly was not feeling well on June 2, 1925, and was scratched from the lineup. Pipp never got his job back as Lou Gehrig, who had pinch-hit the day before, started at first base June 2 against the Washington Senators in what became game No. 2 in Gehrig's record string of 2,130 consecutive games.

PITTSBURGH PIRATES

The only pennant-winning team in major league history (except for the strike-shortened 1981 season) not to have at least one pitcher with 15 victories. The leading winner for the 1979 world champion Pittsburgh Pirates was John Candelaria, who notched 14 victories.

Fernando Valenzuela led the 1981 world champion Los Angeles Dodgers with 13 victories, and Ron Guidry paced the '81 American League champion New York Yankees with 11 triumphs.

JACK QUINN

The oldest player in big-league history to hit a home run. Eight days shy of his 46th birthday, Quinn, a pitcher, homered for the Philadelphia Athletics against Chad Kimsey of the St. Louis Browns on June 27, 1930.

JACK REED

His 22nd-inning home run, a two-run drive off Detroit's Phil Regan and the only homer of Reed's major league career, enabled the New York Yankees to defeat the Tigers, 9-7, on June 24, 1962. It was the latest inning in which a home run has been hit in the big leagues.

ED REULBACH

The only pitcher in big-league history to hurl shutouts in both games of a doubleheader. Pitching for the Chicago Cubs against Brooklyn on September 26, 1908, Reulbach scored a five-hit, 5-0 triumph in the opener and a three-hit, 3-0 victory in the second game. Johnny Kling was Reulbach's catcher for both games.

PAUL, RICK REUSCHEL

The only brothers to combine for a big-league shutout. Pitching for the

The irony of Game 1 of the 1954 World Series was that Cleveland's Vic Wertz (right) hit a 460-foot drive that was caught by Willie Mays and New York's Dusty Rhodes (left) hit a ball approximately 260 feet that resulted in a game-winning home run.

Chicago Cubs against the Los Angeles Dodgers on August 21, 1975, Rick went the first 6⅓ innings and Paul hurled the final 2⅔ innings in a 7-0 triumph.

ALLIE REYNOLDS

The most recent of three pitchers who have won final World Series games in consecutive years. Pitching for the New York Yankees in 1952 and 1953, Reynolds was the winning pitcher in the two clinchers against the Brooklyn Dodgers.

Art Nehf of the New York Giants won the final games of the 1921 and 1922 World Series against the Yankees, and the Yanks' Lefty Gomez beat the Giants in the 1936 and 1937 Series finales.

DUSTY RHODES

New York Giants' pinch-hitter whose three-run, 10th-inning home run off Cleveland's Bob Lemon gave the Giants a 5-2 victory in Game 1 of the 1954 World Series. Rhodes, batting for New York left fielder Monte Irvin, connected two innings after Giants' center fielder Willie Mays made a miraculous catch of a drive hit by Indians' first baseman Vic Wertz.

Again pinch-hitting for Irvin, Rhodes delivered a run-scoring single in the fifth inning of Game 2 that netted the Giants a 1-1 tie and later hit a bases-empty homer (after taking over for Irvin in left) as New York won, 3-1. In Game 3, Rhodes again batted for Irvin—and came through with a bases loaded single in the third inning, making him 4-for-4 in the Series (3-for-3 as a pinch-hitter) with seven runs batted in. Staying in the game, Rhodes struck out in his final two at-bats. Rhodes' services weren't required in Game 4 as the Giants completed a Series sweep.

PETE RICHERT

The only pitcher to strike out four batters in one inning in his first major league game. Pitching for the Los Angeles Dodgers on April 12, 1962, Richert struck out Cincinnati's Frank Robinson, Gordy Coleman, Wally Post and Johnny Edwards in the third inning. Coleman reached first base when catcher John Roseboro dropped a third strike.

FRANK ROBINSON

The only player in history to hit 200 or more home runs in both the National and American leagues. Robinson, who played in the majors from 1956 through 1976, hit 343 homers in the N.L. while playing for Cincinnati and Los Angeles, and 243 in the A.L. while playing for Baltimore, California and Cleveland.

Robinson is also the only player to hit home runs for both the National League and American League in All-Star Game competition. Representing Cincinnati, Robinson homered for the N.L. in the second All-Star Game of 1959; representing Baltimore, he homered for the A.L. in 1971.

FRANK ROBINSON, RUSTY STAUB

The players who hold the major league mark for homering in the most parks, 32, during regular-season play. Both hit home runs at these parks: Atlanta, Atlanta Stadium; Baltimore, Memorial Stadium; Boston, Fenway Park; California, Anaheim Stadium; Chicago, Comiskey Park and Wrigley Field; Cincinnati, Crosley Field and Riverfront Stadium; Cleveland, Municipal Stadium; Detroit, Tiger Stadium; Houston, Colt Stadium; Kansas City, Royals Stadium; Los Angeles, Dodger Stadium; Milwaukee, County Stadium; Minnesota, Metropolitan Stadium; New York, Polo Grounds, Shea Stadium and Yankee Stadium; Oakland, Oakland Coliseum; Philadelphia, Connie Mack Stadium and Veterans Stadium; Pittsburgh, Forbes Field; San Diego, San Diego Stadium; San Francisco, Candlestick Park; Texas, Arlington Stadium.

Additionally, Robinson homered at these parks: Brooklyn, Ebbets Field; Jersey City (where Brooklyn played a total of 15 home games in 1956 and 1957), Roosevelt Stadium; Kansas City, Municipal Stadium; Los Angeles, Memorial Coliseum; St. Louis, old Busch Stadium; San Francisco, Seals Stadium; Washington, Robert F. Kennedy Memorial Stadium.

Additionally, Staub homered at these parks: Houston, Astrodome; Montreal,

Jarry Park and Olympic Stadium; Pittsburgh, Three Rivers Stadium; St. Louis, Busch Memorial Stadium; Seattle, Kingdome; Toronto, Exhibition Stadium.

Hank Aaron slugged home runs in 31 parks during his regular-season career in the big leagues.

BABE RUTH

The only starting pitcher in World Series history to bat anywhere but ninth in the order. In his last Series appearance as a pitcher, Ruth batted sixth in the lineup for the Boston Red Sox in Game 4 of the 1918 Series and grounded out, hit a two-run triple and sacrificed against the Chicago Cubs. After allowing a single and a walk to open the ninth inning, Ruth moved to left field and reliever Joe Bush nailed down the Red Sox's 3-2 victory. Boston went on to win the Series, four games to two.

Catcher Sam Agnew was Boston's ninth-place batter on the day pitcher Ruth hit in the sixth position. Agnew went 0-for-2 before being replaced by Wally Schang.

BABE RUTH

Owns the record for the longest complete-game pitching victory in a World Series. Pitching for the Boston Red Sox against Brooklyn in Game 2 of the 1916 Series, Ruth allowed only six hits in 14 innings and posted a 2-1 triumph in the lengthiest game in Series history.

NOLAN RYAN

Pitching for the California Angels in 1973, he established the modern major league record for most strikeouts in a season with 383. Ryan set the mark in his last start of the season, a September 27 game against the Minnesota Twins in which he struck out 16 batters in 11 innings and won, 5-4.

Rich Reese was Ryan's 383rd victim, enabling the California hurler to surpass the total of 382 strikeouts recorded by Sandy Koufax of the Los Angeles Dodgers in 1965. Five years earlier, Reese also was part of history when he struck out for the final out in Oakland pitcher Jim (Catfish) Hunter's perfect game against the Twins.

RED SCHOENDIENST

St. Louis Cardinals' second baseman whose 14th-inning home run off Ted Gray of the Detroit Tigers boosted the National League past the American League, 4-3, in the 1950 All-Star Game at Chicago's Comiskey Park.

PAT SEEREY

One of only 10 players in big-league history to hit four home runs in one game—accomplishing the feat for the Chicago White Sox on July 18, 1948—but he slugged only eight more homers (all in '48) in the majors, finishing

Dodgers Manager Burt Shotton points out the heroes of the National League's 1950 All-Star Game victory at Comiskey Park in Chicago. Pittsburgh's Ralph Kiner hit a ninth-inning home run to tie the score and St. Louis' Red Schoendienst won the game with a 14th-inning blast.

with a career total of 86. Seerey's big game was the opener of an American League doubleheader against the Philadelphia A's, and his fourth homer of the contest—coming in the 11th inning—gave the White Sox a 12-11 victory. Seerey, obtained from Cleveland earlier in the '48 season, saw his big-league career end the next year with a four-game stint with the White Sox; he was only 26 years old when he left the majors.

Joe Adcock of the Milwaukee Braves established a major league record for total bases, 18, in his four-homer game against Brooklyn in 1954. In addition to his homers, Adcock hit a double in the National League game.

The others to hit four homers in one game: Bobby Lowe, Boston, N.L., 1894; Ed Delahanty, Philadelphia, N.L., 1896; Lou Gehrig, New York, A.L., 1932; Chuck Klein, Philadelphia, N.L., 10 innings, 1936; Gil Hodges, Brooklyn, N.L., 1950; Rocky Colavito, Cleveland, A.L., 1959; Willie Mays, San Francisco, N.L., 1961, and Mike Schmidt, Philadelphia, N.L., 10 innings, 1976.

The Yankees'
Moose Skowron
(above left) hams it
up in the clubhouse
with Johnny Kucks
(above center) and
Yogi Berra after
hitting a grand slam
in the seventh game
of the 1956 World
Series, while
Philadelphia's Dick
Sisler gets a hero's
welcome (right)
after hitting his
pennant-winning
home run on the
final day of the 1950
season.

ROY SIEVERS

One of only two players to sock a pinch-hit, bases-loaded home run in both major leagues. Sievers connected for the American League's Chicago White Sox on June 21, 1961, and for the National League's Philadelphia Phillies on May 26, 1963.

Jimmie Foxx hit a pinch grand slam for the A.L.'s Philadelphia Athletics on September 21, 1931, and one for the N.L.'s Phils on May 18, 1945.

DICK SISLER

Philadelphia left fielder whose three-run, 10th-inning home run off Brooklyn's Don Newcombe on the final day of the 1950 season wrapped up the National League pennant for the Phillies. Robin Roberts, collecting his 20th victory of the season, pitched the 4-1 triumph for the Phils, who entered the day with a one-game lead over the Dodgers. Besides foiling the Dodgers' pennant hopes, Sisler's smash also ruined Newcombe's bid to become a 20-game winner (he finished 19-11).

BILL SKOWRON

The only player to hit a bases-loaded home run in the final game of a World Series. Skowron's grand slam came in the seventh inning of Game 7 of the 1956 Series, capping the New York Yankees' scoring in a 9-0 victory over the Brooklyn Dodgers.

No player has hit a grand slam in the first game of a World Series.

REGGIE SMITH

One of only two men to play for both the American League and National League in the All-Star Game and for A.L. and N.L. teams in the World Series. Smith played for the A.L. in the 1969 and 1972 All-Star Games and for the N.L. in 1974, 1975, 1977, 1978 and 1980. He played in the 1967 Series for the A.L.'s Boston Red Sox and in the 1977, 1978 and 1981 Series for the N.L.'s Los Angeles Dodgers.

Frank Robinson played for the N.L. in 1956, 1957, 1959, 1961, 1962 and 1965 All-Star Games, and for the A.L. in 1966, 1969, 1970, 1971 and 1974. He played for the N.L.'s Cincinnati Reds in the 1961 Series and for the A.L.'s Baltimore Orioles in the 1966, 1969, 1970 and 1971 Series.

REGGIE SMITH

The last of only five big leaguers to hit World Series home runs for both American and National league teams. Smith homered twice for the A.L.'s Boston Red Sox in the 1967 Series, and he hit three for Los Angeles of the N.L. in 1977 and another for the Dodgers in the '78 classic.

Enos Slaughter, Moose Skowron, Frank Robinson and Roger Maris also hit at least one Series homer for both N.L. and A.L. teams. Slaughter homered for the St. Louis Cardinals and New York Yankees, Skowron for the Yankees and Dodgers, Robinson for the Cincinnati Reds and Baltimore Orioles and Maris for the Yankees and Cardinals.

TRIS SPEAKER

The only American Leaguer other than Ty Cobb to lead the league in batting from 1907 through 1919. In that span, Detroit's Cobb won the A.L. hitting championship 12 times and captured the crown nine straight years before Cleveland's Speaker broke the string in 1916 with a .386 average (Cobb was runner-up at .371).

RENNIE STENNETT

The only major leaguer since the turn of the century to collect seven hits in a nine-inning game. Stennett had four singles, two doubles and a triple in seven at-bats on September 16, 1975, leading the Pittsburgh Pirates to a 22-0 victory over the Chicago Cubs in the most lopsided shutout in modern big-league history. Stennett twice had two hits in one inning, tying the major league mark.

The next night, Stennett went 3-for-5 against the Philadelphia Phillies to set a modern record for most hits, 10, in two consecutive nine-inning games.

GENE STEPHENS

The only player in modern major league history to collect three hits in one inning. Playing for Boston against the Detroit Tigers on June 18, 1953, Stephens singled twice and doubled in the Red Sox's 17-run seventh inning (Boston won, 23-3).

BRUCE SUTTER

One of only two pitchers to win two straight major league All-Star Games. Representing the Chicago Cubs in 1978 and 1979, Sutter was the victor as the National League beat the American League, 7-3 and 7-6. In the 1978 game at San Diego Stadium, Sutter retired five straight batters in relief; in the 1979 game at Seattle's Kingdome, he pitched two scoreless innings as the last of seven N.L. pitchers.

Don Drysdale of the Los Angeles Dodgers was the winner for the N.L. in the 1967 and 1968 All-Star Games, pitching two scoreless innings of relief in a 15-inning, 2-1 triumph at Anaheim Stadium in '67 and hurling three scoreless innings as a starter in a 1-0 victory at Houston's Astrodome in '68.

GENE TENACE

The only player to hit home runs in his first two World Series at-bats. Playing for the Oakland A's against the Cincinnati Reds in the first game of the 1972 Series, Tenace walloped a two-run homer off Gary Nolan in the second inning and a bases-empty shot off Nolan in the fifth as the A's won, 3-2.

Pittsburgh's Rennie Stennett emphasizes his lucky number (left) after collecting seven hits against the Cubs, then receives a plaque from National League President Chub Feeney (below) in recognition of the feat.

Max West, who had homered for the National League in the first inning of the 1940 All-Star Game at St. Louis' Sportsman's Park, had to be removed from the game an inning later after crashing into the right-field wall.

LEFTY TYLER

Boston Braves' pitcher who stopped New York, 8-3, in the second game of a September 30, 1916, doubleheader, ending the Giants' major league-record 26-game winning streak. The Giants had won the opener, 4-0, behind pitcher Rube Benton.

The Giants started their streak September 7 when Ferdie Schupp pitched New York past Brooklyn, 4-1.

DIXIE, HARRY WALKER

The only brothers to win major league batting championships. Dixie, playing for the Brooklyn Dodgers in 1944, won the National League title with a .357 figure. Harry, playing most of the 1947 season with the Philadelphia Phillies after starting the year with the St. Louis Cardinals, led the N.L. with a .363 mark.

JOHN MONTGOMERY WARD

The youngest pitcher in major league history to record a perfect game. At age 20, Ward pitched his gem on June 17, 1880, as Providence beat Buffalo, 5-0, in a National League game.

CLAUDELL WASHINGTON

The most recent of three players to slug three home runs in a game in both major leagues. Washington had a three-homer game for the Chicago White Sox in 1979 and repeated the feat for the New York Mets in 1980.

Babe Ruth recorded three-homer games for the New York Yankees in 1930 and for the Boston Braves in 1935 (and also had two three-homer days in World Series competition, in 1926 and 1928).

Johnny Mize, though, is the only player in big-league history to hit three consecutive homers in a game in both the National League and American League. Mize walloped three straight for the St. Louis Cardinals in 1938 and 1940, for the New York Giants in 1947 and for the New York Yankees in 1950. He had two other three-homer (non-consecutive) games for the Cards —in '38 and '40.

MAX WEST

One of only two players to hit a home run in his lone official All-Star Game at-bat. West, Boston Braves' outfielder, hit a three-run homer for the National League in the first inning of the 1940 classic at St. Louis' Sportsman's Park, then left the game in the second inning after crashing into the right-field wall.

Lee Mazzilli is the other player with a homer in his only official All-Star at-bat (through 1982), connecting for a score-tying pinch homer in the eighth inning of the 1979 game at Seattle's Kingdome. Mazzilli, representing the New York Mets, drew a game-winning, bases-loaded walk in the ninth for the National League.

The scoreboard tells the story as Hoyt Wilhelm, nearly 45 years old, works during a 1968 game for the Chicago White Sox.

HOYT WILHELM

Working in relief for the Chicago White Sox in the first game of a July 24, 1968, doubleheader, he set a major league record by making his 907th career appearance as a pitcher. Two days shy of his 45th birthday, Wilhelm took over for Tommy John in the ninth inning and retired the Oakland A's in order (on six pitches).

Wilhelm, whose big-league career began in 1952 and ended in 1972, finished with 1,070 lifetime appearances (Lindy McDaniel ranks second at 987 and Cy Young third at 906).

TED WILLIAMS

Boston Red Sox's left fielder whose two-out, three-run homer off Claude Passeau of the Chicago Cubs in the ninth inning of the 1941 All-Star Game gave the American League a 7-5 victory over the National League at Detroit's Briggs Stadium.

HOOKS WILTSE

One of three pitchers in major league history to hurl a complete-game, no-hit victory that went extra innings. Pitching for the New York Giants against the Philadelphia Phillies on July 4, 1908, Wiltse held the Phils hitless in a 1-0, 10-inning triumph.

Fred Toney and Jim Maloney, both of the Cincinnati Reds, pitched 1-0, no-hit victories against the Chicago Cubs in games that went 10 innings— and were 48 years apart. Toney's came on May 2, 1917, and Maloney's was on August 19, 1965.

RICK WISE

The only man in major league history to pitch a no-hitter and hit two home runs in the same game. Wise, pitching for the Philadelphia Phillies, held the Cincinnati Reds hitless on June 23, 1971, and slugged a two-run homer off Ross Grimsley and a bases-empty shot off Clay Carroll as the Phils won, 4-0.

EARLY WYNN

The only major leaguer to slug a pinch-hit, bases-loaded homer and also surrender one. Batting for Washington Senators' pitcher Roger Wolff on September 15, 1946, Wynn hit a grand slam off Johnny Gorsica of the Detroit Tigers. Pitching for the Chicago White Sox on May 28, 1961, Wynn gave up a pinch grand slam to Bob Cerv of the New York Yankees.

CARL YASTRZEMSKI

The only player in major league history whose record-book totals show more than 3,000 career hits but no 200-hit seasons. Boston's Yastrzemski had 3,318 hits through 1982, with a season high of 191 for the 1962 Red Sox.

Cap Anson, who played for Chicago's National League club from 1876 through 1897, is credited with 3,081 hits and **one** 200-hit season. However, Anson's 200-hit season, 1887, was a year in which bases on balls were credited as hits (and Anson drew 60 walks). By modern standards, Anson would have had 164 hits—not 224—in 1887. And the same standards would leave Anson with 3,021 career hits . . . and no 200-hit seasons (with a high of 187 in 1886).

CARL YASTRZEMSKI

The player with the lowest league-leading batting average in major league history. Yastrzemski hit .301 for the Boston Red Sox in 1968, topping the American League.

RUDY YORK

Detroit Tigers' first baseman who singled in the second inning for the only hit off Claude Passeau of the Chicago Cubs in Game 3 of the 1945 World Series. The Cubs won, 3-0.

CY YOUNG

The only man to pitch major league no-hitters before and after 1900. Young pitched a no-hitter for Cleveland of the National League on September 18, 1897, then threw a perfect game for the Boston Red Sox on May 5, 1904. He pitched another no-hitter for the Red Sox on June 30, 1908.

JOEL YOUNGBLOOD

The only player in major league history to collect hits for two teams in one day. Youngblood started in center field for the New York Mets on August 4, 1982, at Chicago and hit a two-run single in the third inning off the Cubs' Ferguson Jenkins. Removed from the game and told he had been traded to the Montreal Expos, Youngblood left immediately to join his new team in Philadelphia. Arriving in time to be used as a defensive replacement for right fielder Jerry White in the sixth inning, Youngblood later singled off Steve Carlton to gain the additional distinction of being the only player in history to face two pitchers (Carlton, Jenkins) already in the 3,000-strikeout club in one day.

On May 30, 1922, Max Flack of the St. Louis Cardinals and Cliff Heathcote of the Chicago Cubs collected hits in the first game of a doubleheader, then were traded for each other. Each played for his new team in the second game (neither got a hit), making Flack and Heathcote the only two other players to perform for two teams in one day (but only Youngblood played for two teams in two cities).

ROBIN YOUNT

The only man to have two four-hit games in World Series competition—and he did it within one Series. Playing for the Milwaukee Brewers against the St. Louis Cardinals in the 1982 Series, Yount had four hits in Game 1 and again in Game 5.

FIFTH INNING:

Coincidences, oddities and ironies.

HANK AARON

Atlanta right fielder who in 1969 homered in each of his team's League Championship Series games. Aaron, who hit home runs in all three games for the Braves in a sweep by the New York Mets, never played in another Championship Series (which became part of the major leagues' postseason play in '69).

HANK, TOMMIE AARON

Hank, the major leagues' career home-run king, and brother Tommie hit homers in the same game three times in their careers—all in 1962. They connected for the Milwaukee Braves on June 12 against the Los Angeles Dodgers, on July 12 against the St. Louis Cardinals and on August 14 against the Cincinnati Reds. No pitcher ever gave up homers to both brothers in the same game. The Aarons' lifetime homer total of 768 is the best of any brother combination (regardless of number). Hank hit 755, Tommie 13.

ALL-STAR, LCS, WORLD SERIES

No major leaguer has hit a home run in the All-Star Game, the League Championship Series and the World Series in the same season.

JOEY AMALFITANO, HARVEY KUENN

The only men to play on the opposing teams in two of Sandy Koufax's no-hitters. Amalfitano was San Francisco's second baseman and Kuenn was the Giants' left fielder in Koufax's 1963 no-hitter for the Los Angeles Dodgers, and both players were ninth-inning pinch-hitters for the Chicago Cubs in Koufax's 1965 perfect game for the Dodgers.

AMERICAN LEAGUE PLAYOFFS

There have been only two playoffs in American League history to decide a division or pennant winner—and both were one-game playoffs at Boston's Fenway Park. The Cleveland Indians defeated the Red Sox, 8-3, in a 1948 playoff for the A.L. pennant, and the New York Yankees beat Boston, 5-4, in a 1978 playoff for the A.L. East Division title.

NEAL BALL

Cleveland shortstop who was the first player in major league history to make an unassisted triple play—and the only man to turn such a play and hit a home run in the same game. After making an unassisted triple play against the Boston Red Sox in the top of the second inning in the first game of a July 19, 1909 doubleheader, Ball homered off Charlie Chech in the bottom of the second.

Other players to make unassisted triple plays in the majors:

● **Bill Wambsganss,** second baseman, Cleveland Indians, October 10, 1920 (Game 5 of the World Series), fifth inning.

● **George Burns,** first baseman, Boston Red Sox, September 14, 1923, second inning.

● **Ernie Padgett,** shortstop, Boston Braves, October 6, 1923 (second game of doubleheader), fourth inning.

● **Glenn Wright,** shortstop, Pittsburgh Pirates, May 7, 1925, ninth inning.

● **Jimmy Cooney,** shortstop, Chicago Cubs, May 30, 1927, fourth inning.

● **Johnny Neun,** first baseman, Detroit Tigers, May 31, 1927, ninth inning.

● **Ron Hansen,** shortstop, Washington Senators, July 30, 1968, first inning.

All eight unassisted triple plays have occurred with runners on first and second base.

CLYDE BARNHART

The only player in modern major league history to get hits in three games in one day. Barnhart, the Pittsburgh Pirates' third baseman in all three games of an October 2, 1920, tripleheader against the Cincinnati Reds, managed two hits in the opener and one hit in each of the other two games.

Also playing in each game of the lone tripleheader in modern big-league history—and thus joining Barnhart in modern baseball's exclusive three-games-in-one-day club—were Pat Duncan and Morrie Rath of Cincinnati and Fred Nicholson and Cotton Tierney of Pittsburgh.

DICK BATES

Pitcher who appeared in only one big-league game—and that was with the 1969 Seattle Pilots (a club that spent only one season in Seattle before moving to Milwaukee and becoming the Brewers).

Three other players spent their entire major league careers with the Pilots. Miguel Fuentes pitched in eight games, Gary Timberlake pitched in two and Billy Williams appeared in four as a pinch-runner and outfielder.

BUDDY BELL

The only player in American League history to attain 200 or more hits in a season without batting .300. Playing for the Texas Rangers in 1979, Bell had 200 hits in 670 at-bats for a .29851 mark (.299 in the record books).

Five National Leaguers have collected 200 or more hits in one year and not reached .300, with Joe Moore of New York being the first big leaguer to have such statistics. Moore went 201-for-681 (.29515) for the 1935 Giants. Maury Wills was 208-for-695 (.29928) for the 1962 Los Angeles Dodgers; Lou Brock went 206-for-689 (.29898, or .299 rounded off) for the 1967 St. Louis Cardinals, and Matty Alou was 201-for-677 (.29690, or .297) for the 1970 Pittsburgh Pirates. The fewest at-bats a 200-hit man can have and fail to record a .300 average is 668—and those were the exact at-bat and hit figures that Ralph Garr of the Atlanta Braves achieved in 1973 (668-200, .29940).

AL BENTON

The only pitcher to face both Babe Ruth and Mickey Mantle in a major league game. Benton, working for the Philadelphia Athletics, pitched to the Yankees' Ruth in 1934; as a member of the Boston Red Sox, he pitched against the Yanks' Mantle in 1952.

Bobo Newsom, who pitched against Ruth in 1934 while a member of the St. Louis Browns, appeared in a total of 41 games for the Washington Senators and Philadelphia A's in 1952 and 1953—but never faced Mantle (who was playing his second and third American League seasons). Newsom pitched only one inning of relief against the Yankees in those two years, and Mantle was out of the lineup because of an injury.

AL BENTON

The only player in major league history to have two sacrifice hits in one inning. Benton, Detroit Tigers' pitcher, laid down two sacrifice bunts during his club's 11-run third inning against the Cleveland Indians on August 6, 1941.

BEVENS, GIONFRIDDO, LAVAGETTO

Probably the most memorable players in the 1947 World Series (Bill Bevens for his near no-hit game, Al Gionfriddo for his catch of a long drive by Joe DiMaggio and Cookie Lavagetto for ruining Bevens' bid for the first no-hitter in Series history) neither Bevens, Gionfriddo nor Lavagetto played a major league game after the '47 Series.

DAVE BOSWELL

Minnesota Twins' pitcher who on October 5, 1969, lost to the Baltimore Orioles, 1-0, in 10 innings and struck out in all four of his at-bats in his only Championship Series game.

ROGER BRESNAHAN

Hall of Fame catcher whose first appearance in the major leagues was as a pitcher—and he threw a shutout in his debut. Pitching for Washington of the National League on August 27, 1897, Bresnahan stopped St. Louis, 3-0, on six hits.

GEORGE BRUNET

Kansas City Athletics' pitcher who issued five bases-loaded walks and hit another batter with the bases loaded during the Chicago White Sox's one-hit, 11-run inning on April 22, 1959. The White Sox drew 10 walks in the seventh inning off A's pitchers Tom Gorman, Mark Freeman and Brunet—and eight came with the bases loaded.

Preceding the run-scoring walks and hit-batsman RBIs, the White Sox scored their first two runs of the inning on Johnny Callison's single and on an error by A's right fielder Roger Maris. Chicago, a 20-6 winner, left three men on base in the seventh, an inning in which Kansas City also contributed three errors.

GEORGE BURNS

Philadelphia Athletics' player who batted twice as a pinch-hitter in the A's 10-run seventh inning in Game 4 of the 1929 World Series against the Chicago Cubs—and made two of his club's outs. Batting for pitcher Eddie Rommel, Burns made the first out of the inning by popping to shortstop Woody English. He later made the last out of the inning by striking out.

JOE BUSH

The only pitcher in modern major league history to win 25 or more games in a season without pitching a shutout. Compiling a 26-7 record for the 1922 New York Yankees, Bush pitched a pair of two-hitters and two four-hitters —but failed to throw a shutout.

Houston's Cesar Cedeno (right) couldn't avoid double plays—or injury—in the 1980 National League Championship Series.

NORM CASH

First baseman who reached a .300 batting average only once in a big-league career that started in 1958 and ended in 1974—but he won an American League batting championship by hitting .361 in 1961 while playing for Detroit. Cash's next highest average was .286, achieved in 1960 for the Tigers.

PETE CASTIGLIONE

Pittsburgh utilityman who in 1950 made one error all season at first base, two errors at second base, three errors at third base and four while playing shortstop for the Pirates.

PHIL CAVARRETTA

Chicago Cubs' player (and manager) whose National League career ended in **1953** after he had appeared in **1,953** N.L. games. Cavarretta played for the Chicago White Sox in 1954 and 1955.

CESAR CEDENO

Houston Astros' center fielder who in 1980 grounded into double plays against the Philadelphia Phillies in all three of his career Championship Series games (an ankle injury kept Cedeno out of Games 4 and 5 of the N.L. series).

Ten years after he took the mound for the Cleveland Indians, Rocky Colavito delivered a pitch for the New York Yankees in 1968.

CHICAGO CUBS

The only National League team not to have a winning record against the 1962 Mets, who established a modern big-league mark with 120 losses (while notching only 40 victories). The Cubs finished 9-9 against New York.

CHICAGO CUBS, CHICAGO WHITE SOX

Opponents the last time the World Series involved two first-time entrants in the classic—and this was in 1906. The Series, which began in 1903, had all-new teams in 1905 and '06 (there was no Series in '04), but in every year since at least one of the teams has played in the classic previously.

JOE CHRISTOPHER

One of seven players in major league history to appear in two perfect games. Christopher played for Pittsburgh in the 1959 game in which the Pirates' Harvey Haddix pitched 12 perfect innings against the Milwaukee Braves, and he played for the New York Mets in the 1964 game in which Philadelphia's Jim Bunning pitched a perfect game.

Patsy Dougherty, Fred Parent, Ossee Schreckengost, Harry Hooper, Wes Covington and Jim Gilliam also played in two perfect games. Dougherty and Parent played behind Cy Young in 1904 when the Boston pitcher hurled a perfect game against the Philadelphia A's, and they played for Chicago in 1908 when Cleveland's Addie Joss threw a perfect game against the White Sox. Schreckengost played against Young in '04 and against Joss in '08, while Hooper played behind Ernie Shore in the Boston pitcher's 1917 perfect game against Washington and behind Charley Robertson in the Chicago hurler's 1922 perfect game against Detroit. Covington played against Haddix in '59 and behind Bunning in '64. Gilliam played for the Brooklyn Dodgers in the 1956 World Series game in which Don Larsen of the New York Yankees pitched a perfect game, and he played for the Los Angeles Dodgers in 1965 when Sandy Koufax was perfect against the Chicago Cubs.

ROCKY COLAVITO

An outfielder who slugged a total of 374 home runs for five big-league teams, he pitched in two games in the majors—and came up a winner on August 25, 1968, when he worked 2⅔ innings of one-hit relief for the New York Yankees against the Detroit Tigers. Playing for the Cleveland Indians in 1958, Colavito did not allow a hit in a three-inning stint against the Tigers on August 13.

Daryl Patterson of Detroit was the losing pitcher in Colavito's lone big-league pitching victory.

NATE COLBERT, STAN MUSIAL

As an 8-year-old in St. Louis, Colbert went out to old Busch Stadium (formerly Sportsman's Park) on May 2, 1954, to see the Cardinals play a doubleheader against the New York Giants. It proved quite a day—the Cardinals' Musial set a major league record by hitting five home runs in the twin bill.

At age 26, Colbert, playing for San Diego, tied Musial's mark by slugging five homers in an August 1, 1972, doubleheader against Atlanta.

JIMMY COONEY

The lone player in major league history to be involved in two unassisted triple plays. Cooney was playing for the St. Louis Cardinals in 1925 when he was caught off second base in the unaided triple play turned by Glenn Wright of the Pittsburgh Pirates. In 1927, Cooney, playing shortstop for the Chicago Cubs, made an unassisted triple play against the Pirates. Both plays occurred at Forbes Field.

WES COVINGTON, HARRY HOOPER

The only men to play for the winning teams in two perfect games. Amazingly, one of the perfect games involving Covington was pitched by the opposing hurler. Covington played for Milwaukee in 1959 when the Braves overcame Harvey Haddix's 12 perfect innings and beat Haddix and the Pittsburgh Pirates, 1-0, on one hit in the 13th inning (Haddix nevertheless was credited with a perfect game). Covington also played for the Philadelphia Phillies in 1964 when Jim Bunning pitched a 6-0 perfect game against the New York Mets. Hooper played for Boston in 1917 when Ernie Shore tossed a 4-0 perfect game against Washington and he was in the Chicago lineup in 1922 when Charley Robertson pitched a 2-0 perfect game against Detroit.

ALVIN DARK

The only person to manage three brothers in World Series competition. Matty and Felipe Alou played for Dark's San Francisco Giants in the 1962 Series, and Jesus Alou played for Dark's Oakland A's in the 1974 classic.

WILLIE DAVIS, RON FAIRLY, JIM GILLIAM

The only three teammates of Sandy Koufax to play in all four of the Los Angeles Dodger pitcher's no-hitters.

DIZZY DEAN, DENNY McLAIN

McLain was the last major league pitcher to win 30 games in a season, going 31-6 in 1968 for the American League's Detroit Tigers. Dean was the National League's last 30-game winner, posting a 30-7 record in 1934 for the St. Louis Cardinals. Both were righthanders who wore No. 17. In '34, Dean's Cardinals beat the Tigers in seven games in the World Series; in '68, McLain's Tigers defeated the Cardinals in seven games in the World Series.

JOE DiMAGGIO

The only player in big-league history to collect at least one All-Star Game hit at Yankee Stadium, the Polo Grounds and Ebbets Field. DiMaggio, New

Dizzy Dean (left) and Denny McLain had more in common than just pitching skill.

York Yankees' center fielder, homered in Yankee Stadium in the 1939 game, singled twice at the Polo Grounds in 1942 and singled and doubled at Ebbets Field in 1949.

VINCE DiMAGGIO

A National League outfielder for five teams (Boston, Cincinnati, Pittsburgh, Philadelphia and the New York Giants), he batted .249 in 1,110 major league games—compared with the .298 mark achieved by brother Dominic DiMaggio in 1,399 games with the Boston Red Sox and the .325 career figure attained by brother Joe DiMaggio in 1,736 games with the New York Yankees. As All-Star Game participants, Joe hit .255 in 11 games, Dom hit .353 in six games and Vince hit . . . 1.000 in two games (going 3-for-3).

CHUCK ESTRADA

Baltimore's starting and winning pitcher in the five games in which teammate Jim Gentile hit all six of his bases-loaded home runs in the major leagues. (Gentile hit two grand slams for the Orioles in a May 9, 1961, game against the Minnesota Twins.)

RON FAIRLY

The only player to represent both Canadian major league teams in the All-Star Game, playing for the National League in 1973 as a member of the Montreal Expos and for the American League in 1977 as a member of the Toronto Blue Jays.

BILL FAUL

Cubs' pitcher who was on the mound when Chicago turned all three of its triple plays during the 1965 season.

In major league history, only one other pitcher—Will White of Cincinnati's 1882 American Association club—has been on the mound for three triple plays in one season. White took part in his team's second and third triple plays.

RICK, WES FERRELL

When Wes Ferrell of the Cleveland Indians pitched a no-hitter against St. Louis in 1931, one of the players in the Browns' lineup was catcher Rick Ferrell—Wes' brother.

The only other instance of a no-hit pitcher facing his brother occurred in 1904 when Jesse Tannehill of the Boston Red Sox hurled a no-hitter against Chicago. Jesse's brother, Lee, was the White Sox's third baseman that day.

AL FITZMORRIS, BOBBY SHANTZ

The only two-time selections in major league baseball's expansion drafts. Shantz was chosen by the new Washington Senators off the New York Yankees' roster in the 1960 American League expansion draft, and by the Hous-

118

ton Colt .45s off the Pittsburgh Pirates' roster in the 1961 National League expansion draft. Fitzmorris was picked by the Kansas City Royals off the Chicago White Sox's roster in the 1968 A.L. expansion draft, and by the Toronto Blue Jays off the Royals' roster in the 1976 A.L. expansion draft.

GEORGE FOSTER

The San Francisco batter for whom the Giants' Willie Mays pinch-hit on September 22, 1969, when Mays hit his 600th big-league home run.

JIMMIE FOXX, CHUCK KLEIN

The players who gave major league baseball its only Triple Crown "double" (two such winners in the same season)—and they were even from the same city. Playing for the Philadelphia Phillies in 1933, Klein led the National League with a .368 batting average, 28 home runs and 120 runs batted in. Playing for the Philadelphia Athletics in '33, Foxx topped the American League with a .356 average, 48 homers and 163 RBIs.

FRANKIE FRISCH

He played the most games (50) in World Series history without hitting a home run. Frisch played in eight Series with the New York Giants (1921, 1922, 1923 and 1924) and St. Louis Cardinals (1928, 1930, 1931 and 1934) and had 197 at-bats.

JIM GILLIAM

The only player in major league history to appear in both a regular-season perfect game and a World Series perfect game. Gilliam played third base for Los Angeles when the Dodgers' Sandy Koufax pitched a perfect game against the Chicago Cubs in 1965, and he was at second base for Brooklyn when Don Larsen of the New York Yankees hurled a perfect game against the Dodgers in the 1956 World Series.

JOE GORDON

New York Yankees' second baseman who at the end of the 1946 season had played exactly 1,000 major league games and collected exactly 1,000 hits. Traded to Cleveland that fall, Gordon was unable to maintain his hit-a-game pace with the Indians. He finished his big-league career in 1950 with 1,530 hits in 1,566 games.

GOOSE GOSLIN

The only man to play in each of the Washington Senators' 19 World Series games. Goslin played in all seven games of both the 1924 and 1925 Series against the New York Giants and Pittsburgh Pirates, and in all five games of the 1933 Series against the Giants.

TED GRAY

Pitcher who appeared in only 14 games in the major leagues in 1955—but pitched for four teams that season. Gray had no record in two games with the Chicago White Sox, two games with the Cleveland Indians and one game with the New York Yankees, and he was 1-2 in nine games with the Baltimore Orioles.

STEVE GROMEK

Cleveland pitcher who beat the New York Yankees, 4-2, in a July 4, 1945, game at Municipal Stadium in which none of the Indians was credited with an assist. Gromek, who struck out four Yankees and allowed eight hits, permitted 15 flies to the outfield—eight to left fielder Jeff Heath, four to center fielder Felix Mackiewicz and three to right fielder Paul O'Dea—among his club's 27 putouts.

The St. Louis Browns are the only other team in major league history to play a complete nine-inning game without recording an assist. The Browns did it in an August 8, 1943, game also played at Cleveland's Municipal Stadium. As 5-2 losers to the Indians, the Browns took the field only eight times (and had 24 putouts).

JERRY GROTE, BUD HARRELSON, CLEON JONES

The only three Mets to play in all 12 of the New York club's World Series games, appearing in each of the five games of the 1969 Series against the Baltimore Orioles and all seven games of the 1973 classic against the Oakland A's.

LEFTY GROVE

One of two pitchers who gave up both a home run to Babe Ruth during the Yankee slugger's 60-homer season of 1927 and a hit to Joe DiMaggio during DiMaggio's 56-game batting streak in 1941. Pitching for the Philadelphia Athletics, Grove yielded a bases-loaded homer to Ruth on September 27, 1927 (Ruth's 57th homer of the year); pitching for the Boston Red Sox on May 25, 1941, he permitted a single to the Yankees' DiMaggio (the 11th straight game in which he batted safely).

Ted Lyons of Chicago gave up Ruth's 54th homer of the 1927 season on September 18, and the White Sox's pitcher surrendered two singles to DiMaggio in the first game of a doubleheader on July 13, 1941, as DiMaggio extended his string to 52 straight games.

BILLY HAMILTON

Philadelphia outfielder who captured the National League batting championship in 1891 with a figure that proved lower than his final career average. Hamilton, who won the '91 hitting title with a .338 mark, finished his career at .344.

Ron Hansen of the Washington Senators earned star billing on July 30, 1968, when he pulled an unassisted triple play against the Cleveland Indians.

Others winning big-league batting crowns with averages lower than their final lifetime marks:

Player, Club, League	Year	Title Avg.	Career Avg.
Dan Brouthers, Brooklyn, N.L.	1892	.335	.349
Elmer Flick, Cleveland, A.L.	1905	.308	.315
Ty Cobb, Detroit, A.L.	1907	.350	.367
Ty Cobb, Detroit, A.L.	1908	.324	.367
Edd Roush, Cincinnati, N.L.	1919	.321	.325
Ted Williams, Boston, A.L.	1947	.343	.344
Ted Williams, Boston, A.L.	1958	.328	.344
Rod Carew, Minnesota, A.L.	1972	.318	.331*

*Through 1982.

JACK HAMILTON

The only pitcher to surrender a big-league home run to Tommie Aaron but not to Tommie's brother, career home-run king Hank Aaron. Hamilton, pitching for the Philadelphia Phillies on April 26, 1962, gave up the first of Tommie's 13 career homers in the majors.

RON HANSEN

The most recent of eight big-league players to make an unassisted triple play—and the feat started a flurry of memorable activity for Hansen. Playing shortstop for the Washington Senators on July 30, 1968, Hansen turned

Chuck Hiller (right) of the San Francisco Giants became the first National League player to hit a bases-loaded homer in a World Series game, accomplishing the feat in Game 4 of the 1962 classic. Matty Alou (41) was among those offering congratulations.

an unassisted triple play in the first inning against the Cleveland Indians—but struck out four straight times against Sam McDowell. On July 31, Hansen fanned in his only two at-bats against Denny McLain of the Detroit Tigers. After walking in his first at-bat on August 1, Hansen snapped his string of six consecutive strikeouts by belting a fourth-inning, bases-loaded homer off Detroit's Pat Dobson. The following day, Hansen was traded to the Chicago White Sox and that night he played third base against his old club, the Senators.

TOMMY HARPER

The only member of the Seattle Pilots to lead the American League in a major statistical category, topping the A.L. with 73 stolen bases in 1969.

HARRY HEILMANN

Detroit Tigers' outfielder who won American League batting championships in odd-numbered years from 1921 through 1927. Heilmann batted an A.L.-high .394 in 1921, .403 in 1923, .393 in 1925 and .398 in 1927.

WHITEY HERZOG

Kansas City A's right fielder who lined into an all-Cuban triple play on July 23, 1960. After Kansas City's Bill Tuttle and Jerry Lumpe led off the third inning of a game against Washington with singles, Herzog lined a 3-2 pitch to pitcher Pedro Ramos. Ramos caught the drive for out No. 1, then threw to first baseman Julio Becquer to double off Lumpe. Becquer fired the ball to shortstop Jose Valdivielso, who caught Tuttle off second base to complete the triple play.

CHUCK HILLER

Although finishing his eight-year major league career with only 20 home runs, he hit the first bases-loaded homer for a National League team in World Series history. Hiller, San Francisco's second baseman in the 1962 Series, slugged his grand slam in the seventh inning of Game 4 off reliever Marshall Bridges of the New York Yankees. The homer snapped a 2-2 tie and led the Giants to a 7-3 triumph.

Ken Boyer of the St. Louis Cardinals hit the N.L.'s second—and only other—grand slam in the World Series. Boyer connected against Al Downing of the Yankees in the sixth inning of Game 4 of the 1964 classic, boosting the Cards from a 3-0 deficit to a 4-3 victory.

KEN HOLTZMAN

Oakland A's player whose World Series homer production (one) in 1974 surpassed his regular-season output (zero)—one of 13 times the feat has occurred in major league history. Holtzman, a pitcher who didn't have a plate appearance during the 1974 American League season (primarily because of the designated-hitter rule), became the most recent player to top

Oakland pitcher Ken Holtzman, connecting for a home run against the Los Angeles Dodgers in 1974, is the last player to exceed his season homer total in the World Series.

his season homer total in the Series when he connected in Game 4 of the '74 classic against the Los Angeles Dodgers.

Pitcher Bob Gibson of the St. Louis Cardinals is the only player who twice has surpassed his regular-season homer mark in the Series, homering in Game 7 against the Boston Red Sox in 1967 and in Game 4 against the Detroit Tigers in 1968 after failing to connect during either season.

BILL HUNNEFIELD

Shortstop who played for the winning team in two no-hitters in his major league career and made a total of four errors in those games. Playing for the Chicago White Sox on August 21, 1926, Hunnefield committed the White Sox's only error as teammate Ted Lyons tossed a no-hitter against the Boston Red Sox. When Wes Ferrell of the Cleveland Indians pitched the American League's next no-hitter, on April 29, 1931, against the St. Louis Browns, Hunnefield made three errors at shortstop for the Tribe.

IKE, NIXON

It was Ike (Delock) pitching to (Russ) Nixon in the early 1960s for the Boston Red Sox. In 1960 (the last full year of the Dwight Eisenhower-Richard Nixon administration), Ike and Nixon led the Red Sox to a 13-4 victory over the Kansas City A's on June 23. Delock pitched a complete-game nine-hitter, and catcher Nixon went 3-for-5—a single, double and home run—and drove in four runs.

RAY JANSEN

Playing third base for the St. Louis Browns on September 30, 1910, he got four singles in five at-bats in his only major league game.

NIPPY JONES

With the New York Yankees leading Milwaukee, 5-4, after 9½ innings of Game 4 of the 1957 World Series, Jones led off the Braves' 10th as a pinch-hitter for pitcher Warren Spahn. Umpire Augie Donatelli called Tommy Byrne's first pitch to Jones a ball, but Jones insisted he had been struck on the foot—and the Milwaukee player set out to prove his point. Retrieving the baseball, Jones showed Donatelli a smudge of shoe polish on the ball. The umpire awarded him first base, and the Braves went on to score three runs for a 7-5 victory that tied the Series at two games apiece.

Twelve years later, in the fifth and final game of the 1969 World Series, another Jones—Cleon of the New York Mets—was awarded first base on a similar play. Leading off the sixth inning, Jones tried to avoid a pitch in the dirt from Baltimore Orioles hurler Dave McNally. Plate umpire Lou DiMuro called the pitch a ball. Mets Manager Gil Hodges retrieved the baseball and showed DiMuro that the ball contained smudges of shoe polish. The umpire then awarded Jones first base and the next batter, Donn Clendenon, belted a home run, cutting the Orioles' lead to 3-2. The Mets went on to win the

With Donn Clendenon (left) looking on, Mets Manager Gil Hodges shows umpire Lou DiMuro a smudge of shoe polish on the ball during Game 5 of the 1969 World Series. The smudge proved that New York's Cleon Jones had been hit by a pitch from Baltimore's Dave McNally, and Clendenon followed with a home run.

game, 5-3, giving them their fourth straight win and the world championship.

ADDIE JOSS, JOHN LEE RICHMOND

Richmond, pitching for Worcester of the National League in 1880, hurled the big leagues' first perfect game (12 had been thrown through 1982), and Addie Joss pitched the majors' fourth perfect game in 1908 for Cleveland of the American League. Richmond later taught mathematics in a Toledo, Ohio, high school and one of his students was Norman Joss—Addie's son.

AL KALINE

Detroit player who was the only batter to face Rocky Colavito in both major league games in which Colavito, normally an outfielder, pitched. Colavito made one mound appearance for the Cleveland Indians in 1958 and one for the New York Yankees in 1968—and both games were against the Tigers.

JOHN KENNEDY

An infielder with Washington during years (1962, 1963) in which John Kennedy was President of the United States, the baseball-playing Kennedy was born on May 29—and so was the President. Baseball's Kennedy, born in 1941 (as opposed to 1917 for the President), also played for the Senators in 1964, then saw action with the Los Angeles Dodgers, New York Yankees, Seattle Pilots, Milwaukee Brewers and Boston Red Sox in a big-league career that ended in 1974.

DON KESSINGER

The most recent of three players in big-league history to receive either a putout or assist in three triple plays in one season. Kessinger, Chicago Cubs' shortstop, accomplished the feat in 1965.

Tom O'Brien had either an assist or putout in three triple plays for Rochester of the American Association in 1890 (he took part in the first two as a first baseman and the third one as a second baseman), and shortstop Donie Bush of the Detroit Tigers was credited with a putout or assist in three triple plays in 1911.

CHUCK KLEIN

The only player to win a Triple Crown in the major leagues and then be traded the following off-season. Playing for the Philadelphia Phillies in 1933, Klein led the National League with a .368 batting average, 28 home runs and 120 runs batted in. However, the financially strapped Phils traded Klein on November 21, 1933, to the Chicago Cubs for pitcher Ted Kleinhans, infielder Mark Koenig, outfielder Harvey Hendrick and an estimated $65,000.

ED KRANEPOOL

The only player to participate in the major league's longest doubleheader, longest shutout game and longest game played to a decision. Kranepool was the New York Mets' first baseman on May 31, 1964, when the Mets and San Francisco Giants played a doubleheader that totaled 32 innings. He also was at first base for the Mets on April 15, 1968, when New York beat the Houston Astros, 1-0, in 24 innings. And Kranepool pinch-hit for the Mets on September 11, 1974, when New York lost to the St. Louis Cardinals, 4-3, in 25 innings.

While no other player performed in all three games, Ed Sudol did umpire in each of the contests.

JOE KUHEL

The only Washington player to hit a home run in the Senators' home park, Griffith Stadium, in 1945. Kuhel slugged a third-inning, inside-the-park homer off Bob Muncrief of the St. Louis Browns on September 7, 1945. Washington hit only 27 homers in the entire season, with Harlond Clift leading the club with eight.

Visiting players slugged only six homers at Griffith Stadium in '45, with Detroit's Rudy York hitting two. Milt Byrnes and Lou Finney, both of the Browns, Eddie Lake of the Boston Red Sox and Jeff Heath of the Cleveland Indians also homered at the Senators' park.

BILL KUNKEL

The home-plate umpire on August 10, 1971, when Harmon Killebrew of the Minnesota Twins hit his 500th career home run in a game against the Baltimore Orioles. While pitching for the Kansas City A's in 1961, Kunkel allowed three homers to the Twins' Killebrew.

WAYNE LaMASTER

The Philadelphia Phillies' starting pitcher on May 5, 1938, who was the loser against the Chicago Cubs although he didn't finish pitching to the Cubs' first batter. After the Phils failed to score in the top of the first inning, LaMaster worked the count to 2-1 on Chicago leadoff man Stan Hack before leaving the game because of a sore arm. Reliever Tommy Reis completed a base on balls to Hack (the walk was charged to LaMaster), and Hack eventually scored in the Cubs' four-run inning. Since the Phils never caught up—they ended up losing, 21-2—LaMaster was charged with the defeat.

DON LARSEN

His first World Series victory was on October 8, 1956, at Yankee Stadium when he pitched a perfect game for the New York Yankees against the Brooklyn Dodgers, and his last Series triumph came exactly six years later —October 8, 1962—at Yankee Stadium when he beat the Yankees in relief while pitching for the San Francisco Giants. Larsen, who compiled a 4-2 career mark in Series play, pitched only one-third of an inning in Game 4 of the '62 classic but came out a winner when Chuck Hiller hit a bases-loaded homer for the Giants in a 7-3 triumph.

DON, THORNTON LEE

The only father-son combination to surrender home runs to Ted Williams of the Boston Red Sox. Williams, in fact, homered off the Lees as he was coming and going in the major leagues. As a Boston rookie, Williams homered off Thornton Lee of the Chicago White Sox in the first game of a September 17, 1939, doubleheader; playing his final season with the Red Sox, Williams connected off Thornton's son, Don, who was pitching for the Washington Senators in the opener of a September 2, 1960, twin bill.

JIM LEFEBVRE

One-fourth of the all-switch-hitting infield that the Los Angeles Dodgers used during the 1965 and 1966 seasons. Besides second baseman Lefebvre, the Dodgers' other switch-hit infielders were first baseman Wes Parker, shortstop Maury Wills and third baseman Jim Gilliam.

BOB LEMON

When Hall of Fame-bound Bob Feller pitched a no-hitter against the New York Yankees on April 30, 1946, the Cleveland pitcher had a future Hall of Famer playing behind him in center field—Lemon. Lemon, in the process of being converted into a pitcher, singled in four at-bats for the Indians.

DON LEPPERT, JOSE SANTIAGO

Don Eugene Leppert was a lefthanded-hitting second baseman who played in 40 games for the Baltimore Orioles in 1955 and batted .114, while Donald George Leppert was a righthanded-hitting catcher who played in 190 games from 1961 through 1964 with the Pittsburgh Pirates and Washington Sena-

The Los Angeles Dodgers of 1965 and 1966 were able to field an all-switch-hitting infield of (left to right) Maury Wills, Jim Lefebvre, Jim Gilliam and Wes Parker.

tors (for whom he hit three of his 15 career homers in one game in 1963) and had a lifetime average of .229.

Jose Guillermo Santiago was a righthanded pitcher for the Cleveland Indians and Kansas City Athletics from 1954 through 1956, compiling a 3-2 record. Righthanded Jose Rafael Santiago, 34-29 in the majors, also pitched for the Kansas City A's (1963 through 1965) before spending the last five years (1966-70) of his big-league career with the Boston Red Sox.

JOHN LUCADELLO

The first player in major league history to homer from both sides of the plate in one game for his only two homers of the season. Lucadello performed the feat on September 16, 1940, for the St. Louis Browns.

Only Ellis Burton, Larry Milbourne and U.L. Washington have matched Lucadello's accomplishment. Burton, playing for the Chicago Cubs, did it in the first game of a September 7, 1964, doubleheader; Milbourne, of the Seattle Mariners, followed on July 15, 1978, and Washington, as a member of the Kansas City Royals, became No. 4 on September 21, 1979.

For Lucadello and Washington, the homers were the first two of each player's big-league career; for Burton, the two homers were his last in the majors.

CONNIE MACK

The man who managed the Philadelphia Athletics for 50 of the club's 54 seasons in the American League. Mack piloted the A's from their inception in 1901 through 1950, with Jimmie Dykes taking over in 1951 and managing the club through 1953. Eddie Joost managed the A's in 1954, their last season in Philadelphia before relocating in Kansas City.

KEN MacKENZIE

The only pitcher to achieve a winning record for the 1962 New York Mets. MacKenzie, who worked in relief in 41 of the 42 games in which he appeared, posted a 5-4 record.

PAT MALONE

The only man to play in the World Series for teams from both leagues under the same manager. Malone pitched with the National League's Chicago Cubs for Joe McCarthy in the 1929 Series, and for the American League's New York Yankees under McCarthy in the 1936 Series.

BILLY MARTIN

The only man to play in Don Larsen's World Series perfect game in 1956, Rocky Colavito's four-homer game in 1959 and Willie Mays' four-homer game in 1961. Martin was a teammate of Larsen and Colavito (with the New York Yankees and Cleveland Indians, respectively), and played against the San Francisco Giants' Mays while with the Milwaukee Braves.

EDDIE MATHEWS

The only man to play for the Boston Braves, Milwaukee Braves and Atlanta Braves. Mathews played for Boston in 1952, for Milwaukee from 1953 through 1965 and for Atlanta in 1966.

CHARLEY MAXWELL

Boston Red Sox's player who hit three home runs in 1951—the first three of his major league career—and each was a pinch-hit homer off a future Hall of Fame pitcher (Bob Feller of Cleveland, Bob Lemon of the Indians and Satchel Paige of the St. Louis Browns). Maxwell's smash against Paige was a grand slam.

CHARLEY MAXWELL

Outfielder who hit 40 of his 148 career home runs in the majors on Sunday, including four in a 1959 doubleheader against the New York Yankees and three in a 1962 twin bill against the Yanks. In '59, 12 of his 31 homers came on Sunday. Maxwell, who played for the Boston Red Sox, Detroit Tigers and Chicago White Sox from 1950 to 1964, had seven lifetime homers on Monday, 21 on Tuesday, 19 on Wednesday, 13 on Thursday, 22 on Friday and 26 on Saturday. Of Maxwell's 40 Sunday shots, 12 were against New York.

Connie Mack's 50th year as Philadelphia A's manager is noted by his players (above) and by American League President Will Harridge (left) and Dodgers Manager Burt Shotton during spring training.

Duke Snider (left) and Willie Mays met in the 1951 National League playoff between the Brooklyn Dodgers and New York Giants and again in the 1962 N.L. playoff between the Los Angeles Dodgers and San Francisco Giants.

WILLIE MAYS, DUKE SNIDER

The only two players to appear in both the 1951 and 1962 National League playoffs. Mays played for the New York Giants in '51 and for the San Francisco Giants in '62, and Snider played for the Brooklyn Dodgers in '51 and the Los Angeles Dodgers in '62.

JOE McCARTHY

New York Yankees' manager who didn't use any of the six Yankee players on hand for the 1943 All-Star Game at Philadelphia's Shibe Park. Apparently resenting accusations that he favored New York players in earlier All-Star Games and seemingly out to prove his American League team could win without the Yankees, McCarthy kept the six on the bench. And he proved his point—the A.L. defeated the National League, 5-3.

CLIFF MELTON

New York Giants' pitcher who on September 15, 1938, became the only man in major league history to give up back-to-back homers to brothers. In the fifth inning of a game with the Pittsburgh Pirates, Melton yielded consecutive homers to Lloyd and Paul Waner (Lloyd's shot was the 27th and last of his big-league career).

RUDI MEOLI

One of only two teammates of Nolan Ryan to play in as many as three of Ryan's five no-hitters in the major leagues. Meoli was California's shortstop when Ryan pitched his first three no-hitters for the Angels—against the Kansas City Royals and the Detroit Tigers, both in 1973, and against the Minnesota Twins in 1974.

Outfielder Leroy Stanton played for the Angels in Ryan's second, third and fourth no-hitters with California (No. 4 was against the Baltimore Orioles in 1975).

SAM MERTES

A 10-year major leaguer who broke up no-hitters in the 10th inning of both American League and National League games. Mertes singled in the 10th inning off Cleveland's Earl Moore after Moore had pitched no-hit ball for nine innings in an A.L. game against the Chicago White Sox on May 9, 1901. Moore lost, 4-2, in 10 innings, yielding two hits. On June 11, 1904, Mertes singled in the 10th inning off the Chicago Cubs' Robert Wicker after Wicker had pitched no-hit ball for 9⅓ innings in an N.L. game against the New York Giants. Wicker won, 1-0, on a 12-inning one-hitter.

MIKE

The first name of the only three pitchers to defeat Ron Guidry of the New York Yankees in 1978. Guidry, winner of the American League's Cy Young Award in '78 when he compiled a 25-3 record, lost to Mike Caldwell of the

Milwaukee Brewers, Mike Flanagan of the Baltimore Orioles and Mike Willis of the Toronto Blue Jays.

Guidry got revenge against the Mikes that year, beating Boston's Mike Torrez, 5-4, in the one-game playoff for the A.L. East Division championship.

BING MILLER

One of five players in World Series history to end the classic with a game-winning hit. Miller, playing for the Philadelphia Athletics in Game 5 of the 1929 Series, doubled off Pat Malone of the Chicago Cubs with two out in the ninth inning, scoring Al Simmons from second base and giving the A's a 3-2 victory.

Other players with Series-ending hits:

• **Earl McNeely,** Washington Senators, 1924, Game 7. McNeely singled off Jack Bentley of the New York Giants with one out in the 12th inning, scoring Muddy Ruel from second base and giving the Senators a 4-3 triumph.

• **Goose Goslin,** Detroit Tigers, 1935, Game 6. Goslin singled off the Cubs' Larry French with two out in the ninth inning, scoring Mickey Cochrane from second base and boosting the Tigers to a 4-3 win.

• **Billy Martin,** New York Yankees, 1953, Game 6. Martin singled off Clem Labine of the Brooklyn Dodgers with one out in the ninth inning, scoring Hank Bauer from second base in a 4-3 victory.

• **Bill Mazeroski,** Pittsburgh Pirates, 1960, Game 7. Mazeroski homered against the Yankees' Ralph Terry to lead off the Pirates' ninth inning, giving Pittsburgh a 10-9 triumph.

BOB MILLER, BOB MILLER

Pitchers and teammates on the 1962 New York Mets. Robert Lane Miller, primarily a starter, was a righthander who compiled a 1-12 record for the '62 Mets. Robert Gerald Miller, a lefthanded reliever, posted a 2-2 mark for New York.

STU MILLER

San Francisco Giants' pitcher whose wind-caused balk helped the American League tie the National League in the ninth inning of the first All-Star Game of 1961, played in Candlestick Park. With the N.L. ahead, 3-2, in the ninth and Al Kaline on second base and Roger Maris on first for the A.L., Miller relieved Sandy Koufax. With Rocky Colavito at bat, gale-like winds blew Miller off the mound and the reliever was charged with a balk. With runners now on third and second, Colavito grounded to third baseman Ken Boyer. Boyer fumbled the ball, enabling Kaline to score the tying run. The N.L. went on to win, 5-4, in 10 innings—and Miller got the victory.

DALE MITCHELL

The only man to have played in the last World Series game of both the Brooklyn Dodgers and New York Giants. Mitchell pinch-hit for Cleveland

Seeking good luck before the start of the 1935 World Series, Detroit outfielder Goose Goslin used a live rabbit—not just a rabbit's foot—as a charm. Goslin was rewarded, becoming one of only five players in history to end a Series with a game-winning hit.

against the Giants on October 2, 1954 (the day New York completed a sweep of the Indians), and pinch-hit **for** Brooklyn on October 10, 1956 (the day the New York Yankees won Game 7 of that Series).

JOHNNY MIZE

St. Louis Cardinals' first baseman whose ejection from the final game of the 1936 season enabled Walter Alston, future managerial standout with the Brooklyn and Los Angeles Dodgers, to appear in his only major league game. Mize was thrown out in the seventh inning, and Alston was his replacement at first base against the Chicago Cubs. In his lone big-league at-bat, Alston struck out against Lon Warneke.

GEORGE MULLIN

The only pitcher to appear in a World Series after losing 20 games during that year's regular season. Mullin, who compiled a 20-20 record for the Detroit Tigers in 1907, was 0-2 against the Chicago Cubs in the '07 Series.

JOHNNY NEUN

While unassisted triple plays are rare in the big leagues (only eight have been performed), Neun's unassisted triple play for the Detroit Tigers against Cleveland on May 31, 1927, was the second in two days in the majors. On May 30, 1927, shortstop Jimmy Cooney of the Chicago Cubs turned an unassisted triple play in the fourth inning of a game against the Pittsburgh Pirates.

Neun's unaided triple play is the only one to end a game, with the first baseman's ninth-inning heroics wrapping up a 1-0 victory over the Indians for Detroit pitcher Rip Collins and giving Collins his only shutout of the '27 season.

NEW YORK YANKEES, SAN FRANCISCO GIANTS

Teams that traded victories in every other game of the 1962 World Series (one club won all odd-numbered games and the other won all even-numbered games). The Yankees became world champions by winning Games 1, 3, 5, 7; the Giants took Games 2, 4 and 6.

The only other time the sequence occurred in the Series was in 1909 when the Pittsburgh Pirates beat the Detroit Tigers in every other game to win the classic, four games to three.

JOE NIEKRO

Through the 1982 season, he had hit only one home run in his major league career—and that was off his brother, Phil. Houston's Joe outpitched Atlanta's Phil in a May 29, 1976, game, and Joe's seventh-inning homer against his older brother helped the Astros beat the Braves, 4-3.

JIM O'ROURKE

The only man to play in major league baseball's first game and also compete in the majors after the turn of the century. Playing for Boston against Philadelphia in the National League's first game on April 22, 1876, O'Rourke singled off Alonzo Knight for the first hit in big-league history. A minor league manager in 1904 at age 52, O'Rourke longed to play one more time for the New York Giants (a team he helped to N.L. pennants in 1888 and 1889)—and Giants' Manager John McGraw acceded. O'Rourke caught the first game of a September 22 doubleheader against Cincinnati and collected one hit in his career-ending game as the Giants clinched the pennant, winning, 7-5, behind pitcher Joe McGinnity.

JOHN, TOM PACIOREK

John, an outfielder, recorded a 1.000 career batting average. In his only major league game, with the 1963 Houston Colts, he went 3-for-3.

Through 1982, Tom, an outfielder-first baseman and John's brother, had a 1.000 career average in Championship Series play (going 1-for-1 in 1974 for the Los Angeles Dodgers); he also had a 1.000 lifetime mark in All-Star Game competition (going 1-for-1 in 1981 while representing the Seattle Mariners for the American League). Tom's World Series average is .500—he went 1-for-2 in 1974 for the Dodgers.

ERNIE PADGETT

Boston Braves' shortstop who turned an unassisted triple play on October 6, 1923, in only his fourth big-league game—and is the only major leaguer to make an unaided triple play in his club's final game of the season.

JIM PALMER

The only man to appear in all five World Series in which the Baltimore Orioles have played. Palmer pitched for the Orioles against the Los Angeles Dodgers in 1966, against the New York Mets in 1969, against the Cincinnati Reds in 1970, against the Pittsburgh Pirates in 1971 and against the Pirates again in 1979.

JIM PERRY

The losing pitcher in three of the four no-hitters hurled in the American League between the 1970 and 1973 All-Star Games. Pitching for Minnesota, Perry was victimized in September of 1970 when Vida Blue of the Oakland A's threw a no-hitter against the Twins. Pitching for Detroit, Perry was victimized in April of 1973 when Steve Busby of the Kansas City Royals hurled a no-hitter against the Tigers, and in July of 1973 when Nolan Ryan of the California Angels also tossed a no-hitter against Detroit.

Kansas City's Bruce Dal Canton was the losing pitcher in the other A.L. no-hit game during that span, falling victim when California's Ryan threw a no-hitter against the Royals in May of 1973.

While Babe Pinelli (center) ended his umpiring career on the bases in Games 6 and 7 of the 1956 World Series, it was Game 5 for which he will be remembered. Pinelli worked behind the plate for the final time that day when Don Larsen (left) and Yogi Berra formed a perfect-game battery.

JIMMY PIERSALL

After hitting his 100th career home run on June 23, 1963, while playing for the New York Mets, he ran around the bases backward—but in sequence—against the Philadelphia Phillies. Piersall's drive, which came off Dallas Green, was his only National League homer (Piersall hit 103 homers in a 1,694-game American League career that was sandwiched around his 40 games with the Mets).

BABE PINELLI

The umpire whose last game behind the plate in the major leagues was on October 8, 1956—the day Don Larsen of the New York Yankees pitched a perfect game against the Brooklyn Dodgers in Game 5 of the World Series. Pinelli, who began umpiring in the National League in 1935, retired after the 1956 season.

PIRATES, TIGERS, YANKEES

The only three teams in World Series history to come from a three-games-to-one deficit and win the title in a seven-game Series—and the Pirates have done it twice. Pittsburgh rebounded against the Washington Senators in 1925 and against the Baltimore Orioles in 1979, while the Yankees came back from the Milwaukee Braves in 1958 and the Tigers scored victories in Games 5, 6 and 7 to beat the Cardinals in 1968.

HUBERT (SHUCKS) PRUETT

A 29-48 career pitcher who in his first 11 head-to-head meetings with Babe Ruth struck out the Yankee slugger eight times, walked him twice and induced him to hit back to the mound. Pruett, who pitched three years (1922-24) with the St. Louis Browns before finishing his career in the National League, went against Ruth 33 times in 14 games (all in the American League) and struck him out 14 times in 25 official at-bats. Ruth wasn't exactly helpless when facing the lefthander, though, batting .280 against him overall (with two homers among his seven hits). And Ruth went 3-for-5 off Pruett during the pitcher's final season in the A.L.

PEE WEE REESE

Dodgers' shortstop who was the only man to play in all 44 World Series games—spanning seven Series (1941, 1947, 1949, 1952, 1953, 1955 and 1956)—between Brooklyn and the New York Yankees.

WILBERT ROBINSON

Holder for 32 years of the major league record for most runs batted in for one game, 11, Robinson was the opposing manager on September 16, 1924, when Jim Bottomley of the St. Louis Cardinals broke his record. Playing against Robinson's Brooklyn Dodgers, Bottomley drove in 12 runs as the Cards won, 17-3.

Playing for Baltimore of the National League on June 10, 1892, Robinson went 7-for-7 (six singles and a double) against St. Louis and knocked in 11 runs in a 25-4 victory.

COOKIE ROJAS

One of two men to play on teams that were beaten in no-hitters pitched by both Sandy Koufax and Nolan Ryan. Rojas was Philadelphia's center fielder in the 1964 game in which Los Angeles' Koufax hurled a no-hitter against the Phillies, and he was Kansas City's second baseman in the 1973 game in which California's Ryan threw a no-hitter against the Royals.

Robert Lane (Bob) Miller was the New York Mets' starting and losing pitcher in the 1962 no-hitter thrown by the Dodgers' Koufax, and he relieved (but had no decision) for Detroit when the Angels' Ryan fired a no-hitter against the Tigers in '73.

JOHN ROSEBORO

Los Angeles Dodgers' player who caught two of Sandy Koufax's four no-hitters. Roseboro caught Koufax's no-hit game against the New York Mets in 1962 and the lefthander's gem against the San Francisco Giants in 1963.

Doug Camilli was the Dodgers' catcher when Koufax threw a no-hitter against the Philadelphia Phillies in 1964, and Jeff Torborg caught for Los Angeles in Koufax's perfect game against the Chicago Cubs in 1965.

JOSE SANTIAGO

The only pitcher in World Series history to lose a game in which he hit a home run. Santiago, the Boston Red Sox's starting pitcher in Game 1 of the 1967 Series, homered off St. Louis' Bob Gibson in his first Series at-bat but ended up a 2-1 loser to the Cardinals.

Pitchers have homered 13 other times (never more than once in a game) in Series play; they have 11 victories in those games and two no-decision outcomes.

MIKE SCHMIDT

Philadelphia Phillies' third baseman who on June 10, 1974, hit one of the longest singles in major league history. With Dave Cash and Larry Bowa on base in the first inning, Schmidt hit a pitch from Houston's Claude Osteen that seemed to be a tape-measure drive. However, the ball deflected off a speaker hanging in fair territory in center field at the Astrodome. It was the first ball to hit a speaker in fair territory, and the ground rules stated the ball was in play. Neither baserunner scored as the ball caromed back onto the field, leaving Schmidt with a single. (The speaker hangs 117 feet off the ground, 329 feet from home plate.)

OSSEE SCHRECKENGOST

The only man to play in two major league games in which his team was victimized by a perfect game. Schreckengost, a catcher, played for the Philadelphia Athletics in 1904 when Cy Young of Boston pitched a 3-0 perfect game against the A's, and he played for the Chicago White Sox in 1908 when Cleveland's Addie Joss hurled a 1-0 perfect game.

DIEGO SEGUI

The only man to play for both the Seattle Pilots and the Seattle Mariners. Segui compiled a 12-6 pitching record for the Pilots in 1969 (their lone American League season before moving to Milwaukee and becoming the Brewers), but was 0-7 for the first-year Mariners in 1977.

MIKE SHANNON

St. Louis Cardinals' player who collected two hits in four at-bats in the opening game of each of his three World Series appearances (1964, 1967 and 1968).

BOBBY SHANTZ

A major league pitcher for 16 seasons, he hurled only one inning in All-Star Game competition—and struck out all three batters he faced. Relieving for

Bill Sharman was highly visible as a basketball player after his disappearing act on the Brooklyn Dodgers' bench.

the American League in the fifth inning of the 1952 game at Philadelphia's Shibe Park, Shantz struck out Whitey Lockman, Jackie Robinson and Stan Musial. The Philadelphia A's pitcher was denied a chance of matching Carl Hubbell's 1934 All-Star Game feat of five consecutive strikeouts, though, as rain ended the game after five innings. The National League won, 3-2.

BILL SHARMAN

Although he never played in a major league game, Sharman was ejected from one. An outfielder who had batted .286 for Class AA Fort Worth of the Texas League during the 1951 season, Sharman was called up to Brooklyn in September. Riding the bench in a September 27 game at Braves Field in Boston, Sharman suddenly found himself banished when umpire Frank Dascoli ejected Dodger catcher Roy Campanella and pitcher Preacher Roe after a disputed play at the plate and cleared the Brooklyn bench as well. With the Dodgers in a tight pennant race, Sharman never got into a game . . . and he soon turned his attention fully to basketball (a sport in which he made the Hall of Fame after a standout career with the Boston Celtics).

Washington pitcher Dean Stone won the 1954 American League All-Star Game the easy way—he never retired a batter.

ENOS SLAUGHTER

The only player to appear in both the 1946 and 1959 National League play-offs. He played for the St. Louis Cardinals in the '46 playoff against the Brooklyn Dodgers, and for the Milwaukee Braves in the '59 playoff against the Los Angeles Dodgers.

REGGIE SMITH

Outfielder-first baseman who through the 1982 season had hit homers from both sides of the plate in one game four times in the American League and twice in the National League. Smith accomplished the feat for the A.L.'s Boston Red Sox in 1967, 1968, 1972 and 1973, and for the N.L.'s St. Louis Cardinals in 1975 and 1976.

Ted Simmons is the only other player in big-league history to hit homers righthanded and lefthanded in one game in both leagues. Simmons, a catcher, did it for the N.L.'s Cardinals in 1975 and 1979 and for the A.L.'s Milwaukee Brewers in 1982.

WARREN SPAHN

As a rookie pitcher for the Boston Braves in 1942, Spahn was credited with one complete game—but he had a 0-0 record in four appearances. Pitching against the New York Giants in the second game of a September 26 double-header at the Polo Grounds, Spahn was trailing, 5-2, in the bottom of the eighth inning when hundreds of youngsters ran onto the field. The youths refused to return to their seats, so umpire Ziggy Sears forfeited the game to the Braves, 9-0—leaving Spahn with a no-decision outcome, but with his first complete game in the majors.

TIM STODDARD

Baltimore Orioles' pitcher whose World Series single in 1979 came in the only plate appearance of his major league career and made him only the sixth player to collect more hits in a World Series than in that year's regular season. Through the 1982 season, Stoddard had never gone to the plate except for his eighth-inning at-bat in Game 4 of the '79 Series when he grounded a single off Kent Tekulve of the Pittsburgh Pirates.

Other players with one World Series hit and none in the regular season are Joe Hoerner of the St. Louis Cardinals (1968), Bill Lee of the Boston Red Sox (1975) and Will McEnaney of the Cincinnati Reds (1975). Ken Holtzman of the Oakland A's (1974) and Luis Tiant of the Red Sox (1975) had two Series hits and no regular-season hits.

DEAN STONE

The winning pitcher in the 1954 All-Star Game at Cleveland's Municipal Stadium although he didn't retire a batter. Stone, Washington Senators' pitcher, entered the game with two out in the top of the eighth inning and his American League squad trailing, 9-8. With Duke Snider at bat for the National League, Red Schoendienst broke from third base in an attempt to steal home. Stone hurried his motion and threw to catcher Yogi Berra in time to retire Schoendienst. While he left the game in the bottom of the eighth for a pinch-hitter (Larry Doby, who homered), Stone notched the victory as the A.L. broke loose for three runs in that inning and an 11-9 triumph. Virgil Trucks worked the ninth inning for the A.L.

FRANK THOMAS

The only man to play in the New York Giants' last game in history and the New York Mets' first game. Thomas played first base for the Pittsburgh Pirates on September 29, 1957, against the Giants, who were playing their last game before moving to San Francisco in 1958; he was in left field for the Mets on April 11, 1962, when they made their debut against the St. Louis Cardinals.

BOBBY TOLAN

The only man to play in both games of the back-to-back no-hitters of San Francisco's Gaylord Perry and St. Louis' Ray Washburn in 1968 and both games of the consecutive no-hitters by Cincinnati's Jim Maloney and Houston's Don Wilson in 1969. Tolan played left field for St. Louis in the game against Perry and right field behind Washburn, and he was in right field for Cincinnati in the Maloney and Wilson no-hitters.

JEFF TORBORG

The only player to catch no-hitters thrown by both Sandy Koufax and Nolan Ryan. Torborg caught Koufax's last no-hitter, a perfect game for the Los Angeles Dodgers against the Chicago Cubs in September of 1965, and he caught Ryan's first no-hitter—for the California Angels against the Kansas City Royals in May of 1973.

DICK TRACEWSKI

Infielder who played in both Sandy Koufax's 15-strikeout game in the 1963 World Series and Bob Gibson's 17-strikeout game in the 1968 Series (Koufax's total had broken Carl Erskine's Series mark of 14, set in 1953, and Gibson then surpassed Koufax). Tracewski played second base behind the Dodgers' Koufax against the Yankees in '63, and was a late-inning defensive replacement at third base for the Tigers against Gibson and the Cardinals in '68.

Roger Maris was the only other player to appear in both games, playing right field for the Yankees in '63 and the same position for the Cardinals in '68. Maris struck out once against Koufax (Tracewski did not bat against Gibson).

VIRGIL TRUCKS

The only pitcher to win more games in the World Series than in the regular season preceding the classic. In the military service for most of the 1945 season, Trucks didn't pitch for the Detroit Tigers until the final game of the year—and he received no decision in a 5⅓-inning stint. However, Trucks started twice against the Chicago Cubs in the '45 Series and pitched the Tigers to a 4-1 victory in Game 2 (in Game 6, he had no decision).

Only twice have pitchers won as many games in a World Series as during the regular season. Paul Lindblad of the Oakland A's, 1-5 during the 1973 season, was 1-0 against the New York Mets in that year's Series. Blue Moon Odom, also of the A's, matched Lindblad's figures the next year, going 1-5 during the season and 1-0 in the '74 Series against the Los Angeles Dodgers.

RUSS VAN ATTA

New York Yankees' pitcher who threw a five-hit shutout and had four singles in four at-bats against the Washington Senators in his big-league debut on April 25, 1933. Van Atta, who later pitched for the St. Louis Browns, never managed another shutout in the majors (although his career lasted into the 1939 season).

Virgil Trucks (left) and Hank Greenberg celebrate after leading Detroit to a 4-1 victory over the Chicago Cubs in Game 2 of the 1945 World Series. Trucks pitched a seven-hitter for his only triumph of the year (he spent most of the season in the military service), and Greenberg hit a three-run homer.

Yankee shortstop Pee Wee Wanninger left a June 1, 1925, game for pinch-hitter Lou Gehrig—and that at-bat started Gehrig's record streak of playing in 2,130 consecutive games.

BILL VIRDON

The only manager of the New York Yankees since the opening of Yankee Stadium in 1923 never to have managed the Yanks in that ballpark. Virdon was the Yankees' manager in 1974 and part of 1975—years in which the Yanks used New York's Shea Stadium as their home because of the extensive remodeling of Yankee Stadium.

BOBBY WALLACE

The man who spent the most years, 25, in the major leagues as an active player without being on a pennant-winning team. Wallace played from 1894 through 1918 with Cleveland and St. Louis of the National League and for St. Louis of the American League.

LLOYD, PAUL WANER

The only brother combination in big-league history to be involved in an unassisted triple play. In a May 30, 1927, game, Pittsburgh's Paul Waner hit a drive to shortstop Jimmy Cooney of the Chicago Cubs for out No. 1. Cooney caught Lloyd Waner off second base and stepped on the bag, then tagged the Pirates' Clyde Barnhart (who was running from first base).

PAUL (PEE WEE) WANNINGER

New York Yankees' shortstop who had a role in the beginning of Lou Gehrig's consecutive-game streak and who (less than a month earlier) had helped to snap the record string that Gehrig eventually surpassed. Wanninger gave way to pinch-hitter Gehrig in the eighth inning of a June 1, 1925, game against the Washington Senators, thereby starting Gehrig's major league-record streak of playing in 2,130 consecutive games. On May 6, 1925, Wanninger replaced Everett Scott at shortstop for the Yankees, ending Scott's consecutive-game streak at 1,307 (the big-league mark until shattered by Gehrig).

HERB WASHINGTON

A non-pitcher who played in 105 regular-season games in the big leagues—but never batted. A track star at Michigan State, Washington was signed by Oakland A's Owner Charlie Finley for use as a pinch-runner specialist. Washington, who played in 92 games for the A's in 1974 and 13 in 1975, had 31 career steals (in 48 attempts) and scored 33 runs. He pinch-ran in three games of the 1974 World Series against the Los Angeles Dodgers, but stole no bases.

HOYT WILHELM

Pitcher who hit a home run in his first major league at-bat but failed to hit another one in a career that spanned 21 seasons. Batting for the New York Giants in the fourth inning of an April 23, 1952, game against the Boston Braves, Wilhelm connected against rookie Dick Hoover. Wilhelm finished his career with 432 official at-bats.

Hoyt Wilhelm homered in his first big-league at-bat, but the pitcher never connected again in a 21-season career.

The April 23, 1952, game was Hoover's second and last in the majors, and Wilhelm's drive was the only homer he allowed in the big leagues.

HACK WILSON

Chicago Cubs' slugger who in 1930 set a major league record with 190 runs batted in and a National League mark with 56 home runs—but didn't hit a grand slam that season.

WILLIE WILSON

Kansas City Royals' outfielder who hit six home runs in 1979—five of them inside the park. Wilson's only over-the-fence homer in '79 was a June 15 shot at Milwaukee off the Brewers' Mike Caldwell.

SIXTH INNING:

Notable firsts.

FELIPE, JESUS, MATTY ALOU

Brothers who were the first batters in the first regular-season major league games at Busch Memorial Stadium in St. Louis, San Diego Stadium and Atlanta Stadium. Felipe, playing for the Atlanta Braves, was the first hitter at Busch Memorial Stadium on May 12, 1966; Jesus, of the Houston Astros, was the first to bat at San Diego Stadium on April 8, 1969, and Matty, a member of the Pittsburgh Pirates, was the leadoff hitter at Atlanta Stadium on April 12, 1966.

EMMETT ASHFORD

The major leagues' first black umpire, he umpired in the American League from 1966 through 1970.

EARL AVERILL

Cleveland Indians' player who collected the first pinch hit in All-Star Game history, singling in the sixth inning on July 6, 1933.

Jackie Robinson (right), the first black to play in modern big-league baseball, was joined in Brooklyn later in the 1947 season by Dan Bankhead, the
first black pitcher in the majors.

BOB BAILOR

The first player picked by the Toronto Blue Jays in the American League expansion draft of 1976. Bailor, a shortstop, was selected off the Baltimore Orioles' roster.

DAN BANKHEAD

The first black pitcher in major league history. Relieving Brooklyn starter Hal Gregg in the second inning of an August 26, 1947, game against Pittsburgh, Bankhead worked $3\frac{1}{3}$ innings and allowed 10 hits and six earned runs. He did not figure in the decision.

Batting in the bottom of the second inning, the Dodgers' Bankhead homered in his first big-league at-bat. He connected off the Pirates' Fritz Ostermueller.

ROSS BARNES

A second baseman for Chicago's National League team, he slugged the first home run in major league history on May 2, 1876. Barnes connected against Cincinnati's Cherokee Fisher.

GINGER BEAUMONT

Pittsburgh center fielder who was the first batter in World Series history on October 1, 1903. Beaumont flied out for the Pirates against Cy Young of the Boston Red Sox.

ERWIN BECK

Cleveland second baseman who hit the first home run in American League history, connecting off John Skopec of Chicago on April 25, 1901.

YOGI BERRA

New York Yankee who belted the first pinch-hit home run in World Series history, connecting off Ralph Branca of the Brooklyn Dodgers in the seventh inning of Game 3 of the 1947 Series.

JOE BLACK

First black pitcher to win a World Series game. After starting only two of the 56 regular-season games in which he pitched for the Brooklyn Dodgers in 1952, Black started Game 1 of the '52 Series and beat the New York Yankees, 4-2, on a six-hitter.

PAUL BLAIR

Baltimore center fielder who was the first man to bat in a night World Series game. As the leadoff hitter in Game 4 of the 1971 Series, Blair singled for the Orioles against the Pittsburgh Pirates.

RON BLOMBERG

The first designated hitter in major league history. Playing in the April 6, 1973, American League game between New York and Boston, the Yankees' Blomberg drew a bases-loaded walk off Luis Tiant in the first inning and finished the day with one hit in three official at-bats. The Red Sox won, 15-5.

JOE BOWMAN

Philadelphia Phillies' pitcher who lost the first night game in major league history, May 24, 1935, at Cincinnati.

EDDIE BRESSOUD

The Houston Colt .45s' first pick in the National League expansion draft of 1961. Bressoud, an infielder, was selected from the San Francisco Giants' roster.

KEN BRETT

Pitching for the Chicago White Sox against the Toronto Blue Jays on April 7, 1977, Brett was the loser in the first American League game played in Canada.

LOU BROCK

St. Louis Cardinals' outfielder who was the first player to bat in a major league game in Canada, April 14, 1969, against the Montreal Expos.

OLLIE BROWN

Outfielder who was the first choice of the San Diego Padres in the National League's 1968 expansion draft. Brown was taken from the San Francisco Giants' roster.

WILLARD BROWN

The first black player in American League history to hit a home run. Pinch-hitting for Joe Schultz of the St. Louis Browns on August 13, 1947, Brown drilled an inside-the-park homer off Hal Newhouser of the Detroit Tigers in the second game of a doubleheader.

WILLARD BROWN, HANK THOMPSON

The first two black players to appear together in a modern major league game. Brown played right field and Thompson second base for the St. Louis Browns in a July 20, 1947, game against the Boston Red Sox.

BYRON BROWNE, DON YOUNG

Chicago Cubs' outfielders who in their first major league game faced Sandy Koufax of the Los Angeles Dodgers on September 9, 1965—the night Koufax

Hank Thompson (above left) and Willard Brown, the first black players to appear together in a modern major league game, sit with St. Louis Browns' Manager Muddy Ruel after signing to play with the Browns in July of 1947. Ron Blomberg (left) became the first designated hitter in major league history on April 6, 1973.

pitched a perfect game and won, 1-0. Browne batted sixth and played left field; Young led off and played center field.

BILLY BRUTON

Braves' player who hit the first major league home run at Milwaukee's County Stadium. Playing in his second big-league game on April 14, 1953, Bruton slugged a 10th-inning homer off Gerry Staley of the St. Louis Cardinals to give Milwaukee a 3-2 triumph. Bruton's drive, which bounced off the glove of St. Louis right fielder Enos Slaughter and over the fence, was the only homer for the Braves' outfielder in 151 games that season.

JIM BUNNING

The first man to pitch for both leagues in All-Star Games. After appearing for the American League in 1957, 1959, 1961 (twice), 1962 and 1963, Bunning pitched for the National League in the 1964 classic (and again in 1966).

BEN CHAPMAN

New York Yankees' outfielder who was the first man to bat for the American League in an All-Star Game. Chapman grounded out to third baseman Pepper Martin of the St. Louis Cardinals on July 6, 1933.

CHICAGO CUBS

The first National League team to draw one million fans in one year, attracting 1,159,168 in 1927.

LOU CHIOZZA

Philadelphia Phillies' second baseman who was the first player to bat in a major league night game. Chiozza grounded out to shortstop Billy Myers of the Cincinnati Reds in the May 24, 1935, game at Cincinnati's Crosley Field.

COMISKEY PARK

Chicago stadium where the National League first won an All-Star Game at an American League site. After losing eight consecutive games in A.L. parks, the N.L. won, 4-3, in 14 innings in 1950 at Comiskey Park, home of the A.L.'s Chicago White Sox.

MORT COOPER

Pitcher for the St. Louis Cardinals who lost the first night All-Star Game in history, July 13, 1943, at Philadelphia's Shibe Park.

RAY CULP

Philadelphia Phillies' pitcher who gave up Hank Aaron's first home run as a member of the Atlanta Braves on April 20, 1966. The homer was the 399th of Aaron's major league career.

BILL DAHLEN

The first player in World Series history to steal home. Playing for the New York Giants against the Philadelphia Athletics in 1905, Dahlen stole home in the fifth inning of Game 3.

CLAY DALRYMPLE

Philadelphia player whose two-out, pinch single in the eighth inning was the only hit off San Francisco's Juan Marichal in the pitcher's first major league game, played July 19, 1960. Marichal and the Giants beat the Phillies, 2-0.

DIZZY DEAN

St. Louis Cardinals' standout who in 1936 became the first National League pitcher to win an All-Star Game.

PAUL DERRINGER

Reds' pitcher who started and won the first night game in major league history on May 24, 1935, at Cincinnati against the Philadelphia Phillies.

VINCE DiMAGGIO

Pittsburgh Pirates' center fielder who hit the National League's first home run in a night All-Star Game, connecting off Tex Hughson in the ninth inning of the 1943 contest.

BILL DINNEEN

Pitcher for the Boston Red Sox who tossed the first shutout in World Series competition, blanking the Pittsburgh Pirates in Game 2 of the 1903 classic.

BILL DINNEEN

The first former World Series player to umpire in a Series. A pitcher for the Boston Red Sox in the 1903 classic, Dinneen umpired his first Series in 1911 when the Philadelphia A's played the New York Giants.

LARRY DOBY, HANK THOMPSON

The first black players to oppose each other in a major league game. In the first game of an August 9, 1947, doubleheader between the Indians and Browns, Doby appeared as a pinch-hitter for Cleveland and Thompson played second base for St. Louis.

BOBBY DOERR

Boston Red Sox's second baseman who hit the first home run in a night All-Star Game, connecting against Mort Cooper in the second inning of the 1943 classic.

PATSY DOUGHERTY

Boston right fielder who was the first player to hit two home runs in one World Series game, accomplishing the feat against Pittsburgh in Game 2 of the 1903 Series.

DAN DRIESSEN

The National League's first designated hitter. With the N.L. using a designated hitter only in even-numbered World Series (a format that began in 1976), Driessen got his chance with Cincinnati in the '76 Series against the New York Yankees. Driessen, who flied out in his first at-bat in the second inning of Game 1, batted .357 in the Series as the Reds' DH.

DON DRYSDALE

Los Angeles Dodgers' pitcher who threw the first All-Star Game and World Series pitches on the West Coast, both in 1959 (when the second All-Star Game of the year was played August 3 at the Los Angeles Memorial Coliseum and Game 3 of the '59 Series was played at the Coliseum on October 4).

DON DRYSDALE

The man who threw the first pitch in the first indoor All-Star Game, 1968, at Houston's Astrodome.

HOWARD EHMKE

Philadelphia Athletics' pitcher who on April 15, 1927, yielded the first of Babe Ruth's 60 home runs that season.

GLENN ELLIOTT

Boston Braves' pitcher who gave up Jackie Robinson's first major league hit. Robinson, playing for the Brooklyn Dodgers on April 17, 1947, collected a bunt single.

GEORGE FALLON

St. Louis Cardinals' shortstop who was the first batter to face Cincinnati's Joe Nuxhall when the Reds' pitcher made his debut in the majors at age 15 on June 10, 1944. Fallon grounded out against the youngest player in big-league history.

HOBE FERRIS

Boston second baseman who committed the first error in World Series history, fumbling a ball hit by Pittsburgh's Kitty Bransfield in the first inning of Game 1 of the 1903 classic.

Longtime Milwaukee Braves slugger Joe Adcock made his major league debut in a Cincinnati Reds uniform in 1950. Adcock played three seasons with the Reds before being traded to the Braves as part of a four-club deal in 1953.

FIRST TEAMS

Many players have not achieved their greatest fame in the majors with their original big-league teams. Included among such players are:

Player	First Club	Debut Year
Joe Adcock	Cincinnati Reds	1950
Gus Bell	Pittsburgh Pirates	1950
Roger Bresnahan	Washington Senators	1897
Lou Brock	Chicago Cubs	1961
Mordecai Brown	St. Louis Cardinals	1903
Lew Burdette	New York Yankees	1950
Jesse Burkett	New York Giants	1890
Johnny Callison	Chicago White Sox	1958
Dolph Camilli	Chicago Cubs	1933

Player	First Club	Debut Year
Norm Cash	Chicago White Sox	1957
Stan Coveleski	Philadelphia A's	1912
Sam Crawford	Cincinnati Reds	1899
Joe Cronin	Pittsburgh Pirates	1926
Mike Cuellar	Cincinnati Reds	1959
Al Dark	Boston Braves	1946
Paul Derringer	St. Louis Cardinals	1931
Elmer Flick	Philadelphia Phillies	1898
Curt Flood	Cincinnati Reds	1956
George Foster	San Francisco Giants	1969
Nellie Fox	Philadelphia A's	1947
Woodie Fryman	Pittsburgh Pirates	1966
Al Gionfriddo	Pittsburgh Pirates	1944
Burleigh Grimes	Pittsburgh Pirates	1916
Jesse Haines	Cincinnati Reds	1918
Bob Hazle	Cincinnati Reds	1955
Waite Hoyt	New York Giants	1918
Randy Hundley	San Francisco Giants	1964
Joe Jackson	Philadelphia A's	1908
Ferguson Jenkins	Philadelphia Phillies	1965
Tommy John	Cleveland Indians	1963
Deron Johnson	New York Yankees	1960
Don Larsen	St. Louis Browns	1953
Dick Littlefield	Boston Red Sox	1950
Ernie Lombardi	Brooklyn Dodgers	1931
Al Lopez	Brooklyn Dodgers	1928
Dolf Luque	Boston Braves	1914
Bill Madlock	Texas Rangers	1973
Roger Maris	Cleveland Indians	1957
Bing Miller	Washington Senators	1921
Manny Mota	San Francisco Giants	1962
Art Nehf	Boston Braves	1915
Bobo Newsom	Brooklyn Dodgers	1929
Bill Nicholson	Philadelphia A's	1936
Lefty O'Doul	New York Yankees	1919
Claude Osteen	Cincinnati Reds	1957
Amos Otis	New York Mets	1967
Roger Peckinpaugh	Cleveland Indians	1910
Herb Pennock	Philadelphia A's	1912
Billy Pierce	Detroit Tigers	1945
Lou Piniella	Baltimore Orioles	1964
Babe Ruth	Boston Red Sox	1914
Bob Turley	St. Louis Browns	1951
Dazzy Vance	Pittsburgh Pirates	1915
Dixie Walker	New York Yankees	1931
Bucky Walters	Philadelphia Phillies	1934
Bill White	New York Giants	1956
Ken Williams	Cincinnati Reds	1915
Hack Wilson	New York Giants	1923

The 1947 Philadelphia A's had a young-looking second baseman named Nellie Fox.

FRANKIE FRISCH

St. Louis Cardinals' second baseman who hit the first National League home run in an All-Star Game, belting a sixth-inning homer off Alvin Crowder of the Washington Senators on July 6, 1933.

RALPH GARR

Outfielder for the Chicago White Sox who in an April 7, 1977, game against the Toronto Blue Jays became the first American League player to bat in Canada.

LOU GEHRIG

New York Yankees' first baseman who committed the first error in All-Star Game history when he dropped a foul fly ball in the fifth inning on July 6, 1933.

LEFTY GOMEZ

New York Yankee and American League hurler who threw the first pitch in All-Star Game competition on July 6, 1933, was the winning pitcher in the first classic and had the first run batted in.

JACK GRANEY

Cleveland Indians' left fielder who was the first player to bat against Babe Ruth (then a pitcher with the Boston Red Sox) in a major league game, July 11, 1914.

ELI GRBA

The Los Angeles Angels' first choice in the American League expansion draft in 1960. Grba, a pitcher, was picked from the New York Yankees' roster.

STAN HACK

Chicago Cubs' third baseman who was the first batter in a night All-Star Game, leading off the 1943 classic with a single.

CHICK HAFEY

Cincinnati Reds' left fielder who singled in the second inning for the first hit in All-Star Game history, July 6, 1933.

BILL HALLAHAN

St. Louis Cardinal who was the first man to pitch for the National League in the All-Star Game and also the losing pitcher in the first classic, July 6, 1933.

LUKE HAMLIN

Brooklyn Dodgers' pitcher who lost to the Cincinnati Reds in the majors' first televised game, August 26, 1939.

TOMMY HARPER

The first batter in Seattle Pilots' history. Harper, a second baseman, led off the Pilots' first game on April 8, 1969, at Anaheim by doubling off Jim McGlothlin of the California Angels.

JOE HARRIS

Washington right fielder who became the first player to hit a home run in his first World Series at-bat. Harris homered for the Senators against the Pittsburgh Pirates in the second inning of Game 1 of the 1925 Series.

EARL HARRIST

The first pitcher to face Larry Doby of Cleveland when Doby became the first black player to appear in an American League game on July 5, 1947. Pitching for the Chicago White Sox, Harrist struck out the Indians' Doby (who was pinch-hitting for pitcher Bryan Stephens in the seventh inning).

FRANK HAYES

Athletics' catcher who hit the first home run in an American League night game, connecting against Cleveland at Philadelphia on May 16, 1939.

MIKE HEGAN

The first player to hit a home run for the Seattle Pilots, connecting off Jim McGlothlin of the California Angels on April 8, 1969.

BABE HERMAN

Cincinnati Reds' player whose home run against the Brooklyn Dodgers on July 10, 1935, was the first in a major league night game.

BILL HOFFER

Cleveland pitcher who lost the first game in American League history, against Chicago on April 24, 1901.

BOBO HOLLOMAN

The only pitcher in modern major league history to toss a no-hitter in his first starting assignment. After four relief appearances earlier in the 1953 season, Holloman started for the St. Louis Browns against the Philadelphia Athletics on May 6. The rookie held the A's hitless in a 6-0 triumph, walking five batters and striking out three. Holloman also had two hits and three runs batted in (the only hits and RBIs of his big-league career). Holloman won only two more games, and on July 23 he owned a 3-7 record. At that juncture, he was sold to Toronto of the International League—never to return to the majors.

CARL HUBBELL

Pitching for the New York Giants against the Boston Braves on April 16, 1935, Hubbell gave up Babe Ruth's first National League home run. The homer was Ruth's 709th career shot in the major leagues.

JOHNNY HUMPHRIES

Cleveland Indians' pitcher who beat the Athletics in the American League's first night game, May 16, 1939, at Philadelphia.

LARRY JASTER

Montreal Expos' hurler who threw the first major league pitch in Canada on April 14, 1969, against the St. Louis Cardinals.

JERRY JOHNSON

Toronto Blue Jays' pitcher who won the first American League game played in Canada, defeating the Chicago White Sox on April 7, 1977.

MACK JONES

Playing for the Montreal Expos against the St. Louis Cardinals on April 14, 1969, he hit the first major league home run in Canada.

RUPPERT JONES

The first selection of the Seattle Mariners in the American League's 1976 expansion draft. Jones, an outfielder, was chosen off the Kansas City Royals' roster.

SAM JONES

The first black pitcher in major league history to toss a no-hitter, throwing a 4-0 gem for the Chicago Cubs against the Pittsburgh Pirates on May 12, 1955.

Jones also was the first black hurler to lose a game in which an opponent pitched a no-hitter. Warren Spahn of the Milwaukee Braves tossed a 1-0 no-hitter against Jones and the San Francisco Giants on April 28, 1961.

BRUCE KISON

Pittsburgh Pirates' reliever who was the winning pitcher against the Baltimore Orioles on October 13, 1971, in the first night game in World Series history. Kison worked $6\frac{1}{3}$ innings of one-hit, scoreless relief.

St. Louis Browns pitcher Bobo Holloman holds the game ball he received for his 1953 no-hitter against the Philadelphia A's and expresses his hope for the future with crossed fingers. The old crossed-finger trick did not work.

BILL KLEM

The home-plate umpire at Cincinnati on May 24, 1935, when the Reds and Philadelphia Phillies played the first night game in big-league history.

DAVE KOSLO

New York Giants' pitcher who gave up the first home run by a black player in major league history. Facing the Brooklyn Dodgers on April 18, 1947, Koslo surrendered a homer to Jackie Robinson.

HOBIE LANDRITH

Catcher who was the first player selected by the New York Mets in the National League expansion draft of 1961. Landrith was drafted off the San Francisco Giants' roster.

DON LARSEN

The starting and losing pitcher for Baltimore in its return to the American League in 1954 (the city's 1901-02 franchise became the New York Yankees). Larsen and the Orioles lost, 3-0, to the Detroit Tigers on April 13.

TOMMY LEACH

Pittsburgh Pirates' third baseman who collected the first hit in World Series play, tripling in the first inning off Cy Young of the Boston Red Sox on October 1, 1903.

BOB LEMON

Cleveland Indians' pitcher who hurled the American League's first night no-hitter, beating the Detroit Tigers, 2-0, on June 30, 1948, at Briggs Stadium.

Johnny Vander Meer's second of two straight no-hitters in 1938 was the National League's first night no-hit game.

EMIL (DUTCH) LEONARD

Washington Senators' hurler who was the winning pitcher in the first night All-Star Game, played July 13, 1943, at Shibe Park in Philadelphia.

LOS ANGELES DODGERS

The first—and, through the 1982 season, the only—major league club to attain three million in attendance in one year, attracting 3,347,845 fans in 1978. The Dodgers also reached 3,000,000 in 1980 (3,249,287) and in 1982 (a record total of 3,608,881).

CONNIE MACK

The first manager of an American League squad in All-Star Game history, piloting the A.L. in 1933.

FRED MARBERRY

Washington Senators' pitcher who on July 23, 1925, surrendered the first of Lou Gehrig's record 23 bases-loaded home runs in the major leagues.

PEPPER MARTIN

St. Louis Cardinals' third baseman who was the first batter in All-Star Game history on July 6, 1933. Martin grounded out to American League shortstop Joe Cronin of the Washington Senators.

DAL MAXVILL

Playing for the St. Louis Cardinals against the Montreal Expos, Maxvill slugged the major leagues' first bases-loaded homer in Canada on April 14, 1969.

VON McDANIEL

After two relief appearances, this St. Louis Cardinal pitcher (just out of high school) shut out the Brooklyn Dodgers, 2-0, on two hits in his first major league start on June 21, 1957. In his seventh start, he beat the Pittsburgh Pirates, 4-0, on a one-hitter and allowed one baserunner. The 18-year-old McDaniel, brother of longtime relief specialist Lindy, finished the season with a 7-5 record and a 3.21 earned-run average. But, losing his pitching rhythm, Von pitched in only two more big-league games (both in 1958) and was through as a major leaguer at age 19.

DAN McGINN

Montreal Expos' relief pitcher who won the first big-league game played in Canada, beating the St. Louis Cardinals on April 14, 1969.

JIM McGLOTHLIN

The first man to pitch against the Seattle Pilots—and he lasted only one-third of an inning for the California Angels, taking the loss in a 4-3 game played on April 8, 1969.

JOHN McGRAW

The first manager of a National League team in All-Star Game history, piloting the N.L. in 1933.

MILWAUKEE BRAVES

The first National League club to hit two million in attendance in one season, drawing 2,131,388 fans in 1954.

DON MINCHER

First baseman who was the first pick of the Seattle Pilots in the 1968 American League expansion draft. Mincher was selected off the California Angels' roster.

DON MINCHER

The first—and only—member of the Seattle Pilots to appear in the All-Star Game. Mincher, pinch-hitting for Denny McLain in the fourth inning of the 1969 game, struck out against Bob Gibson.

WILLIE MITCHELL

Cleveland Indians' hurler who lost to Babe Ruth of the Boston Red Sox on July 11, 1914, when Ruth pitched and won his first big-league game.

RICK MONDAY

The first player selected in major league baseball's first amateur free-agent draft, chosen by the Kansas City Athletics in June of 1965.

MANNY MOTA

Infielder-outfielder who was the first player taken by the Montreal Expos in the National League's expansion draft in 1968. Mota was selected off the Pittsburgh Pirates' roster.

LES MUELLER

Detroit Tigers' pitcher who on April 17, 1945, surrendered the first hit, a single, in the major league career of Pete Gray, the St. Louis Browns' one-armed outfielder.

BILLY MYERS

Cincinnati shortstop who made the first hit in a major league night game. Leading off the first inning for the Reds against the Philadelphia Phillies in a May 24, 1935, game, Myers doubled.

ROGER NELSON

The first selection of the Kansas City Royals in the American League's expansion draft of 1968. Nelson, a pitcher, was picked off the Baltimore Orioles' roster.

NEW YORK YANKEES

The first big-league club to draw one million (1,289,422 in 1920) and two million (2,265,512 in 1946) in attendance in one season.

MICKEY OWEN

Brooklyn Dodgers' catcher who slugged the first pinch-hit home run in All-Star Game history, connecting in the 1942 classic. Owen did not homer in 133 regular-season games that year.

SATCHEL PAIGE

The first black pitcher to take the mound in the World Series. Paige worked two-thirds of an inning for the Cleveland Indians in Game 5 of the 1948 World Series against the Boston Braves, allowing no hits or walks.

Dan Bankhead of the Brooklyn Dodgers was the first black pitcher to appear in a World Series, but he was used only as a pinch-runner in Game 6 of the 1947 classic.

CLARENCE (ACE) PARKER

Future Pro Football Hall of Famer who in the first at-bat of a two-year career in big-league baseball slammed a pinch-hit home run for the Philadelphia Athletics. Parker connected against Wes Ferrell of the Boston Red Sox on April 30, 1937.

ROY PARMELEE

Philadelphia Athletics' pitcher who lost to the Cleveland Indians in the first night game in American League history, May 16, 1939, at Philadelphia.

ROY PATTERSON

Chicago hurler who made the first pitch in American League history on April 24, 1901, against Cleveland and was the winning pitcher in the A.L.'s first game.

MARTY PATTIN

The first pitcher in the history of the Seattle Pilots. Pattin was the starter and winner—he worked five innings—in the Pilots' 4-3 triumph over the California Angels on April 8, 1969.

HERB PENNOCK

Pitcher for the Boston Red Sox who gave up Babe Ruth's first home run as a New York Yankee on May 1, 1920. It was Ruth's 50th lifetime homer.

GAYLORD PERRY

Cleveland Indians' pitcher who gave up Hank Aaron's first American League home run (the 734th homer of Aaron's big-league career). Aaron connected on April 18, 1975, as a member of the Milwaukee Brewers.

EDDIE PHELPS

Pittsburgh Pirates' catcher who in Game 1 of the 1903 World Series became the first man to strike out in Series play. Phelps fanned in the first inning against Cy Young of the Boston Red Sox, but reached first base when the ball got away from catcher Lou Criger.

DEACON PHILLIPPE

The winning pitcher in the first World Series game in history. Pitching for the Pittsburgh Pirates on October 1, 1903, Phillippe hurled a six-hit, 7-3 victory against the Boston Red Sox.

OLLIE PICKERING

Cleveland right fielder who was the first batter in American League history, going to the plate against Chicago on April 24, 1901.

LOU PINIELLA

The first designated hitter in World Series history. Playing for the New York Yankees against the Cincinnati Reds in Game 1 of the '76 Series, Piniella led off the second inning with a double.

JAMIE QUIRK, DAN QUISENBERRY

The majors' first "Q" battery. With Quirk catching for the Kansas City Royals in an April 13, 1980, game against the Detroit Tigers, Quisenberry came on as a relief pitcher in the seventh inning.

VIC RASCHI

Pitching for the St. Louis Cardinals against the Milwaukee Braves on April 23, 1954, he gave up the first home run of Hank Aaron's major league career.

ROBIN ROBERTS

The first man to pitch under artificial-turf conditions in the major leagues, hurling for the Houston Astros in an April 18, 1966, game against the Los Angeles Dodgers at the Astrodome. The Astrodome, which opened in 1965 and had natural grass during its first season, began the 1966 season with only an AstroTurf infield, but its outfield was covered with synthetic grass later in the year.

FRANK ROBINSON

The first black manager in major league history, making his debut as Cleveland's pilot on April 8, 1975, when the Indians played their American League season opener against the New York Yankees. In the Tribe's lineup as a designated hitter, Robinson homered against Doc Medich in the first inning.

Robinson also was the first black manager in National League history, making his debut for the San Francisco Giants on April 9, 1981.

BILL ROHR

Boston pitcher who in his first big-league game in 1967 went 8⅔ innings without allowing a hit before Elston Howard of the Yankees—on a 3-2 pitch

Frank Robinson gets a cold greeting from John Lowenstein after hitting a first-inning home run in his debut as Cleveland's player-manager.

Boston pitcher Bill Rohr's 1967 debut was memorable as he held the Yankees hitless until Elston Howard singled with two out in the ninth inning.

Yankee slugger Babe Ruth trots home after hitting the first home run in All-Star Game history in 1933 at Chicago's Comiskey Park.

—singled. Rohr, whose batterymate (Russ Gibson) also was making his debut in the majors, finished with a one-hit, 3-0 triumph in New York's home opener—but he pitched in only nine more games for the Red Sox and 17 for the Cleveland Indians before bowing out of the big leagues in 1968 at age 23.

SCHOOLBOY ROWE

The first player to appear for both leagues in All-Star Game competition. Rowe, representing the Detroit Tigers, pitched for the American League in 1936; as a member of the Philadelphia Phillies, he pinch-hit for the National League's Warren Spahn in 1947.

JOE RUDI

Left fielder who played his first game for Oakland on May 8, 1968—the night that Jim (Catfish) Hunter of the A's pitched a perfect game against the Minnesota Twins. Rudi had played 19 games for the Kansas City A's in 1967.

BABE RUTH

New York Yankees' right fielder who hit the first home run in All-Star Game competition, connecting in the third inning off Bill Hallahan of the St. Louis Cardinals on July 6, 1933.

JOHNNY SAIN

The first pitcher to face Jackie Robinson in the majors. Sain, pitching for the Boston Braves against the Brooklyn Dodgers on April 15, 1947, got Robinson—in his first at-bat as the first black player in modern big-league history—to ground out to third baseman Bob Elliott in the first inning.

JOE SCHULTZ

The first—and only—manager of the American League's Seattle Pilots, who moved to Milwaukee and became the Brewers after one season, 1969, in Seattle.

JIMMY SEBRING

Right fielder for the Pittsburgh Pirates who hit the first home run in World Series competition, connecting against Cy Young of the Boston Red Sox in the seventh inning of Game 1 of the 1903 Series.

BOBBY SHANTZ

Pitcher who was the first choice of the Washington Senators (second club) in the American League expansion draft of 1960. Shantz was selected off the New York Yankees' roster.

SHIBE PARK

Philadelphia stadium that was the site of the first night All-Star Game in major league history, July 13, 1943.

BILL SINGER

Facing the Chicago White Sox on April 7, 1977, the Toronto Blue Jays' Singer threw the first pitch in the first American League game played in Canada.

ELMER SMITH

Cleveland Indians' right fielder who was the first player to hit a bases-loaded home run in World Series play. Smith walloped his grand slam against the Brooklyn Dodgers in the first inning of Game 5 of the 1920 Series.

KARL SPOONER

One of only nine players to pitch shutouts in their first two big-league games, Spooner made perhaps the most dramatic debut by striking out a total of 27 batters. Called up by the Brooklyn Dodgers from Fort Worth late in the 1954 season, Spooner shut out the New York Giants, 3-0, on three hits September 22 and blanked the Pittsburgh Pirates, 1-0, on four hits September 26. Spooner, who struck out 15 Giants and 12 Pirates, went 8-6 in 1955 and then bowed out of the majors at age 24 because of arm trouble.

DON SUTTON

The winning pitcher in the first major league game played on artificial turf, hurling the Los Angeles Dodgers past the Houston Astros in an April 18, 1966, game at the Astrodome.

IRA THOMAS

Detroit Tigers' player who notched the first pinch hit in World Series history, singling against the Chicago Cubs in the ninth inning of Game 1 of the 1908 Series.

HANK THOMPSON

The first black player for two major league teams. Thompson, an infielder-outfielder who played nine big-league seasons, was the St. Louis Browns' first black player in 1947 and the New York Giants' first in 1949.

HECTOR TORRES

Playing for the Toronto Blue Jays against the New York Yankees on June 27, 1977, Torres hit the first bases-loaded home run in Canada in American League history.

GUS TRIANDOS

The first man to catch no-hitters in both major leagues. Triandos caught for Baltimore in 1958 when the Orioles' Hoyt Wilhelm pitched a no-hit game against the New York Yankees, and he caught for Philadelphia in 1964 when the Phillies' Jim Bunning threw a perfect game against the New York Mets.

ARKY VAUGHAN

Shortstop for the Pittsburgh Pirates who in 1941 became the first player to hit two home runs in an All-Star Game.

LUKE WALKER

Pittsburgh Pirates' pitcher who delivered the first pitch in a World Series night game, October 13, 1971, against the Baltimore Orioles.

MOSES (FLEET) WALKER

The first black player in major league history. Walker, a catcher, made his debut on May 1, 1884, when he caught for Toledo against Louisville in an American Association game.

BUCKY WALTERS

Cincinnati Reds' pitcher who won big-league baseball's first televised game, beating the Brooklyn Dodgers on a two-hitter on August 26, 1939.

JACK WARHOP

Pitching for the New York Yankees against the Boston Red Sox on May 6, 1915, he surrendered the first home run of Babe Ruth's major league career.

GARY WASLEWSKI

Pitcher for the St. Louis Cardinals who was the loser in the first big-league game played in Canada, beaten by the Montreal Expos on April 14, 1969.

EDDIE WATT

Baltimore Orioles' reliever who was the losing pitcher against the Pittsburgh Pirates on October 13, 1971, in the first night game in World Series history.

ROY WEATHERLY

Cleveland Indians' center fielder who was the first man to bat in an American League night game, May 16, 1939, in Philadelphia.

BILLY WERBER

Cincinnati third baseman who was the first batter in major league baseball's first televised game, the Reds' August 26, 1939, game against the Dodgers at Brooklyn.

WALLY WESTLAKE

Playing for the Pittsburgh Pirates on June 18, 1948, he hit a home run off the Philadelphia Phillies' Robin Roberts—the first of a major league-record 502 homers surrendered by Roberts during his career.

ART WILLIAMS

The first black umpire in the National League. Williams umpired in the N.L. from 1973 through 1977.

MAURY WILLS

Los Angeles Dodgers' player who was the first man to bat on an artificial surface in a big-league game, leading off against the Houston Astros on April 18, 1966, at the Astrodome.

CY YOUNG

The losing pitcher in the first World Series game in history. Pitching for the Boston Red Sox on October 1, 1903, Young was a 7-3 loser to the Pittsburgh Pirates. He went the distance, allowing 12 hits.

ROSS YOUNGS

New York Giant who was the first player in World Series competition to collect two hits in one inning. Youngs accomplished the feat against the New York Yankees in 1921, doubling and tripling in the seventh inning of Game 3.

RICHIE ZISK

The first American Leaguer to belt a home run in Canada, connecting for the Chicago White Sox against the Toronto Blue Jays on April 7, 1977.

SEVENTH INNING:

Notable lasts.

HANK AARON, JOE TORRE

The last members of the Milwaukee Braves to play in an All-Star Game, both playing the entire game for the National League in 1965 at Bloomington, Minn. Torre slugged a two-run homer for the N.L. in the first inning.

BABE ADAMS

Pittsburgh pitcher who was beaten, 1-0, by Boston's Cy Young in Young's 511th and last major league victory, September 22, 1911.

BOB ALLISON

The last player to hit a home run for Washington's original American League franchise, connecting for the Senators on September 28, 1960.

WALTER ALSTON

The last manager of the Brooklyn Dodgers, piloting the team in 1957. Alston also managed the club in the three previous seasons, and he guided the Los Angeles Dodgers from 1958 through 1976.

LUKE APPLING

The last manager of the Kansas City Athletics, succeeding Alvin Dark on August 21, 1967, and guiding the club for the rest of the season.

JIM BIVIN

The last man to pitch to Babe Ruth in a major league game. Bivin, pitching for the Philadelphia Phillies against the Boston Braves in the first game of a May 30, 1935, doubleheader at Baker Bowl, retired Ruth in the first inning on a grounder to first baseman Dolph Camilli. Ruth left the game shortly after his first at-bat and never played again.

TINY BONHAM

Pitcher for the New York Yankees who on September 16, 1945, surrendered the last major league hit by Pete Gray, one-armed outfielder of the St. Louis Browns.

BOSTON BRAVES

Facing the Dodgers at Ebbets Field on September 28, 1952, Boston played Brooklyn to a 5-5 tie in the Braves' last game before moving to Milwaukee in 1953. The 12-inning game was called because of darkness. Boston's last National League victory came on September 27, 1952, when pitcher Virgil Jester notched his third and last big league triumph by beating Joe Black and the Dodgers, 11-3.

LOU BOUDREAU

The last player-manager in the major leagues to lead his team to a pennant. Boudreau, a shortstop, batted .355 with 18 home runs and 106 runs batted in for his 1948 Cleveland Indians, American League champions and World Series titlists.

BOBBY BRAGAN

The last manager of the Milwaukee Braves, piloting the club in 1965. Bragan, who took over as the Braves' manager in 1963, continued to manage the club when it moved to Atlanta in 1966—but he was dismissed in August of '66.

BROOKLYN DODGERS

Playing their final game before moving to Los Angeles in 1958, the Dodgers lost to the Phillies, 2-1, on September 29, 1957, at Philadelphia. Seth Morehead, collecting the first of only five career victories in the majors, outdueled Roger Craig, the last pitcher of record in Brooklyn history.

MORDECAI BROWN, CHRISTY MATHEWSON

Future Hall of Famers whose pitching matchup on September 4, 1916, marked the last major league playing appearance for both men. Mathewson, Cincinnati's manager, hurled his only game for the Reds that day and beat Brown and the Chicago Cubs, 10-8, in the second game of a doubleheader. Both pitchers went the distance, with Mathewson yielding 15 hits and Brown allowing 19.

GUY BUSH

Pittsburgh pitcher who surrendered the final two home runs of Babe Ruth's big-league career. Playing for the Boston Braves against the Pirates on May 25, 1935, Ruth slugged three homers in the game—the first off Red Lucas and the last two (No. 713 and No. 714, lifetime) against Bush.

STEVE CARLTON

The last pitcher to collect a hit in the All-Star Game. Carlton, St. Louis Cardinals' pitcher, started for the National League in the 1969 game and hit a run-scoring double off Blue Moon Odom in the third inning.

SYD COHEN

Washington Senators' pitcher who yielded a home run to Babe Ruth of the New York Yankees on September 29, 1934—the 708th and last American League homer for Ruth.

RAY CULP

Philadelphia Phillies' pitcher who surrendered Hank Aaron's 398th and last home run for the Milwaukee Braves on September 20, 1965.

EDDIE DENT

Brooklyn pitcher who beat Boston's Cy Young in Young's final appearance in the majors, an October 6, 1911, National League game.

DICK DRAGO

Pitching for the California Angels against the Milwaukee Brewers on July 20, 1976, he allowed Hank Aaron's 755th and last major league home run.

DAVE DUNCAN

The last player to hit a home run for the Kansas City A's, connecting on October 1, 1967.

STEVE DUNNING

The last American League pitcher to hit a bases-loaded home run. Playing for the Cleveland Indians in a May 11, 1971, game against the Oakland A's, Dunning walloped his grand slam off Diego Segui in the second inning.

Camera Day proved a big attraction at Ebbets Field on August 24, 1957—exactly a month from the day that the last big-league game was played at the Brooklyn ballpark.

RAWLY EASTWICK

Pitching for the Cincinnati Reds against the Atlanta Braves on October 2, 1974, Eastwick gave up Hank Aaron's 733rd and last National League home run.

EBBETS FIELD

Pitching for Brooklyn on September 24, 1957, in the last big-league game at Ebbets Field, Danny McDevitt of the Dodgers blanked Pittsburgh, 2-0. The Pirates' losing pitcher was Bennie Daniels, who was making his debut in the majors.

BOB ELLIOTT

The last member of the Boston Braves to play in an All-Star Game, competing in the 1951 classic in Detroit. Elliott hit a two-run homer for the National League.

LARRY FRENCH

Brooklyn Dodgers' pitcher who in the last appearance of his major league career faced the minimum 27 batters, hurling a one-hit, 6-0 triumph against the Philadelphia Phillies on September 23, 1942. Nick Etten got the lone hit off French, a second-inning single, but was erased in a double play. French, who turned 35 a little more than a month after the regular season concluded, soon went into the Navy and his big-league career was at an end.

MIGUEL FUENTES

Making his eighth and last appearance in the major leagues, reliever Fuentes pitched the final inning in the history of the Seattle Pilots. Fuentes worked the ninth inning against the Oakland A's on October 2, 1969.

JIM GANTNER

Milwaukee player who pinch-ran for the Brewers' Hank Aaron in Aaron's last big-league game, October 3, 1976, against the Detroit Tigers.

JIM GOSGER

The last batter to face Satchel Paige in a major league game. Batting for the Boston Red Sox against the Kansas City A's with two out in the third inning of a September 25, 1965, game, Gosger grounded out against the 59-year-old Paige.

BURLEIGH GRIMES

The last of 17 legalized spitball pitchers in the majors, making his final appearance on September 20, 1934, for the Pittsburgh Pirates against the Brooklyn Dodgers. Grimes pitched one inning, the eighth, and surrendered no hits or walks, striking out one batter (Joe Stripp, the last man he faced in the big leagues).

On February 10, 1920, a rules change barred the spitball. Recognizing that some pitchers were in effect making a living by using the spitter, baseball officials certified 17 hurlers as legalized spitballers—meaning those pitchers could throw the pitch for the remainder of their careers; otherwise, the spitter was outlawed. The 17 pitchers, their 1920 clubs and the years that their big-league careers spanned:

American League	National League
Doc Ayers, Detroit, 1913-21	Bill Doak, St. Louis, 1912-29
Ray Caldwell, Cleveland, 1910-21	Phil Douglas, New York, 1912-22
Stan Coveleski, Cleveland, 1912-28	Dana Fillingim, Boston, 1915-25
Urban Faber, Chicago, 1914-33	Ray Fisher, Cincinnati, 1910-20
Hub Leonard, Detroit, 1913-25	Marv Goodwin, St. Louis, 1916-25
Jack Quinn, New York, 1909-33	Grimes, Brooklyn, 1916-34
Allan Russell, Boston, 1915-25	Clarence Mitchell, Brooklyn, 1911-32
Urban Shocker, St. Louis, 1916-28	Dick Rudolph, Boston, 1910-27
Allen Sothoron, St. Louis, 1914-26	

CHARLEY GRIMM

The last manager of the Boston Braves. Grimm replaced Tommy Holmes early in the 1952 season, the Braves' final year in Boston, and then managed the Milwaukee Braves from 1953 until mid-June of 1956.

BUMP HADLEY

Washington Senators' pitcher who gave up Ty Cobb's final major league hit. Cobb, pinch-hitting for Philadelphia A's shortstop Joe Boley, doubled off Hadley on September 3, 1928.

CARROLL HARDY

Boston player who went in defensively for Ted Williams in the ninth inning of a September 28, 1960, game against the Baltimore Orioles after the Red Sox's left fielder had homered an inning earlier in his last major league at-bat.

GAIL HARRIS

The last player to hit a home run for the New York Giants, connecting in the second game of a doubleheader on September 21, 1957. Harris slugged two homers in that game.

RORIC HARRISON

The last American League pitcher to hit a regular-season home run, connecting for the Baltimore Orioles against Ray Lamb of the Cleveland Indians in the second game of an October 3, 1972, doubleheader.

Ken Holtzman is the last A.L. pitcher to hit a home run, belting one for the Oakland A's in the 1974 World Series.

JIM HICKMAN

The last player to hit a home run at New York's Polo Grounds, connecting for the New York Mets against the Philadelphia Phillies on September 18, 1963.

GIL HODGES

The last representative of the Brooklyn Dodgers to play in an All-Star Game, pinch-hitting in the bottom of the ninth inning in 1957 for Brooklyn teammate Clem Labine (who had pitched the top of the ninth). Gino Cimoli of the Dodgers pinch-hit in the eighth inning for the National League in the game played at St. Louis.

FRANK HOWARD

The last representative of Washington's second American League franchise to play in an All-Star Game, appearing in the 1971 game at Detroit.

FRANK HOWARD

The last player to hit a home run for Washington's second American League franchise, connecting for the Senators on September 30, 1971.

BILLY HUNTER

The last player to hit a home run for the St. Louis Browns, connecting on September 26, 1953.

JIM (CATFISH) HUNTER

The last representative of the Kansas City Athletics to appear in an All-Star Game, pitching the final five innings for the American League in the 15-inning game played at Anaheim in 1967. Hunter was the losing pitcher as the N.L. won, 2-1.

RANSOM JACKSON

The last player to hit a home run for the Brooklyn Dodgers, connecting on September 28, 1957.

HENRY JOHNSON

New York Yankees' pitcher who retired Ty Cobb of the Philadelphia Athletics in Cobb's final major league at-bat. Pinch-hitting for A's third baseman Jimmie Dykes against Johnson on September 11, 1928, Cobb popped out to New York shortstop Mark Koenig.

Owner Connie Mack
(above left) signs
Eddie Joost (above
right) as the
Athletics' manager
for 1954—the A's
last season in
Philadelphia. Joost
succeeded Jimmie
Dykes (right), who
managed the club
from 1951 through
1953 after taking
over for Mack.

EDDIE JOOST

The last manager of the Philadelphia Athletics, guiding the club in 1954.

RIP JORDAN

Pitching for the Washington Senators in the fifth and last game of his big-league career, Jordan surrendered Babe Ruth's final home run as a member of the Boston Red Sox on September 27, 1919. The homer was the 49th of Ruth's major league career.

KANSAS CITY ATHLETICS

Jim (Catfish) Hunter was the last pitcher of record for the Kansas City A's, dropping a 4-3 decision to the Yankees at New York on October 1, 1967. Mel Stottlemyre was the winning pitcher against the A's, who were playing their final game before moving to Oakland in 1968.

DON KESSINGER

The major leagues' last player-manager. Kessinger managed the Chicago White Sox from the start of the 1979 American League season until August 2, when he resigned, and made his last appearance as a player on July 31 when he entered a game against the New York Yankees as a late-inning defensive replacement at shortstop.

BOB KLINE

Pitcher for the Boston Red Sox who was defeated by Babe Ruth of the New York Yankees in Ruth's last big-league pitching appearance, October 1, 1933.

GARY KOLB

St. Louis player who ran for the Cardinals' Stan Musial on September 29, 1963, after Musial singled in his last at-bat in the majors. Musial collected the hit—the 3,630th of his big-league career—off Cincinnati's Jim Maloney in the sixth inning of the season finale.

HARVEY KUENN

The last batter in two of Sandy Koufax's four career no-hitters with the Los Angeles Dodgers. Kuenn, San Francisco's left fielder on May 11, 1963, grounded back to Koufax for the final out in the Dodger pitcher's no-hitter against the Giants; pinch-hitting for Chicago pitcher Bob Hendley on September 9, 1965, he struck out to end Koufax's perfect game against the Cubs.

PETE LaCOCK

Pinch-hitting for the Chicago Cubs against the St. Louis Cardinals on September 3, 1975, LaCock collected the last big-league hit given up by Bob Gibson—a bases-loaded home run.

LAST OUTS IN PERFECT GAMES

June 12, 1880
John Richmond, Worcester (N.L.), 1-0.
Losing pitcher—Jim McCormick, Cleveland.
LAST OUT—Left fielder Ned Hanlon.

June 17, 1880
John Montgomery (Monte) Ward, Providence (N.L.), 5-0.
Losing pitcher—Jim (Pud) Galvin, Buffalo.
LAST OUT—Galvin.

May 5, 1904
Cy Young, Boston (A.L.), 3-0.
Losing pitcher—Rube Waddell, Philadelphia.
LAST OUT—Waddell.

October 2, 1908
Addie Joss, Cleveland (A.L.), 1-0.
Losing pitcher—Ed Walsh, Chicago.
LAST OUT—John Anderson, pinch-hitting for Walsh.

**June 23, 1917
(first game)**
Ernie Shore, Boston (A.L.), 4-0.
Losing pitcher—Doc Ayers, Washington.
LAST OUT—Mike Menosky, pinch-hitting for Ayers.

April 30, 1922
Charley Robertson, Chicago (A.L.), 2-0.
Losing pitcher—Herman Pillette, Detroit.
LAST OUT—John Bassler, pinch-hitting for Pillette.

October 8, 1956
Don Larsen, New York (A.L.), 2-0, World Series.
Losing pitcher—Sal Maglie, Brooklyn.
LAST OUT—Dale Mitchell, pinch-hitting for Maglie.

May 26, 1959
Harvey Haddix, Pittsburgh (N.L.), 0-1, lost in 13th inning
on one hit.
Winning pitcher—Lew Burdette, Milwaukee.
LAST BATTER—First baseman Joe Adcock, Milwaukee.
Adcock hit a run-scoring double in the 13th inning.

**June 21, 1964
(first game)**
Jim Bunning, Philadelphia (N.L.), 6-0.
Losing pitcher—Tracy Stallard, New York.
LAST OUT—John Stephenson, pinch-hitting for relief
pitcher Tom Sturdivant.

September 9, 1965
Sandy Koufax, Los Angeles (N.L.), 1-0.
Losing pitcher—Bob Hendley, Chicago.
LAST OUT—Harvey Kuenn, pinch-hitting for Hendley.

May 8, 1968
Jim (Catfish) Hunter, Oakland (A.L.), 4-0.
Losing pitcher—Dave Boswell, Minnesota.
LAST OUT—Rich Reese, pinch-hitting for relief pitcher
Ron Perranoski.

May 15, 1981
Len Barker, Cleveland (A.L.), 3-0.
Losing pitcher—Luis Leal, Toronto.
LAST OUT—Ernie Whitt, pinch-hitting for catcher Buck
Martinez.

Jim Bunning (above), the father of six at the time, celebrated Father's Day in 1964 by pitching a perfect game against the Mets, getting John Stephenson on a strikeout to end the game. Jim (Catfish) Hunter (left) receives a victory ride in 1968 after striking out Minnesota's Rich Reese for the final out in his perfect game.

LAST TEAMS

Many notable players ended their major league careers on teams with whom they are seldom associated. Included among such players are:

Player	Last Club	Final Year
Hank Aaron	Milwaukee Brewers	1976
Joe Adcock	California Angels	1966
Grover Alexander	Philadelphia Phillies	1930
Richie Allen	Oakland A's	1977
Felipe Alou	Milwaukee Brewers	1974
Jesus Alou	Houston Astros	1979
Matty Alou	San Diego Padres	1974
Luis Aparicio	Boston Red Sox	1973
Richie Ashburn	New York Mets	1962
Earl Averill	Boston Braves	1941
Chief Bender	Chicago White Sox	1925
Wally Berger	Philadelphia Phillies	1940
Yogi Berra	New York Mets	1965
Bobby Bonds	Chicago Cubs	1981
Jim Bottomley	St. Louis Browns	1937
Lou Boudreau	Boston Red Sox	1952
Ken Boyer	Los Angeles Dodgers	1969
Roger Bresnahan	Chicago Cubs	1915
Ken Brett	Kansas City Royals	1981
Lew Burdette	California Angels	1967
Jesse Burkett	Boston Red Sox	1905
Johnny Callison	New York Yankees	1973
Dolph Camilli	Boston Red Sox	1945
Max Carey	Brooklyn Dodgers	1929
Phil Cavarretta	Chicago White Sox	1955
Orlando Cepeda	Kansas City Royals	1974
Frank Chance	New York Yankees	1914
Ben Chapman	Philadelphia Phillies	1946
Jack Chesbro	Boston Red Sox	1909
Ty Cobb	Philadelphia A's	1928
Rocky Colavito	New York Yankees	1968
Jocko Conlan	Chicago White Sox	1935
Stan Coveleski	New York Yankees	1928
Mike Cuellar	California Angels	1977
Kiki Cuyler	Brooklyn Dodgers	1938
Al Dark	Milwaukee Braves	1960
Tommy Davis	Kansas City Royals	1976
Willie Davis	San Diego Padres	1976
Dizzy Dean	St. Louis Browns	1947
Paul Dean	St. Louis Browns	1943
Ed Delahanty	Washington Senators	1903
Paul Derringer	Chicago Cubs	1945
Hugh Duffy	Philadelphia Phillies	1906
Del Ennis	Chicago White Sox	1959
Johnny Evers	Boston Braves	1929
Roy Face	Montreal Expos	1969
Ron Fairly	California Angels	1978
Wes Ferrell	Boston Braves	1941
Curt Flood	Washington Senators	1971

Dizzy Dean's last appearance in the majors came in 1947 with St. Louis—the Browns, that is. Dean, a former Cardinal great, faced the Chicago White Sox as a publicity stunt in the '47 season finale—and pitched four scoreless innings.

Player	Last Club	Final Year
Nellie Fox	Houston Astros	1965
Jimmie Foxx	Philadelphia Phillies	1945
Larry French	Brooklyn Dodgers	1942
Bob Friend	New York Mets	1966
Lefty Gomez	Washington Senators	1943
Goose Goslin	Washington Senators	1938
Hank Greenberg	Pittsburgh Pirates	1947
Burleigh Grimes	Pittsburgh Pirates	1934
Dick Groat	San Francisco Giants	1967
Don Gutteridge	Pittsburgh Pirates	1948
Harvey Haddix	Baltimore Orioles	1965
Granny Hamner	Kansas City A's	1962
Tommy Harper	Oakland A's	1975
Bucky Harris	Detroit Tigers	1931
Gabby Hartnett	New York Giants	1941
Bob Hazle	Detroit Tigers	1958
Harry Heilmann	Cincinnati Reds	1932
Billy Herman	Pittsburgh Pirates	1947
Gil Hodges	New York Mets	1963
Tommy Holmes	Brooklyn Dodgers	1952
Rogers Hornsby	St. Louis Browns	1937
Willie Horton	Seattle Mariners	1980
Elston Howard	Boston Red Sox	1968
Frank Howard	Detroit Tigers	1973
Waite Hoyt	Brooklyn Dodgers	1938
Randy Hundley	San Diego Padres	1975
Ron Hunt	St. Louis Cardinals	1974
Monte Irvin	Chicago Cubs	1956
Julian Javier	Cincinnati Reds	1972
Deron Johnson	Boston Red Sox	1976
George Kell	Baltimore Orioles	1957
George Kelly	Brooklyn Dodgers	1932
Harmon Killebrew	Kansas City Royals	1975
Ralph Kiner	Cleveland Indians	1955
Ted Kluszewski	Los Angeles Angels	1961
Harvey Kuenn	Philadelphia Phillies	1966
Nap Lajoie	Philadelphia A's	1916
Don Larsen	Chicago Cubs	1967
Fred Lindstrom	Brooklyn Dodgers	1936
Dick Littlefield	Milwaukee Braves	1958
Mickey Lolich	San Diego Padres	1979
Al Lopez	Cleveland Indians	1947
Sherry Magee	Cincinnati Reds	1919
Sal Maglie	St. Louis Cardinals	1958
Heinie Manush	Pittsburgh Pirates	1939
Juan Marichal	Los Angeles Dodgers	1975
Roger Maris	St. Louis Cardinals	1968
Billy Martin	Minnesota Twins	1961
Eddie Mathews	Detroit Tigers	1968
Christy Mathewson	Cincinnati Reds	1916
Carl Mays	New York Giants	1929
Willie Mays	New York Mets	1973
Sam McDowell	Pittsburgh Pirates	1975
Stuffy McInnis	Philadelphia Phillies	1927

Harmon Killebrew hit the last 14 of his 573 career home runs for the Kansas City Royals, with whom he finished his career in 1975.

Well-traveled Bobo Newsom closed out his big-league career with a second stint as a member of the Philadelphia Athletics.

Player	Last Club	Final Year
Denny McLain	Atlanta Braves	1972
Roy McMillan	New York Mets	1966
Dave McNally	Montreal Expos	1975
Bob Meusel	Cincinnati Reds	1930
Bing Miller	Boston Red Sox	1936
Art Nehf	Chicago Cubs	1929
Don Newcombe	Cleveland Indians	1960
Hal Newhouser	Cleveland Indians	1955
Bobo Newsom	Philadelphia A's	1953
Lefty O'Doul	New York Giants	1934
Claude Osteen	Chicago White Sox	1975
Mickey Owen	Boston Red Sox	1954
Camilo Pascual	Cleveland Indians	1971
Roger Peckinpaugh	Chicago White Sox	1927
Herb Pennock	Boston Red Sox	1934
Joe Pepitone	Atlanta Braves	1973
Jim Perry	Oakland A's	1975
Johnny Pesky	Washington Senators	1954
Billy Pierce	San Francisco Giants	1964
Vada Pinson	Kansas City Royals	1975
Eddie Plank	St. Louis Browns	1917
Wally Post	Cleveland Indians	1964
Boog Powell	Los Angeles Dodgers	1977
Pete Reiser	Cleveland Indians	1952
Sam Rice	Cleveland Indians	1934
Robin Roberts	Chicago Cubs	1966
Frank Robinson	Cleveland Indians	1976
Red Ruffing	Chicago White Sox	1947
Babe Ruth	Boston Braves	1935
Ron Santo	Chicago White Sox	1974

Paul Waner managed only one hit as a New York Yankee—and it was the 3,152nd and last of his major league career.

Player	Last Club	Final Year
Hank Sauer	San Francisco Giants	1959
Ray Schalk	New York Giants	1929
Curt Simmons	California Angels	1967
George Sisler	Boston Braves	1930
Moose Skowron	California Angels	1967
Enos Slaughter	Milwaukee Braves	1959
Duke Snider	San Francisco Giants	1964
Warren Spahn	San Francisco Giants	1965
Tris Speaker	Philadelphia A's	1928
Casey Stengel	Boston Braves	1925
Junior Stephens	Chicago White Sox	1955
Dick Stuart	California Angels	1969
Bobby Thomson	Baltimore Orioles	1960
Virgil Trucks	New York Yankees	1958
Bob Turley	Boston Red Sox	1963
Mickey Vernon	Pittsburgh Pirates	1960
Joe Vosmik	Washington Senators	1944
Rube Waddell	St. Louis Browns	1910
Dixie Walker	Pittsburgh Pirates	1949
Bucky Walters	Boston Braves	1950
Paul Waner	New York Yankees	1945
Vic Wertz	Minnesota Twins	1963
Zack Wheat	Philadelphia A's	1927
Hoyt Wilhelm	Los Angeles Dodgers	1972
Billy Williams	Oakland A's	1976
Ken Williams	Boston Red Sox	1929
Hack Wilson	Philadelphia Phillies	1934
Jimmy Wynn	Milwaukee Brewers	1977
Rudy York	Philadelphia A's	1948
Cy Young	Boston Braves	1911

Pittsburgh's Roberto Clemente displays the ball he hit on September 30, 1972, for his 3,000th and last regular-season hit in the majors. Clemente died three months later in a plane crash.

COOKIE LAVAGETTO

The last manager for Washington's first American League franchise, piloting the Senators in 1960. Lavagetto, who took over as the Senators' manager on May 7, 1957, continued to manage the club when it moved to Minnesota in 1961—but he lasted only 74 games at the Twins' helm.

HAL LEE

Boston Braves' player who replaced Babe Ruth in left field against the Philadelphia Phillies on May 30, 1935, when Ruth—making his last big-league appearance—left the first game of a doubleheader shortly after batting in the first inning.

JIM LEMON

The last representative of Washington's first American League franchise to play in an All-Star Game, participating in the first game in 1960 at Kansas City.

EMIL LEVSEN

Cleveland pitcher who was the last major leaguer to hurl two complete-game victories in one day. Levsen and the Indians beat the Boston Red Sox, 6-1 and 5-1, on August 28, 1926.

LOU LIMMER

The last player to hit a home run for the Philadelphia A's, connecting on September 25, 1954. The homer was the last of 19 for Limmer in the major leagues.

MARTY MARION

The last manager of the St. Louis Browns. Marion, who took over the job during the 1952 season, managed the Browns for all of 1953 (their final year).

EDDIE MATHEWS

The last player to hit a home run for the Boston Braves, connecting on September 27, 1952. The homer was one of three that Mathews slugged that day.

JON MATLACK

New York Mets' pitcher who surrendered Roberto Clemente's 3,000th and last regular-season major league hit (a double) in a September 30, 1972, game against the Pittsburgh Pirates.

Pete Gray of the St. Louis Browns displays his batting form in 1945.

WILLIE MAYS

The last member of the New York Giants to play in an All-Star Game, hitting a single and triple in four at-bats for the National League in 1957 at St. Louis.

MILWAUKEE BRAVES

Playing the Dodgers on October 3, 1965, in Los Angeles, the Milwaukee Braves lost their final National League game, 3-0. Bob Miller was the winning pitcher, while Bob Sadowski took the loss for the Atlanta-bound Braves.

Playing the outfield took some ingenuity, but the one-armed Gray found just the right technique.

HAL NEWHOUSER

The last major league pitcher to face one-armed Pete Gray of the St. Louis Browns. Pitching to Gray in the eighth inning of a September 30, 1945, game between the Detroit Tigers and the Browns, Newhouser induced the outfielder to hit into a fielder's choice.

Gray played 77 games (all in 1945) in the majors, batting .218 with no homers and 13 runs batted in.

The New York Giants and Pittsburgh Pirates head for the locker rooms at the Polo Grounds on September 29, 1957, after the Giants played their final game as a New York-based club.

NEW YORK GIANTS

Playing the Pirates at the Polo Grounds on September 29, 1957, New York lost to Pittsburgh, 9-1, in the Giants' last game before relocating in San Francisco in 1958. Bob Friend was the winning pitcher, beating Johnny Antonelli.

GENE OLIVER

The last player to hit a home run for the Milwaukee Braves, connecting on October 2, 1965.

SATCHEL PAIGE

The last representative of the St. Louis Browns to play in an All-Star Game, pitching the eighth inning of the 1953 game for the American League. In the seventh inning, Billy Hunter of the Browns ran for Mickey Mantle in the game played at Cincinnati.

BEN PASCHAL

The last man to pinch-hit for Babe Ruth. Paschal batted for Ruth in the sixth inning of the 1927 season opener after Ruth had gone 0-for-3 (striking out twice), and he delivered a single.

PHILADELPHIA ATHLETICS

Playing their final game before moving to Kansas City in 1955, the A's defeated the New York Yankees, 8-6, at Yankee Stadium on September 26, 1954. Art Ditmar posted his first major league pitching victory, while Tommy Byrne took the loss for the Yankees.

With nothing at stake in the season finale against the A's, the Yankees played three men out of position. Yogi Berra was at third base for the only time in his big-league career; Bill Skowron played second base (which he did only one other time in the majors), and Mickey Mantle was at shortstop for one of only seven times in the big leagues.

JOE PIGNATANO

New York Mets' catcher who hit into a triple play in his last at-bat in the major leagues. Batting with Sammy Drake on second base and Richie Ashburn on first in the eighth inning of a September 30, 1962, game against the Chicago Cubs, Pignatano popped the ball into short right field. Second baseman Ken Hubbs made a spectacular catch, and throws from Hubbs to first baseman Ernie Banks and from Banks to shortstop Andre Rodgers caught Ashburn and Drake off base. All three Mets involved in the play—Pignatano, Ashburn and Drake—were playing in their last major league game.

POLO GROUNDS

Facing the New York Mets on September 18, 1963, Chris Short of the Philadelphia Phillies was a 5-1 winner in the last major league game in Polo Grounds history. The losing pitcher was Craig Anderson.

BILL RIGNEY

The last manager of the New York Giants, leading the club in 1957. Rigney also managed the team in 1956, and he piloted the San Francisco Giants from 1958 until mid-June of 1960.

DAVE ROBERTS

Pitching for the Detroit Tigers against the Milwaukee Brewers on October 3, 1976, he was the last man to face Hank Aaron in the major leagues. Roberts gave up a sixth-inning single to Aaron in the Milwaukee designated hitter's final at-bat.

EDDIE ROBINSON

The last member of the Philadelphia Athletics to play in an All-Star Game, pinch-hitting in the eighth inning of the 1953 classic at Cincinnati. Gus Zernial of the A's started the game in left field for the American League, going 1-for-2 before being replaced.

LEE ROSS

Philadelphia A's pitcher who on August 20, 1938, gave up a bases-loaded

The Cubs' Dale Long (left), the last of the lefthanded-throwing catchers in the National League, checks out a lefthanded catcher's mitt in 1958 as Sammy Taylor, Chicago's No. 1 catcher, looks on. Long, who caught in two games, used his first baseman's glove in his catching debut.

home run to Lou Gehrig of the New York Yankees—the last of a major league-record 23 grand slams by Gehrig.

ST. LOUIS BROWNS

About 6½ months away from taking the field as the Baltimore Orioles, the Browns played their last game on September 27, 1953, in St. Louis against the Chicago White Sox. Billy Pierce was the winning pitcher and Duane Pillette was charged with the defeat as the White Sox prevailed, 2-1, in 11 innings.

SEATTLE PILOTS

An expansion team that spent only one season in Seattle before shifting to Milwaukee and becoming the Brewers, the Pilots played their final game on October 2, 1969—and lost to the Oakland A's, 3-1. Steve Barber took the loss in the game played at Seattle, while Jim Roland was the winning pitcher.

DUKE SNIDER

The last player to hit a home run at Brooklyn's Ebbets Field, connecting on September 22, 1957. Snider hit two homers that day.

MIKE SQUIRES

The last lefthanded-throwing catcher in the majors. Squires, normally a first baseman, replaced Bruce Kimm behind the plate for the Chicago White Sox late in American League games of May 4 and 7, 1980 (and caught for Ed Farmer and then Randy Scarbery).

Dale Long, also a first baseman by trade, was the National League's last lefthanded-throwing catcher. He caught in two games (August 20, September 21) in 1958 for the Chicago Cubs.

WILLIE STARGELL

Playing for the Pittsburgh Pirates against the Chicago Cubs on September 3, 1966, Stargell slugged the last of a major league-record 502 home runs surrendered by Robin Roberts.

BILL TERRY

New York Giants' first baseman who was the last National Leaguer to bat .400 in one season, hitting .401 in 1930.

WASHINGTON SENATORS (FIRST A.L. CLUB)

The American League's original-franchise Washington Senators played their last game on October 2, 1960, dropping a 2-1 decision to the Baltimore Orioles at Washington. Milt Pappas was the winning pitcher; Pedro Ramos took the loss for the Senators, who became the Minnesota Twins in 1961.

WASHINGTON SENATORS (SECOND A.L. CLUB)

The American League's second Washington Senators played their final game on September 30, 1971—and it turned into a 9-0 forfeit. With the Senators leading the New York Yankees, 7-5, with two out in the ninth inning at Washington, souvenir hunters swarmed the field—and the game could not be resumed. Since a forfeit results in no pitchers of record, Jim Shellenback —a 6-3 loser to the Yankees' Mel Stottlemyre the night before—was the last Washington pitcher to get a decision. The franchise became the Texas Rangers in 1972.

STEVE WHITAKER

The last player to hit a home run for the Seattle Pilots, connecting on October 2, 1969.

TED WILLIAMS

The last major leaguer to record a season batting average of .400, hitting .406 for the American League's Boston Red Sox in 1941.

TED WILLIAMS

The last manager for Washington's second American League franchise, heading the Senators in 1971. Williams, who became the Senators' manager in 1969, moved with the club to Texas—but he managed the Rangers for only one season, 1972.

TAFT WRIGHT

Right fielder for the Chicago White Sox who grounded out for the final out when Bob Feller of the Cleveland Indians pitched a no-hitter on opening day in 1940.

Satchel Paige (29) leaves the mound with Manager Haywood Sullivan on September 25, 1965, after working three innings for the Kansas City A's at age 59. Paige allowed only one hit, a first-inning double by Boston's Carl Yastrzemski.

CARL YASTRZEMSKI

The last player to collect a hit off Satchel Paige in a major league game. Becoming the oldest player in big-league history at age 59, Paige started and pitched three innings for the Kansas City A's against the Boston Red Sox on September 25, 1965—and allowed only one hit, a two-out double by Yastrzemski in the first inning. Paige made only 28 pitches, walking no one and striking out one batter (opposing pitcher Bill Monbouquette). Leading 1-0, Paige was replaced by Diego Segui at the start of the fourth inning. Boston won, 5-2, with Monbouquette notching the victory and Don Mossi being saddled with the loss.

EIGHTH INNING:

Promotions, innovations and gimmicks.

YELLOW BASEBALL

In the first game of a doubleheader at Ebbets Field on August 2, 1938, St. Louis and Brooklyn experimented with a yellow baseball throughout the contest to see if it would be easier to follow than a white ball. Terry Moore of the Cardinals was the first to bat against the yellow ball, and St. Louis' Johnny Mize hit the only home run of the game. The Dodgers won, 6-2, behind the pitching of Freddie Fitzsimmons. A conventional white ball was used in the nightcap (use of a yellow ball never gained support in the majors), and Brooklyn prevailed, 9-3.

SMALL STRIKE ZONE

Eddie Gaedel, a 26-year-old midget, pinch-hit for the St. Louis Browns in the second game of an August 19, 1951, doubleheader against Detroit at Sportsman's Park. Bill Veeck, owner of the Browns, used Gaedel as part of a promotional stunt. However, Gaedel was released the next day when American League President Will Harridge refused to approve his contract (Harridge said the use of a midget was not in the best interests of baseball).

Gaedel, standing 3 feet, 7 inches and wearing uniform number 1/8, batted for right fielder Frank Saucier to lead off the Browns' first inning.

Supporting Cast:

● **Bob Cain.** Detroit pitcher who walked Gaedel on four pitches.

● **Jim Delsing.** St. Louis player who ran for Gaedel after his inning-opening walk.

● **Ed Hurley.** The home-plate umpire when Gaedel went to bat.

● **Bob Swift.** Cain's batterymate for the Tigers.

● **Zack Taylor.** Manager of the Browns who was questioned by Hurley about the legality of Gaedel's participation in an American League game. Taylor produced an official, signed contract, and Gaedel became the smallest player in major league history.

GAEDEL MAKES 'COMEBACK'

Nearly 10 years after appearing as a pinch-hitter for the St. Louis Browns, midget Eddie Gaedel was back in the news at a big-league ballpark. Bill Veeck, owner of the Chicago White Sox, took note of fans' constant complaints about vendors blocking their view and he hired Gaedel and seven other midgets in 1961 to work as vendors in the box-seat sections of Comiskey Park on opening day.

As another first-game highlight, Veeck asked John F. Kennedy to throw out the first ball in '61. And Kennedy did. One not-so-small point, though: This JFK was a fan from suburban Oak Lawn, not the President of the United States.

"Ball," says umpire Ed Hurley as Bob Swift catches the high pitch to Eddie Gaedel.

When midget Eddie Gaedel popped out of a cake between games of the August 19, 1951, doubleheader at Sportsman's Park, Browns' fans laughed at Bill Veeck's latest stunt. Little did they know, however, that the best was yet to come.

Before taking his place in baseball history by stepping to the plate, Gaedel received a little help from Browns Manager Zack Taylor and words of encouragement from coach Johnny Tobin (right).

BURYING THE PENNANT

On September 23, 1949, with the Cleveland Indians out of the American League pennant race after winning the A.L. flag and World Series the year before, Owner Bill Veeck held a pregame ceremony during which he buried the 1948 pennant at Municipal Stadium. Wearing a top hat, Veeck guided a horse-drawn hearse at the head of the funeral procession to the gravesite behind the center-field fence. Cleveland Manager Lou Boudreau and his coaches served as pallbearers, and Rudie Schaffer, the club's business manager, read the last rites from the "bible of baseball"—The Sporting News. The cardboard tombstone read simply, "1948 Champs." The Indians went on to lose that night, 5-0, to the Detroit Tigers.

The funeral procession approaches the gravesite behind the center-field fence at Cleveland's Municipal Stadium. In uniform at the head of the casket are coach Bill McKechnie and Manager Lou Boudreau (wearing jacket). Indians Vice President Hank Greenberg is third from the left.

With heavy hearts and respect befitting the sad occasion, Indians players, coaches, managers, officials and Owner Bill Veeck (center above) listened to club business manager Rudie Schaffer read the last rites from The Sporting News, the "bible of baseball." A young fan (left) pays his last respects to the memory of a season lost.

Kansas City's Ken Harrelson emerges from a chauffeured limousine that

The Pennant Porch complete with sheep grazing beyond the right-field wall.

delivered the starting lineup in one of Charlie Finley's promotional stunts.

CHARLIE FINLEY

The Kansas City Athletics played at a .405 clip (458 victories, 672 losses) during Finley's seven-year reign (1961-67) as owner of the Kansas City club —but things seldom were dull at Municipal Stadium. With a subpar on-field product, Finley tried to compensate with attractions aimed at luring fans to the ballpark.

Saying that the dimensions of Yankee Stadium gave a distinct advantage to New York hitters and helped make the Yankees a powerhouse, Finley built a "Pennant Porch" at Municipal Stadium to rival the right-field configuration at New York. The A's owner moved the right-field foul pole from 338 feet to 325 (the big-league minimum for recently constructed ballparks), then angled the fence to a point that was 296 feet from the plate—the same distance as Yankee Stadium's "porch." The structure was up for two exhibition games before Commissioner Ford Frick and American League President Joe Cronin ordered it dismantled. In its place, Finley put up a "One-Half Pennant Porch" that was 325 feet down the line. Foiled in his effort to help A's hitters with dramatically shorter distances (a bleacher roof that also cut the right-field distance to 296 feet was banned, too), Finley took another tack. He erected a 40-foot-high screen in right field in an attempt to stymie opposing power hitters. That didn't last, either.

Not all of Finley's stunts were aimed at influencing what occurred on the field; entertainment was emphasized. Finley introduced "Harvey," a mechanical rabbit who popped out of the ground and delivered baseballs to the home-plate umpire. The A's owner brought sheep to Municipal Stadium—and a shepherd to tend them. The sheep grazed between the right-field fence and the outer wall, keeping the grass short. There also was Charlie O., a mule who served as a team mascot, and a zoo was provided for children in the picnic area down the left-field line.

Finley also installed a clock to time pitchers (to make sure a game kept moving), and he hired a woman commentator—a television weather reporter from Chicago—to work on the A's radio team. Kansas City's starting lineup once rode into Municipal Stadium as a "mule train," and on another occasion A's players arrived via limousines. And when Kansas City's Rocky Colavito was closing in on his 300th career homer in the majors, Finley parked a Brink's truck beyond the left-field wall so he could reward Colavito when he reached the milestone. Colavito hit No. 300 on the road, though, and a belated presentation was made in Kansas City.

Whatever the promotion or gimmick, Finley still had trouble attracting fans (the A's best season attendance during Finley's years in Kansas City was 773,929, in 1966). And by 1968, Finley and the A's were off to Oakland.

Harvey popped out of the ground to deliver balls to the umpire and Charlie O. the mule was a frequent companion of Charlie O. the man.

After the Pennant Porch came a 40-foot right-field screen, being surveyed above by A's players (left to right) Manny Jimenez, Bill Bryan, Wayne Causey and Jim Dickson.

One of Finley's more memorable gimmicks was bringing in the A's starting lineup by mule train. Leading the procession is Ken Harrelson, followed by Wayne Causey, Rene Lachemann, Ed Charles, Bert Campaneris, Nelson Mathews and Jim Landis.

BROADCASTING FROM ASTRODOME ROOF

On April 28, 1965, broadcaster Lindsey Nelson of the New York Mets called the Mets-Astros game from a gondola 208 feet above second base at Houston's Astrodome. Nelson and Joel Nixon, the executive producer of the Mets' broadcasts, ascended in the gondola to the apex of the dome—and they were there about 4 hours (the game lasted 3 hours, 24 minutes). Astrodome ground rules specified that a ball hitting any part of the roof was in play, so Nelson and Nixon were included in the ground rules. The two men had walkie-talkie contact to the Mets' radio booth and a direct telephone line to their director, Joe Gallagher. Nelson described the play-by-play only in the seventh and eighth innings, but provided color commentary to announcing partners Ralph Kiner and Bob Murphy the rest of the time. Nelson took only a scorecard and binoculars with him, but didn't keep score in fear a dropped pen might become a dangerous missile to the players below. The game, won by Houston, 12-9, was the seventh regular-season contest in Astrodome history.

PITCHER-AN-INNING STUNT

St. Louis hurler Dick Starr completed a pitcher-an-inning gimmick for the Browns on the final day of the 1949 season. Ned Garver, Joe Ostrowski, Cliff Fannin, Tom Ferrick, Karl Drews, Bill Kennedy, Al Papai, Red Embree and Starr faced the Chicago White Sox in the opener of a doubleheader—and the White Sox won, 4-3. Kennedy took the loss.

The Browns had another attraction in the second game, announcing the major league debut of Eddie Albrecht, a 20-year-old pitcher from St. Louis County. Albrecht, up from Pine Bluff of the Class C Cotton States League (where he won 29 games in '49), started against Chicago and was a 5-3 winner, allowing only one hit in five innings before the game was called because of darkness. The game was one of only three for Albrecht in his big-league career.

NIGHTCLUB SINGER BELTS BALL

During a July 31, 1935, game at Cincinnati's Crosley Field, nightclub singer Kitty Burke grabbed a bat from the Reds' Babe Herman and stepped to the plate for an unofficial at-bat against Paul Dean of the St. Louis Cardinals. The incident occurred with one out in the eighth inning, St. Louis leading, 2-1, and the Reds' Sammy Byrd on first base. Burke motioned to Dean to pitch, and he threw hard the first time. Dean then made an underhand toss, and Burke grounded back to the mound. After being "thrown out" at first base, Burke returned to the crowd (a larger turnout than the Reds' security force could handle was lured to the sixth night game in Cincinnati history, with fans spilling onto the field and making plays impossible in foul territory). Burke's desire to bat stemmed from a kidding-around session involving the Cards' Joe Medwick, with the singer insisting she could hit a pitched ball.

Good Old Joe Earley and his wife were well rewarded by Bill Veeck.

'GOOD OLD JOE EARLEY' NIGHT

In 1948, a Cleveland fan named Joe Earley wrote a letter to a newspaper suggesting that he—as an average follower of the Indians—deserved a night in his honor, claiming players weren't the only ones worthy of such tributes. When Bill Veeck, owner of the Indians, heard about the letter, he thought the idea would make a great promotion—and he was right, as a crowd of 60,405 for "Good Old Joe Earley" Night proved on September 28. Earley, a 26-year-old veteran of World War II who worked as a night guard at an auto plant, and his wife were called to an on-field microphone at the start of pregame festivities. Earley was presented with a new convertible, clothes, luggage, books and numerous appliances. In addition, livestock, poultry and other gifts were given to fans, and Veeck spent $30,000 to have orchids flown in from Hawaii to be presented to the first 20,000 women entering the stadium.

'PITCHER' STAN MUSIAL

Frankie Baumholtz of the Chicago Cubs was the only man to bat against Musial in a major league game. Musial made the lone pitching appearance of his big-league career on September 28, 1952, facing Baumholtz in a season-ending stunt at Sportsman's Park that matched the National League's top two hitters in the '52 batting-crown race. Musial, who led Baumholtz, .336 to .326, came in from center field to pitch in the first inning of the Cardinals-Cubs game after St. Louis starter Harvey Haddix walked leadoff batter Tommy Brown (Haddix went to right field, and right fielder Hal Rice

211

Cardinal great Stan Musial delivers a pitch to Chicago's Frankie Baumholtz, normally a lefthanded batter, during the final game of the 1952 season at Sportsman's Park in St. Louis. Bill Sarni is St. Louis' catcher.

switched to center). Baumholtz, a lefthanded hitter, batted righthanded against Musial and grounded to Solly Hemus at third base. Hemus, the Cardinals' regular shortstop, bobbled the ball, allowing Baumholtz to reach first base on the error. Musial then returned to center field, Rice went back to right and Haddix resumed his pitching duties. Musial went 1-for-3 during the game, keeping his title-winning average at .336; Baumholtz's 1-for-4 day dropped his figure to .325. The Cubs won, 3-0.

JERSEY CITY DODGERS

The Brooklyn Dodgers played seven home games in 1956 and eight in 1957 at Roosevelt Stadium in Jersey City, N.J. By playing the 15 home games away from Brooklyn, the Dodgers seemingly were threatening to move from the borough unless its civic leaders helped to provide a new stadium to replace aging—and small—Ebbets Field.

The big-league contests were the first in Jersey City since the New York Giants played two games there (but not in Roosevelt Stadium) to open the 1889 season.

Players and teams involved in firsts, lasts and other notable occurrences at Roosevelt Stadium included:

Supporting Cast:

● **Harry Anderson.** Philadelphia player who hit the final major league home run at Roosevelt Stadium, connecting for the Phillies on September 3, 1957.

● **Richie Ashburn.** The first man to bat in a big-league game at Roosevelt Stadium, leading off for the Phils on April 19, 1956.

● **Roy Campanella.** Brooklyn catcher who collected his 1,000th hit in the

212

majors in the first big-league game at Roosevelt Stadium, doubling in the 10th inning.

- **Gino Cimoli.** Brooklyn left fielder who made his major league debut in the Dodgers' first game at Jersey City.
- **Murry Dickson.** The losing pitcher for Philadelphia in the first big-league game at Roosevelt Stadium when the Dodgers defeated the Phillies, 5-4, in 10 innings.
- **Don Drysdale.** Dodger pitcher who hurled the first of his 49 big-league shutouts at Roosevelt Stadium, beating the Chicago Cubs, 4-0, on June 5, 1957. He also was the losing pitcher in the last major league game at Jersey City, dropping a 3-2, 12-inning decision to Philadelphia on September 3, 1957. (The defeat left Brooklyn with an 11-4 record in the Jersey City "experiment.")
- **Dick Farrell.** Philadelphia pitcher who was the winner of the final major league game at Roosevelt Stadium.
- **Carl Furillo.** The first Brooklyn player to hit a home run at Jersey City, connecting on July 25, 1956.
- **Clem Labine.** The Dodgers' winning pitcher in the first big-league game at Roosevelt Stadium.
- **Eddie Mathews.** Playing for the Milwaukee Braves, he was the only visiting player to hit two home runs at Roosevelt Stadium. He belted one in 1956 and one in '57.
- **Wally Moon.** St. Louis Cardinal who slugged the first major league homer at Jersey City, accomplishing the feat on May 16, 1956.
- **Charlie Neal.** Brooklyn second baseman who collected his first big-league hit at Roosevelt Stadium on April 19, 1956.
- **Don Newcombe.** Brooklyn pitcher who was the biggest winner and loser at Roosevelt Stadium, compiling a 4-3 record.
- **New York Giants.** The only National League team to defeat the Dodgers twice at Roosevelt Stadium. Johnny Antonelli's two-hit pitching and Willie Mays' home run beat the Dodgers, 1-0, on August 15, 1956, and the Giants scored an 8-5 victory over Brooklyn on August 7, 1957. Newcombe lost both games.
- **Philadelphia Phillies.** The only visiting team to play three games against Brooklyn at Roosevelt Stadium. Besides losing the first big-league game at the park and winning the last game there, the Phils also played the Dodgers on April 22, 1957, at Roosevelt Stadium—and Brooklyn prevailed, 5-1.
- **Duke Snider.** The lone Brooklyn player to hit two home runs at Roosevelt Stadium. Both were hit in 1956.

COUNTY STADIUM—HOME OF SOX

The Chicago White Sox played a total of 20 home games (winning eight) in 1968 and 1969 at Milwaukee's County Stadium. Milwaukee had been without major league baseball since the Braves left the city at the end of the 1965 season. In 1970, the Seattle Pilots moved to Milwaukee and became the Brewers.

Houston's all-rookie lineup on September 27, 1963, included (front row, left to right) Jay Dahl, Jerry Grote; (second row) Glenn Vaughan, Sonny Jackson, Joe Morgan, Rusty Staub; (back row) Brock Davis, Aaron Pointer and Jim Wynn.

ALL-ROOKIE LINEUP FAILS

Jay Dahl was the starting pitcher for Houston in the all-rookie lineup that the Colts fielded against the New York Mets on September 27, 1963, at Colt Stadium. Others in the Colts' lineup: Brock Davis, left field; Jimmy Wynn, center field; Aaron Pointer, right field; Rusty Staub, first base; Joe Morgan, second base; Glenn Vaughan, third base; Sonny Jackson, shortstop, and Jerry Grote, catcher. The Mets won, 10-3, over Dahl, whose three-inning stint marked his lone appearance in the majors.

FANS MANAGE BROWNS

Owner Bill Veeck of the St. Louis Browns let 1,115 fans—so-called "grandstand managers"—guide his club during an August 24, 1951, game against the Philadelphia Athletics. As part of a Veeck promotion, the managers sat behind the Browns' dugout and decided strategy by flashing "Yes" or "No" cards after coaches posed questions at key junctures. The grandstanders chose to bench catcher Matt Batts and first baseman Ben Taylor, replacing them with Sherm Lollar and Hank Arft. Lollar had three hits (including what proved a game-winning home run) and two runs batted in, and Arft contributed two RBIs. After five of the first six A's hit safely in the first inning, the fans were asked, "Shall We Warm Up a New Pitcher?" The response was no, and St. Louis starter Ned Garver allowed only two hits the rest of the way in a 5-3 triumph. While the strategy-deciding process may have appeared time-consuming, the game was played in 2 hours, 11 minutes.

When strategy questions were posed at key junctures of an August 24, 1951, game between the St. Louis Browns and Philadelphia Athletics, the majority ruled as 1,115 "grandstand managers" answered with a yes or no. The promotion was another in the large arsenal of Browns Owner Bill Veeck.

Bill Veeck's 1979 Disco Demolition promotion backfired (above) when White Sox fans became unruly and forced the forfeiture of the second game of the team's doubleheader against Detroit. Cleveland fan Charley Lupica (right) finally left his flagpole on September 25, after his beloved Indians had been eliminated from the 1949 American League pennant race.

DISCO DEMOLITION NIGHT

More than 50,000 fans—many of them teen-agers—showed up at Comiskey Park on July 12, 1979, for Disco Demolition Night. Between games of a doubleheader between the Detroit Tigers and Chicago White Sox, disco records were to be burned—much to the delight of rock fans who paid 98 cents (disc jockey Steve Dahl of 98 WLUP-FM helped arrange the festivities) to get into the park. Many fans started to sling the records Frisbee-style onto the field during the first game, a contest that was delayed a number of times and finally won by Detroit, 4-1. During the record-burning, an estimated 5,000 fans raced onto the field and wouldn't return to their seats despite an appeal from Bill Veeck, owner of the White Sox. Umpire-in-chief Dave Phillips determined the crowd was too difficult to control—furthermore, the field had become a mess—and he called off the second game. Later, American League President Lee MacPhail ordered the game forfeited to Detroit.

FLAGPOLE SITTER SITS AND SITS

Cleveland fan Charley Lupica took up residence on a platform atop a flagpole on May 31, 1949, vowing not to come down until his beloved Indians moved into first place in the American League. On September 25, Owner Bill Veeck of the Indians had the platform moved to Municipal Stadium for a ceremony during which Lupica gave up his fruitless, 117-day vigil. The Indians, 1948 World Series champions who were in seventh place when Lupica's stunt began, were in fourth place when Lupica came down and they finished third.

FEATHERED FRIEND

The man who entertains baseball fans as The Chicken (formerly the San Diego Chicken) is Ted Giannoulas.

BERT CAMPANERIS—MR. VERSATILITY

Playing against the California Angels on September 8, 1965, Kansas City's Campaneris became the first man in major league history to play all nine positions in one game. In order, Campaneris played a full inning at shortstop (his normal position), second base, third base, left field, center field, right field (where he made his only error of the game), first base and pitcher. Campaneris then caught part of the ninth inning for the A's before leaving the game because of an injury.

Supporting Cast:

● **Bill Bryan.** A's catcher who caught pitcher Campaneris in the eighth when Campaneris allowed one run on one hit and two walks.

● **Jose Cardenal.** The first California player to bat against Campaneris. Cardenal, Campaneris' second cousin, popped out.

● **Ed Kirkpatrick.** California baserunner who was tagged out by catcher Campaneris in a home-plate collision in the ninth. The play forced Campan-

Bert Campaneris had his good and bad moments when he displayed his versatility in a September 8, 1965, promotion in Kansas City. Campaneris pitched the eighth inning (right) and caught the ninth until a home-plate collision with California's Ed Kirkpatrick (below) forced him to leave the game.

Minnesota's Cesar Tovar duplicated Campaneris' feat in a September 22, 1968, game against Oakland.

eris out of the game with a shoulder injury.

● **Rene Lachemann.** A's player who replaced Campaneris behind the plate in the ninth.

● **Aurelio Monteagudo.** A's pitcher who had Campaneris for a batterymate in the ninth inning of the game that the Angels won, 5-3, in 13 innings.

CESAR TOVAR MATCHES CAMPANERIS

Tovar, Minnesota infielder-outfielder, became the second major leaguer in history to play all nine positions in one game. Tovar's performance, which started with an inning of pitching, came in the Twins' 2-1 triumph over the Oakland A's on September 22, 1968.

Supporting Cast:

● **Bert Campaneris.** The first big leaguer to accomplish the all-positions playing feat (1965), Campaneris led off the game against Tovar and fouled out. Reggie Jackson then struck out, Danny Cater walked and Sal Bando fouled out.

● **Tom Hall.** Minnesota pitcher who replaced Tovar, hurling 6⅓ innings of relief and earning the victory.

● **Jerry Zimmerman.** Twins' catcher who caught Tovar in the first inning.

Players often are easily identified by their uniform numbers—but not always. Joe DiMaggio wore No. 9 at the outset of his career with the New York Yankees before switching to No. 5.

NINTH INNING:

Numbers.

0

Number of grand slams hit by Roger Maris during his record 61-home run year of 1961.

0

Number of intentional walks received by Roger Maris during his 61-home run year of 1961. Pitchers were reluctant to give up free passes to Maris because the Yanks' next batter in the lineup was Mickey Mantle, who hit 54 homers that season.

0

The number of changes in the alignment of the major leagues from 1903 through 1952. In each of those 50 years, the American League consisted of Boston, Chicago, Cleveland, Detroit, New York, Philadelphia, St. Louis and Washington; the National League was made up of Boston, Brooklyn, Chicago, Cincinnati, New York, Philadelphia, Pittsburgh and St. Louis.

George McQuinn gave St. Louis Browns fans something to cheer about when he homered in the 1944 World Series.

0

Number of grand slams hit in All-Star Game history.

⅛

Uniform number worn by midget Eddie Gaedel when he batted for the St. Louis Browns in 1951, thereby becoming the smallest player in big-league history.

1

The number of World Series home runs hit by the St. Louis Browns. First baseman George McQuinn connected for the Browns in Game 1 of the 1944 Series against the St. Louis Cardinals (the '44 Series marked the Browns' only appearance in postseason play).

2

Number of grand slams hit by Babe Ruth during his 60-home run year of 1927.

2

Fewest pitchers used by one team in a World Series. The Philadelphia Athletics used only Chief Bender and Jack Coombs in defeating the Chicago Cubs, four games to one, in the 1910 Series.

2¾

The maximum number of inches in diameter of a bat at its thickest part.

3

Uniform number of Oakland A's designated runner Herb Washington in 1974-75.

3

Number of pitchers who gave up hits in four games to Joe DiMaggio during his 56-game hitting streak in 1941. Thornton Lee and Johnny Rigney of the Chicago White Sox and Eldon Auker of the St. Louis Browns were the three.

3.20

The highest earned-run average figure that was the lowest in a league for a season. Early Wynn of the 1950 Cleveland Indians led the American League with the 3.20 ERA.

Minnie Minoso (above) appeared in big-league games in five decades, while Early Wynn (right) was a four-decade player in the majors.

4

The number of decades in which these players competed in the major leagues:

Player	First Club	Last Club
Jim O'Rourke	Boston, N.L., 1876	New York, N.L., 1904
Dan Brouthers	Troy, N.L., 1879	New York, N.L., 1904
Jack O'Connor	Cincinnati, A.A., 1887	St. Louis, A.L., 1910
Deacon McGuire	Toledo, A.A., 1884	Detroit, A.L., 1912
Kid Gleason	Philadelphia, N.L., 1888	Chicago, A.L., 1912
John Ryan	Louisville, A.A., 1889	Washington, A.L., 1913
Eddie Collins	Philadelphia, A.L., 1906	Philadelphia, A.L., 1930
Jack Quinn	New York, A.L., 1909	Cincinnati, N.L., 1933
Bobo Newsom	Brooklyn, N.L., 1929	Philadelphia, A.L., 1953
Mickey Vernon	Washington, A.L., 1939	Pittsburgh, N.L., 1960
Ted Williams	Boston, A.L., 1939	Boston, A.L., 1960
Early Wynn	Washington, A.L., 1939	Cleveland, A.L., 1963
Tim McCarver	St. Louis, N.L., 1959	Philadelphia, N.L., 1980
Willie McCovey	San Francisco, N.L., 1959	San Francisco, N.L., 1980
Jim Kaat	Washington, A.L., 1959	*St. Louis, N.L., 1982

*Still active in 1983.

4:11

The time of the afternoon when Bobby Thomson hit his three-run, pennant-clinching home run for the New York Giants on October 3, 1951.

4-2

The score by which the Mudville nine lost in Ernest Thayer's "Casey at the Bat."

4.74

The 1960 earned-run average of Boston Red Sox pitcher Ike Delock, who, ironically, compiled a .474 won-lost percentage that year. Delock had a 9-10 record and allowed 68 earned runs in 129 innings for the twin "474" figures.

5

The number of decades in which these players competed in the major leagues:

Player	First Club	Last Club
Nick Altrock	Louisville, N.L., 1898	Washington, A.L., 1933
Minnie Minoso	Cleveland, A.L., 1949	Chicago, A.L., 1980

5

Number of outs accounted for by Brooklyn Dodgers pitcher Clarence Mitchell in his two at-bats during the fifth game of the 1920 World Series. Mitchell lined into the only triple play in Series history in the fifth inning, and he

Hall of Famer Ed Delahanty obviously was the best of the five Delahanty brothers, but Jim Delahanty (above) had his moments. In fact, Jim batted .339 for the Detroit Tigers in 1911.

grounded into a double play in the eighth.

5

The number of Delahanty brothers who played in the majors. The brothers, with their first and last seasons in the big leagues: Edward J., 1888, 1903; Thomas J., 1894, 1897; James C., 1901, 1912; Frank G., 1905, 1908, and Joseph N., 1907, 1909. Ed, a .346 lifetime hitter, is a member of the Hall of Fame.

5, 5¼

The minimum and maximum weight, in ounces, of a baseball.

6

The lowest victory total for a Cy Young Award winning pitcher. Bruce Sutter of the Chicago Cubs had a 6-6 record with 37 saves when he won the award in 1979, and Rollie Fingers of the Milwaukee Brewers had a 6-3 record with 28 saves when he won in the strike-shortened 1981 season.

6

Number of hits a team could possibly get in one inning without scoring a run. The first three batters load the bases with infield singles. The opposing pitcher picks the runners off third and second. Two more infield singles reload the bases and the final batter hits a ball that strikes a baserunner. The runner is out while the batter is credited with a hit.

6

The most hits given up by a pitcher to Joe DiMaggio during his 56-game hitting streak of 1941. Thornton Lee of the Chicago White Sox gave up the six hits in a span of four games.

6

The number of World Series sweeps (1927, 1928, 1932, 1938, 1939 and 1950) by the New York Yankees. No other team has won more than one four-game Series.

7

Uniform number of Cesar Gutierrez when the Detroit Tigers' shortstop became the first player in modern major league history to get seven hits in seven at-bats in a game. Gutierrez collected six singles and a double in the 12-inning second game of a June 21 doubleheader in 1970.

7

The number of times Roger Maris hit two home runs in a game during his 61-homer year of 1961.

Joe Jackson (above left) and Swede Risberg (above right) were two of the eight so-called "Black Sox" of 1919 who were barred from the major leagues. Also banned were Claude (Lefty) Williams and Ed Cicotte (left and right, respectively, in right photo), who flank Bill James. James was not involved in the scandal.

8

The number of times Babe Ruth hit two home runs in a game during his 60-homer year of 1927.

8

The number of major league players who have turned unassisted triple plays.

8

The number of Chicago White Sox players who were barred for life in 1920 by Commissioner Kenesaw Mountain Landis for allegedly fixing the 1919 World Series. Although the players—Ed Cicotte, Joe Jackson, Claude (Lefty) Williams, Oscar (Happy) Felsch, Buck Weaver, Swede Risberg, Chick Gandil and Fred McMullin—later were acquitted by the courts, Landis refused to allow them back into baseball.

9:07

The time of night when Hank Aaron of the Atlanta Braves hit his 715th major league home run, breaking Babe Ruth's all-time record.

11

The most pitchers used by one team in a World Series. The Boston Red Sox used 11 hurlers in losing four out of the seven games played against the St. Louis Cardinals in 1946.

11

The largest number enshrined in baseball's Hall of Fame in one year. The following entered the Hall in 1946: Jesse Burkett, Frank Chance, Jack Chesbro, Johnny Evers, Clark Griffith, Tom McCarthy, Joe McGinnity, Eddie Plank, Joe Tinker, Rube Waddell and Ed Walsh. All 11 were named by the committee on old-timers; no players were elected by the Baseball Writers' Association of America.

12

The number of home runs hit by Roger Maris off lefthanded pitchers in his 61-homer season of 1961.

12:32

Time of the afternoon in which Bob Watson of the Houston Astros scored the millionth run in major league history. Watson scored from second base on a three-run homer by teammate Milt May at San Francisco's Candlestick Park on May 4, 1975. Jose Cruz scored from first on the play. May hit his home run off Giants hurler John Montefusco.

Ralph Branca, wearing his familiar No. 13, defied superstition on Friday, April 13, 1951, by flaunting the number and holding a black cat . . .

12

The uniform number worn by Ralph Branca in 1952. The Brooklyn Dodgers' pitcher had forsaken No. 13 after giving up Bobby Thomson's pennant-winning homer in 1951. Branca resumed wearing No. 13 in 1953.

... but the Brooklyn pitcher changed his tune during spring training of 1952. Having yielded Bobby Thomson's pennant-winning homer the previous October, Branca was ready to discard his old uniform top.

14

The uniform number worn by Pete Gray when the one-armed outfielder played for the St. Louis Browns in 1945.

15

The number of home runs hit by Joe DiMaggio during his 56-game hitting streak in 1941.

15

The width and length, in inches, of the bags at first, second and third base.

15

The lowest stolen base total to lead a league. Dominic DiMaggio of the Boston Red Sox stole only 15 bases in 1950, but still led the American League.

16

The most Gold Glove fielding awards won by any player. Pitcher Jim Kaat won 14 in the American League and two in the National League from 1962 through 1977, while Brooks Robinson won the award at third base in the American League from 1960 through 1975.

17

The width, in inches, of home plate.

17

Uniform number worn by Andy Messersmith when he signed as a free agent with the Atlanta Braves in 1976. When Messersmith, who wore number 47 for the Los Angeles Dodgers the year before, came to the Braves, Owner Ted Turner gave him uniform No. 17 because, in Turner's words, "That is the channel at my TV station (Turner owned WTBS, a so-called superstation that broadcasts via satellite and cable out of Atlanta). Super 17, that's Andy." But Turner carried things a bit further and, instead of putting Messersmith's name on the back of his uniform, he gave his new pitcher the nickname "Channel." Shortly after, in June of '76, National League President Chub Feeney lectured Turner on his uniform advertising ploy and made Turner remove the word "Channel" from Messersmith's uniform.

17

Largest number of players involved in one major league trade. The deal, between the Baltimore Orioles and New York Yankees, started on November 18, 1954, when Baltimore sent pitcher Bob Turley, pitcher Don Larsen and shortstop Billy Hunter to New York for pitcher Harry Byrd, pitcher Jim McDonald, outfielder Gene Woodling, catcher Hal Smith, short-

When Atlanta's Ted Turner, owner of WTBS, Channel 17, signed Andy Messersmith to a Braves contract in 1976, he had a uniform ready for his new pitcher. However, N.L. President Chub Feeney didn't approve.

stop Willie Miranda and catcher-first baseman Gus Triandos. The deal was completed on December 1 when the Orioles sent pitcher Mike Blyzka, catcher Darrell Johnson, first baseman Dick Kryhoski, outfielder Jim Fridley and outfielder Ted Del Guercio to the Yankees for pitcher Bill Miller, third baseman Kal Segrist and second baseman Don Leppert.

18

Uniform number of Don Larsen when he pitched his perfect World Series game in 1956.

18⅓

The most innings worked by a relief pitcher in one major league game, with Zip Zabel of the Chicago Cubs setting the record on June 17, 1915, against Brooklyn. Zabel allowed nine hits and only one walk, emerging as the winning pitcher in the Cubs' 4-3, 19-inning triumph.

19

The number of home runs Babe Ruth hit off lefthanded pitchers during his 60-homer year of 1927.

22

The record number of World Series titles won by the American League's New York Yankees.

23

The number of World Series titles won by other American League clubs.

28

The number of home runs hit by Babe Ruth at Yankee Stadium during his 60-home run year of 1927.

29

The uniform number worn by Satchel Paige when he threw three scoreless innings for the Kansas City A's in 1965, Satch's final appearance in the major leagues.

30

The number of home runs hit by Roger Maris at Yankee Stadium during his 61-homer year of 1961.

31

The number of home runs hit by Roger Maris on the road during his 61-homer year of 1961.

The famed Green Monster (the left-field wall) in Boston's Fenway Park long has provided an inviting target for American League hitters.

32

The number of home runs hit by Babe Ruth on the road during his 60-homer year of 1927.

33

The record number of World Series appearances by the New York Yankees.

33

The number of different pitchers who gave up home runs to Babe Ruth during his 60-homer year of 1927.

37

Height, in feet, of the famous left-field wall in Boston's Fenway Park. The wall is nicknamed the "Green Monster."

39

The most home runs hit at one ballpark by a player in one season. Hank Greenberg of the Detroit Tigers hit 39 at Detroit's Briggs Stadium in 1938.

40

Height, in feet, of the left-field screen in the Los Angeles Memorial Coliseum, the Dodgers' first California home.

41

The number of home runs hit by Babe Ruth off righthanded pitchers during his 60-homer year of 1927.

42

The major league-record number of times Rickey Henderson was caught stealing in 1982, when the Oakland A's speedster set a modern major league record of 130 stolen bases.

42

The maximum length, in inches, of a bat.

43

Height, in inches, of St Louis Browns' midget Eddie Gaedel.

44

Uniform number worn by Hank Aaron when he hit his major league record-setting 715th home run. Ironically, the pitcher he victimized that night, Los Angeles Dodgers hurler Al Downing, was also wearing No. 44.

46

The number of different pitchers who gave up home runs to Roger Maris during his 61-homer year of 1961.

46

The most home runs allowed by a pitcher during one season. Robin Roberts of the Philadelphia Phillies allowed 46 in 1956.

49

The number of home runs hit by Roger Maris off righthanded pitchers during his 61-homer year of 1961.

50

The length, in days, of the 1981 players' strike.

50

The major league-record number of times Ron Hunt of the Montreal Expos was hit by a pitch in 1971. The Pittsburgh Pirates were the only team that did not hit him. Jim Bunning of the Philadelphia Phillies was the first to hit Hunt (April 10) and Milt Pappas of the Chicago Cubs was the last (September 29). Nolan Ryan of the New York Mets hit him the most times overall, four.

Montreal's Ron Hunt often found a painful route to first base during the 1971 season.

51

The total of retired numbers in the majors (excluding the Angels' number 26, retired in honor of the club's "26th man," Owner Gene Autry):

No.	Player	Team
1	Richie Ashburn	Phillies
1	Fred Hutchinson	Reds
1	Billy Meyer	Pirates
2	Nellie Fox	White Sox
3	Earl Averill	Indians
3	Harmon Killebrew	Twins
3	Babe Ruth	Yankees
4	Luke Appling	White Sox
4	Lou Gehrig	Yankees
4	Mel Ott	Giants
4	Duke Snider	Dodgers
4	Earl Weaver	Orioles
5	Lou Boudreau	Indians
5	Joe DiMaggio	Yankees
5	Brooks Robinson	Orioles
6	Al Kaline	Tigers
6	Stan Musial	Cardinals
7	Mickey Mantle	Yankees
8	Yogi Berra & Bill Dickey	Yankees
8	Willie Stargell	Pirates
9	Ted Williams	Red Sox
11	Carl Hubbell	Giants
14	Ernie Banks	Cubs
14	Gil Hodges	Mets
15	Thurman Munson	Yankees
16	Whitey Ford	Yankees
17	Dizzy Dean	Cardinals
19	Bob Feller	Indians
19	Jim Gilliam	Dodgers
20	Lou Brock	Cardinals
20	Frank Robinson	Orioles
20	Pie Traynor	Pirates
21	Roberto Clemente	Pirates
21	Warren Spahn	Braves
24	Walter Alston	Dodgers
24	Willie Mays	Giants
27	Juan Marichal	Giants
32	Sandy Koufax	Dodgers
32	Jim Umbricht	Astros (Colt .45s)
33	Honus Wagner	Pirates
36	Robin Roberts	Phillies
37	Casey Stengel	Mets & Yankees
39	Roy Campanella	Dodgers
40	Danny Murtaugh	Pirates
40	Don Wilson	Astros
41	Eddie Mathews	Braves
42	Jackie Robinson	Dodgers
44	Hank Aaron	Braves & Brewers
44	Willie McCovey	Giants
45	Bob Gibson	Cardinals

Lou Gehrig's uniform No. 4 was retired by the New York Yankees.

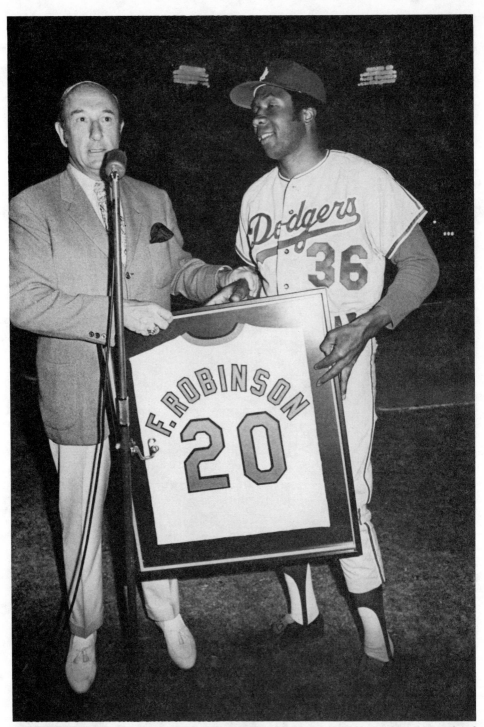

Orioles President Jerry Hoffberger presents a framed uniform No. 20, retired by the Baltimore club, to Frank Robinson before the 1972 season. Robinson spent '72 with the Los Angeles Dodgers.

53

The number of players to play for the Seattle Pilots in 1969—the club's only year of existence.

53

One of only three numbers between 0 and 61 that has never been totaled by a major league home run hitter during a season. The other two numbers are 55 and 57.

54

The number of hits a team could possibly get during a nine-inning game and still be shut out.

56

The number of singles collected and runs scored by Joe DiMaggio during his 56-game hitting streak of 1941.

56

The day-by-day batting performance of Joe DiMaggio during his major league-record 56-game hitting streak:

Opposing Pitcher and Club	AB.	R.	H.	2B.	3B.	HR.	RBI.
May 15—Smith, Chicago	4	0	1	0	0	0	1
16—Lee, Chicago	4	2	2	0	1	1	1
17—Rigney, Chicago	3	1	1	0	0	0	0
18—Harris (2), Niggeling (1), St. Louis	3	3	3	1	0	0	1
19—Galehouse, St. Louis	3	0	1	1	0	0	0
20—Auker, St. Louis	5	1	1	0	0	0	1
21—Rowe (1), Benton (1), Detroit	5	0	2	0	0	0	1
22—McKain, Detroit	4	0	1	0	0	0	1
23—Newsome, Boston	5	0	1	0	0	0	2
24—Johnson, Boston	4	2	1	0	0	0	2
25—Grove, Boston	4	0	1	0	0	0	0
27—Chase (1), Anderson (2), Carrasquel (1), Washington	5	3	4	0	0	1	3
28—Hudson, Washington (Night)	4	1	1	0	1	0	0
29—Sundra, Washington	3	1	1	0	0	0	0
30—Johnson, Boston	2	1	1	0	0	0	0
30—Harris, Boston	3	0	1	1	0	0	0
June 1—Milnar, Cleveland	4	1	1	0	0	0	0
1—Harder, Cleveland	4	0	1	0	0	0	0
2—Feller, Cleveland	4	2	2	1	0	0	0
3—Trout, Detroit	4	1	1	0	0	1	1
5—Newhouser, Detroit	5	1	1	0	1	0	1
7—Muncrief (1), Allen (1), Caster (1), St. Louis	5	2	3	0	0	0	1
8—Auker, St. Louis	4	3	2	0	0	2	4
8—Caster (1), Kramer (1), St. Louis	4	1	2	1	0	1	3
10—Rigney, Chicago	5	1	1	0	0	0	0

Opposing Pitcher and Club	AB.	R.	H.	2B.	3B.	HR.	RBI.
12—Lee, Chicago (Night)	4	1	2	0	0	1	1
14—Feller, Cleveland	2	0	1	1	0	0	1
15—Bagby, Cleveland	3	1	1	0	0	1	1
16—Milnar, Cleveland	5	0	1	1	0	0	0
17—Rigney, Chicago	4	1	1	0	0	0	0
18—Lee, Chicago	3	0	1	0	0	0	0
19—Smith (1), Ross (2), Chicago	3	2	3	0	0	1	2
20—Newsom (2), McKain (2), Detroit	5	3	4	1	0	0	1
21—Trout, Detroit	4	0	1	0	0	0	1
22—Newhouser (1), Newsom (1), Detroit.	5	1	2	1	0	1	2
24—Muncrief, St. Louis	4	1	1	0	0	0	0
25—Galehouse, St. Louis	4	1	1	0	0	1	3
26—Auker, St. Louis	4	0	1	1	0	0	1
27—Dean, Philadelphia	3	1	2	0	0	1	2
28—Babich (1), Harris (1), Philadelphia ...	5	1	2	1	0	0	0
29—Leonard, Washington	4	1	1	1	0	0	0
29—Anderson, Washington	5	1	1	0	0	0	1
July 1—Harris (1), Ryba (1), Boston	4	0	2	0	0	0	1
1—Wilson, Boston	3	1	1	0	0	0	1
2—Newsome, Boston	5	1	1	0	0	1	3
5—Marchildon, Philadelphia	4	2	1	0	0	1	2
6—Babich (1), Hadley (3), Philadelphia..	5	2	4	1	0	0	2
6—Knott, Philadelphia	4	0	2	0	1	0	2
10—Niggeling, St. Louis (Night)	2	0	1	0	0	0	0
11—Harris (3), Kramer (1), St. Louis	5	1	4	0	0	1	2
12—Auker (1), Muncrief (1), St. Louis	5	1	2	1	0	0	1
13—Lyons (2), Hallett (1), Chicago	4	2	3	0	0	0	0
13—Lee, Chicago	4	0	1	0	0	0	0
14—Rigney, Chicago	3	0	1	0	0	0	0
15—Smith, Chicago	4	1	2	1	0	0	2
16—Milnar (2), Krakauskas (1), Cleve.	4	3	3	1	0	0	0
Totals for 56 games	223	56	91	16	4	15	55

Stopped July 17 at Cleveland, New York won, 4 to 3. First inning, Alfred J. Smith pitching, thrown out by Keltner; fourth inning, Smith pitching, received base on balls; seventh inning, Smith pitching, thrown out by Keltner; eighth inning, James C. Bagby, Jr., pitching, grounded into double play.

60

Babe Ruth's 60 home runs in 1927:

HR No.	Game No.	Date	Opposing Pitcher and Club	City
1	4	April 15	Howard J. Ehmke (R), Phila.	New York
2	11	April 23	George E. Walberg (L), Phila.	Philadelphia
3	12	April 24	Hollis Thurston (R), Wash.	Washington
4	14	April 29	Bryan W. Harriss (R), Boston	Boston
5	16	May 1	John P. Quinn (R), Phila.	New York
6	16	May 1	George E. Walberg (L), Phila.	New York
7	24	May 10	Milton Gaston (R), St. Louis	St. Louis
8	25	May 11	Ernest Nevers (R), St. Louis	St. Louis
9	29	May 17	H. Warren Collins (R), Detroit	Detroit
10	33	May 22	Benj. J. Karr (R), Cleveland	Cleveland

Joe DiMaggio matches Willie Keeler's 44-game batting streak on the way to establishing the major league record of hitting safely in 56 consecutive games.

HR No.	Game No.	Date	Opposing Pitcher and Club	City
11	34	May 23	Hollis Thurston (R), Wash.	Washington
12	37	May 28*	Hollis Thurston (R), Wash.	New York
13	39	May 29	Daniel K. MacFayden (R), Boston	New York
14	41	May 30‡	George E. Walberg (L), Phila.	Philadelphia
15	42	May 31*	John P. Quinn (R), Phila.	Philadelphia
16	43	May 31†	Howard J. Ehmke (R), Phila.	Philadelphia
17	47	June 5	Earl O. Whitehill (L), Detroit	New York
18	48	June 7	Alphonse T. Thomas (R), Chi.	New York
19	52	June 11	Garland M. Buckeye (L), Cleve.	New York
20	52	June 11	Garland M. Buckeye (L), Cleve.	New York
21	53	June 12	George E. Uhle (R), Cleveland	New York
22	55	June 16	Jonathan T. Zachary (L), St. L.	New York
23	60	June 22*	Harold J. Wiltse (L), Boston	Boston
24	60	June 22*	Harold J. Wiltse (L), Boston	Boston
25	70	June 30	Bryan W. Harriss (R), Boston	New York
26	73	July 3	Horace O. Lisenbee (R), Wash.	Washington
27	78	July 8†	Donald W. Hankins (R), Detroit	Detroit
28	79	July 9*	Kenneth E. Holloway (R), Detroit	Detroit
29	79	July 9*	Kenneth E. Holloway (R), Detroit	Detroit
30	83	July 12	Joseph B. Shaute (L), Cleve.	Cleveland
31	94	July 24	Alphonse T. Thomas (R), Chi.	Chicago
32	95	July 26*	Milton Gaston (R), St. Louis	New York
33	95	July 26*	Milton Gaston (R), St. Louis	New York
34	98	July 28	Walter C. Stewart (L), St. L.	New York
35	106	Aug. 5	George S. Smith (R), Detroit	New York
36	110	Aug. 10	Jonathan T. Zachary (L), Wash.	Washington
37	114	Aug. 16	Alphonse T. Thomas (R), Chi.	Chicago
38	115	Aug. 17	George W. Connally (R), Chi.	Chicago
39	118	Aug. 20	J. Walter Miller (L), Cleveland	Cleveland
40	120	Aug. 22	Joseph B. Shaute (L), Cleve.	Cleveland
41	124	Aug. 27	Ernest Nevers (R), St. Louis	St. Louis
42	125	Aug. 28	J. Ernest Wingard (L), St. Louis	St. Louis
43	127	Aug. 31	Tony Welzer (R), Boston	New York
44	128	Sept. 2	George E. Walberg (L), Phila.	Philadelphia
45	132	Sept. 6*	Tony Welzer (R), Boston	Boston
46	132	Sept. 6*	Tony Welzer (R), Boston	Boston
47	133	Sept. 6†	Jack Russell (R), Boston	Boston
48	134	Sept. 7	Daniel K. MacFayden (R), Boston	Boston
49	134	Sept. 7	Bryan W. Harriss (R), Boston	Boston
50	138	Sept. 11	Milton Gaston (R), St. Louis	New York
51	139	Sept. 13*	G. Willis Hudlin (R), Cleveland	New York
52	140	Sept. 13†	Joseph B. Shaute (L), Cleveland	New York
53	143	Sept. 16	Ted Blankenship (R), Chicago	New York
54	147	Sept. 18†	Theodore A. Lyons (R), Chicago	New York
55	148	Sept. 21	Samuel B. Gibson (R), Detroit	New York
56	149	Sept. 22	Kenneth E. Holloway (R), Detroit	New York
57	152	Sept. 27	Robert M Grove (L), Phila.	New York
58	153	Sept. 29	Horace O. Lisenbee (R), Wash.	New York
59	153	Sept. 29	Paul Hopkins (R), Washington	New York
60	154	Sept. 30	Jonathan T. Zachary (L), Wash.	New York

*First game of doubleheader. †Second game of doubleheader.
‡Afternoon game of split doubleheader.

61

The game-by-game home run performance of Roger Maris in 1961:

HR No.	Game No.	Date	Opposing Pitcher and Club	City
1	11	April 26	Paul Foytack (R), Detroit	Detroit
2	17	May 3	Pedro Ramos (R), Minnesota	Minneapolis
3	20	May 6	Eli Grba (R), Los Angeles	Los Angeles
4	29	May 17	Peter Burnside (L), Washington	New York
5	30	May 19	James Perry (R), Cleveland	Cleveland
6	31	May 20	Gary Bell (R), Cleveland	Cleveland
7	32	May 21	Charles Estrada (R), Baltimore	New York
8	35	May 24	D. Eugene Conley (R), Boston	New York
9	38	May 28	Calvin McLish (R), Chicago	New York
10	40	May 30	D. Eugene Conley (R), Boston	Boston
11	40	May 30	Miguel Fornieles (R), Boston	Boston
12	41	May 31	Billy Muffett (R), Boston	Boston
13	43	June 2	Calvin McLish (R), Chicago	Chicago
14	44	June 3	Robert Shaw (R), Chicago	Chicago
15	45	June 4	Russell Kemmerer (R), Chicago	Chicago
16	48	June 6	Edwin Palmquist (R), Minnesota	New York
17	49	June 7	Pedro Ramos (R), Minnesota	New York
18	52	June 9	Raymond Herbert (R), Kan. City	New York
19	55	June 11†	Eli Grba (R), Los Angeles	New York
20	55	June 11†	John James (R), Los Angeles	New York
21	57	June 13	James Perry (R), Cleveland	Cleveland
22	58	June 14	Gary Bell (R), Cleveland	Cleveland
23	61	June 17	Donald Mossi (L), Detroit	Detroit
24	62	June 18	Jerry Casale (R), Detroit	Detroit
25	63	June 19	James Archer (L), Kansas City	Kansas City
26	64	June 20	Joseph Nuxhall (L), Kansas City	Kansas City
27	66	June 22	Norman Bass (R), Kansas City	Kansas City
28	74	July 1	David Sisler (R), Washington	New York
29	75	July 2	Peter Burnside (L), Washington	New York
30	75	July 2	John Klippstein (R), Washington	New York
31	77	July 4†	Frank Lary (R), Detroit	New York
32	78	July 5	Frank Funk (R), Cleveland	New York
33	82	July 9*	William Monbouquette (R), Bos.	New York
34	84	July 13	Early Wynn (R), Chicago	Chicago
35	86	July 15	Raymond Herbert (R), Chicago	Chicago
36	92	July 21	William Monbouquette (R), Bos.	Boston
37	95	July 25*	Frank Baumann (L), Chicago	New York
38	95	July 25*	Don Larsen (R), Chicago	New York
39	96	July 25†	Russell Kemmerer (R), Chicago	New York
40	96	July 25†	Warren Hacker (R), Chicago	New York
41	106	Aug. 4	Camilo Pascual (R), Minnesota	New York
42	114	Aug. 11	Peter Burnside (L), Washington	Washington
43	115	Aug. 12	Richard Donovan (R), Wash.	Washington
44	116	Aug. 13*	Bennie Daniels (R), Washington	Washington
45	117	Aug. 13†	Marion Kutyna (R), Washington	Washington
46	118	Aug. 15	Juan Pizarro (L), Chicago	New York
47	119	Aug. 16	W. William Pierce (L), Chicago	New York
48	119	Aug. 16	W. William Pierce (L), Chicago	New York
49	124	Aug. 20	James Perry (R), Cleveland	Cleveland

HR No.	Game No.	Date	Opposing Pitcher and Club	City
50	125	Aug. 22	Kenneth McBride (R), L. Angeles	Los Angeles
51	129	Aug. 26	Jerry Walker (R), Kansas City	Kansas City
52	135	Sept. 2	Frank Lary (R), Detroit	New York
53	135	Sept. 2	Henry Aguirre (L), Detroit	New York
54	140	Sept. 6	Thomas Cheney (R), Washington	New York
55	141	Sept. 7	Richard Stigman (L), Cleveland	New York
56	143	Sept. 9	James Grant (R), Cleveland	New York
57	151	Sept. 16	Frank Lary (R), Detroit	Detroit
58	152	Sept. 17	Terrence Fox (R), Detroit	Detroit
59	155	Sept. 20	Milton Pappas (R), Baltimore	Baltimore
60	159	Sept. 26	John Fisher (R), Baltimore	New York
61	163	Oct. 1	E. Tracy Stallard (R), Boston	New York

*First game of doubleheader. †Second game of doubleheader.

65

The weight, in pounds, of St. Louis Browns midget pinch-hitter Eddie Gaedel.

72

The major league-record number of times Babe Ruth hit two or more home runs in one game during his regular-season career. He did it another four times in the World Series, for a total of 76.

96

Uniform number worn by Bill Voiselle starting in 1947 after he was traded from the New York Giants to the Boston Braves. Voiselle was from the town of Ninety Six, S.C., and his uniform number reflected that fact.

96

The number of home runs that Frank (Home Run) Baker hit in a big-league career that began in 1908 and ended in 1922. Baker never slugged more than 12 homers in one season.

97

The number of pitches thrown by Don Larsen of the New York Yankees in his 1956 World Series perfect game.

98.2

The highest percentage of votes received by a player elected to the Baseball Hall of Fame. Ty Cobb collected votes on 222 of the 226 ballots cast when he was elected in 1936.

103

The most wins achieved in a season by the New York Yankees in the

Pitcher Bill Voiselle of the Boston Braves was from Ninety Six, S.C.—and obviously proud of it.

10-year period between 1949 and 1958. The Yankees won 103 games in 1954, but finished second to Cleveland's 111 wins that season. Ironically, they won the pennant in each of the other nine years, but never won as many as 100 games in any season.

108

The number of double stitches in a regulation baseball.

158

The number of lifetime home runs Roger Maris had after he hit his record 61st of 1961.

186

The distance, in feet, from the playing field to the highest point of the ceiling in Minnesota's Metrodome.

208

The distance, in feet, from the playing field to the highest point of the ceiling in Houston's Astrodome.

250

The distance, in feet, from the playing field to the highest point of the ceiling in Seattle's Kingdome.

251

The distance, in feet, from home plate to the left-field foul pole in the Los Angeles Memorial Coliseum, the Dodgers' first California home.

257

The distance, in feet, from home plate to the right-field foul pole in New York's Polo Grounds.

275

The number of career home runs hit by single-season homer king Roger Maris, who hit 61 in 1961.

279

The distance, in feet, from home plate to the left-field foul pole in New York's Polo Grounds.

297

The distance, in feet, from home plate to the right-field foul pole in Brooklyn's Ebbets Field.

The configuration of the Los Angeles Memorial Coliseum (above, packed for Game 3 of the 1959 World Series) wasn't meant for baseball, as evidenced by the 251-foot distance from home plate to the left-field flagpole (left). The left-field screen became a favorite home-run target.

The 483-foot marker in deepest center field at the Polo Grounds is barely visible as players stand at attention for flag-raising ceremonies.

300

The distance, in feet, from home plate to the right-field foul pole in the Los Angeles Memorial Coliseum, the Dodgers' first California home. However, right field proved a tough area in which to hit a home run because the fence curved out dramatically from the foul pole.

323

The highest number of home runs hit by one player in one park during a career. Mel Ott had 323 homers for the New York Giants at the Polo Grounds.

348

The distance, in feet, from home plate to the left-field foul pole in Brooklyn's Ebbets Field.

416

The number of lifetime home runs Babe Ruth had after he hit his 60th of the 1927 season.

483

The distance, in feet, from home plate to the deepest part of center field in New York's Polo Grounds.

500-HOMER CLUB

Twelve players in major league history have hit 500 or more lifetime home runs. The first, 500th and last victims of each follow:

	Hank Aaron (755)	**Babe Ruth** (714)	**Willie Mays** (660)
First Victim	Vic Raschi St. Louis, N.L. April 23, 1954 At St. Louis	Jack Warhop New York, A.L. May 6, 1915 At New York	Warren Spahn Boston, N.L. May 28, 1951 At New York
500th Victim	Mike McCormick San Francisco, N.L. July 14, 1968 At Atlanta	Willis Hudlin Cleveland, A.L. August 11, 1929 At Cleveland	Don Nottebart Houston, N.L. September 13, 1965 At Houston
Last Victim	Dick Drago California, A.L. July 20, 1976 At Milwaukee	Guy Bush Pittsburgh, N.L. May 25, 1935 At Pittsburgh	Don Gullett Cincinnati, N.L. August 17, 1973 At New York

	Frank Robinson (586)	**Harmon Killebrew** (573)	**Mickey Mantle** (536)
First Victim	Paul Minner Chicago, N.L. April 28, 1956 At Cincinnati	Billy Hoeft Detroit, A.L. June 24, 1955 At Washington	Randy Gumpert Chicago, A.L. May 1, 1951 At Chicago
500th Victim	Fred Scherman Detroit, A.L. September 13, 1971 At Baltimore	Mike Cuellar Baltimore, A.L. August 10, 1971 At Minnesota	Stu Miller Baltimore, A.L. May 14, 1967 At New York
Last Victim	Sid Monge California, A.L. July 6, 1976 At California	Ed Bane Minnesota, A.L. September 18, 1975 At Minnesota	Jim Lonborg Boston, A.L. September 20, 1968 At New York

	Jimmie Foxx (534)	**Ted Williams** (521)	**Willie McCovey** (521)
First Victim	Urban Shocker New York, A.L. May 31, 1927 At Philadelphia	Bud Thomas Philadelphia, A.L. April 23, 1939 At Boston	Ron Kline Pittsburgh, N.L. August 2, 1959 At San Francisco
500th Victim	George Caster Philadelphia, A.L. September 24, 1940 At Philadelphia	Wynn Hawkins Cleveland, A.L. June 17, 1960 At Cleveland	Jamie Easterly Atlanta, N.L. June 30, 1978 At Atlanta
Last Victim	Johnny Lanning Pittsburgh, N.L. September 9, 1945 At Pittsburgh	Jack Fisher Baltimore, A.L. September 28, 1960 At Boston	Scott Sanderson Montreal, N.L. May 3, 1980 At Montreal

Harmon Killebrew entered the 500-homer club on August 10, 1971, and added another for good measure.

	Eddie Mathews **(512)**	**Ernie Banks** **(512)**	**Mel Ott** **(511)**
First Victim	Ken Heintzelman Philadelphia, N.L. April 19, 1952 At Philadelphia	Gerry Staley St. Louis, N.L. September 20, 1953 At St. Louis	Hal Carlson Chicago, N.L. July 18, 1927 At New York
500th Victim	Juan Marichal San Francisco, N.L. July 14, 1967 At San Francisco	Pat Jarvis Atlanta, N.L. May 12, 1970 At Chicago	Johnny Hutchings Boston, N.L. August 1, 1945 At New York
Last Victim	Sammy Ellis California, A.L. May 27, 1968 At California	Jim McGlothlin Cincinnati, N.L. August 24, 1971 At Chicago	Oscar Judd Philadelphia, N.L. April 16, 1946 At New York

600-HOMER CLUB

Only three players have hit 600 or more major league home runs. The players and their 600th victims follow:

Player, Club	**Victim, Club**	**Date, Place**
Babe Ruth, New York, A.L.	George Blaeholder, St. Louis	August 21, 1931 At St. Louis
Willie Mays, San Francisco, N.L.	Mike Corkins, San Diego	September 22, 1969 At San Diego
Hank Aaron, Atlanta, N.L.	Gaylord Perry, San Francisco	April 27, 1971 At Atlanta

Willie Mays (right) trots home after slugging career homer No. 600 in a 1969 game against the San Diego Padres.

Red Barber interviews Dodgers Manager Leo Durocher (center) after W2XBS presented the first telecast of a big-league game in 1939. Reds Manager Bill McKechnie (1) also was interviewed.

672

The highest number of at-bats compiled by one player during a season without hitting a home run. Rabbit Maranville of the Pittsburgh Pirates reached this figure in 1922.

691

The major league-record number of games in which Hank Aaron hit one or more home runs in his regular-season career. In addition, he hit homers in eight post-season and All-Star Games.

700-HOMER CLUB

The only two players to hit 700 big-league home runs, and their 700th victims:

Player, Club	Victim, Club	Date, Place
Babe Ruth, New York, A.L.	Tommy Bridges, Detroit	July 13, 1934 At Detroit
Hank Aaron, Atlanta, N.L.	Ken Brett, Philadelphia	July 21, 1973 At Atlanta

Baseball comedian Max Patkin apparently is puzzled over what uniform number he should wear.

712

The number of games canceled in the major leagues during the 1981 players' strike. There were 328 games canceled in the N.L. and 384 in the A.L.

755

The record number of career home runs hit by Hank Aaron. Including All-Star Games and post-season contests, Aaron hit 763.

W2XBS

The experimental television station in New York which aired the first televised major league game on August 26, 1939 from Ebbets Field, between the Cincinnati Reds and Brooklyn Dodgers. The Reds won the game, 5-2. Only three commercials were shown during the game: Ivory Soap, Mobil Oil and Wheaties. The contest was the first game of a doubleheader played between the two teams that day.

?

The uniform "number" of baseball comedian Max Patkin.

The comedy team of Bud Abbott and Lou Costello brought baseball into its act and smiles to faces in the audience.

TENTH INNING:

Touching other bases.

1	2	3	4	5	6	7	8	9	**10**
1	2	3		5	6	7	8	9	**10**

BILL WILSON

AND IN RIGHT FIELD . . .

In the "Who's on First?" comedy sketch that Bud Abbott and Lou Costello made famous, the name of one player—the right fielder—was routinely omitted. Names in the rest of the lineup:

- **First baseman**—Who.
- **Second baseman**—What.
- **Third baseman**—I Don't Know.
- **Shortstop**—I Don't Care.
- **Left fielder**—Why.
- **Center fielder**—Because.
- **Catcher**—Today.
- **Pitcher**—Tomorrow.

EARL AVERILL

Cleveland outfielder who hit a line drive off the foot of pitcher Dizzy Dean of the St. Louis Cardinals in the 1937 All-Star Game at Washington. Averill was thrown out, but Dean suffered a broken toe on the play.

Pittsburgh Manager Bobby Bragan's orange drink-sipping routine in 1957 may have cost him his job.

Dean, 26 years old at the time of the toe injury, apparently tried to come back too soon after the fracture and put stress on his arm. Having entered the 1937 All-Star Game with a 12-7 season record and a 133-72 career mark in the majors, the sore-armed Dean won only 17 more games in the big leagues (losing three of his four post-All-Star decisions in '37 to begin the slip from stardom).

BOBBY BRAGAN

Pittsburgh manager who after being thrown out of a July 31, 1957, game at Milwaukee returned to the field later in the game sipping an orange drink. Bragan, who offered a sip to the umpiring crew, had intended to be munching on a hot dog as well (but the sandwich never arrived after Bragan ordered it). National League President Warren Giles fined and reprimanded Bragan for "repeated farcical acts," and two days after the incident the Pirates dismissed the manager.

258

TOM BROWN

The only man to play major league baseball and also appear in football's Super Bowl. Brown, from the University of Maryland, was a first baseman-outfielder who played in 61 games for Washington in 1963 and batted .147 with one home run. He then played with Green Bay of the National Football League from 1964 through 1968, starting at safety for the Packers in Super Bowls I and II, and finished his NFL career with the Washington Redskins in 1969.

STEVE CARLTON

The only man to win the Cy Young Award while pitching for a last-place team. Carlton was honored after compiling a 27-10 record for the 1972 Philadelphia Phillies, whose 59-97 mark (.378) was the worst in the National League.

RAY CHAPMAN

Cleveland shortstop who was fatally injured when struck by a pitch from the New York Yankees' Carl Mays on August 16, 1920, at the Polo Grounds. Chapman led off the fifth inning for the Indians and was hit in the head by Mays' first pitch of the inning. Mays, at first thinking the ball had struck the handle of Chapman's bat, fielded the ball and threw to first base. Chapman was rushed to New York's St. Lawrence Hospital, where he died the next morning of massive head injuries at age 29.

Harry Lunte, who played in only 54 regular-season games in his big-league career, is the man who replaced Chapman in the game.

HAL CHASE

Of the 51 men receiving votes in the first Hall of Fame balloting in 1936, only eight have failed to make it to Cooperstown over the years—and Chase is one of them. Five of the 51 were elected the first year, and 38 more eventually were inducted. Unable to win election: Chase (11 votes in '36), Johnny Kling (8), Lou Criger (7), Joe Jackson (2), Bill Bradley (1), Nap Rucker (1), Jake Daubert (1) and Kid Elberfeld (1).

TY COBB

The leading vote-getter among the five first-year Hall of Fame inductees when balloting for the shrine began in 1936. Needing 75 percent of the 226 ballots cast for election to the Hall of Fame, Cobb received 222 votes.

Other first-time Hall choices and their vote totals: Babe Ruth and Honus Wagner, 215; Christy Mathewson, 205, and Walter Johnson, 189.

ROCKY COLAVITO, HARVEY KUENN

Colavito, Cleveland outfielder who shared the American League homer championship in 1959, and Kuenn, Detroit outfielder who won the '59 A.L.

Rocky Colavito (left), who shared American League home run honors in 1959, and 1959 batting champion Harvey Kuenn talk things over after being traded for each other prior to the 1960 season.

batting title, were dealt away two days before their clubs were to open the 1960 season—and they were traded for each other. The stunning swap took on added drama since the Tigers and Colavito—one of the most popular players in Cleveland history—were scheduled to begin the '60 season with two games against the Indians in Cleveland. With 52,756 fans on hand for the opener, Detroit beat the Indians, 4-2, in 15 innings—but Colavito had a dismal "homecoming," going 0-for-6 and striking out four times. Kuenn went 2-for-7. Colavito rebounded the next day, though, slugging a three-run homer in Detroit's 6-4 triumph. Kuenn was sidelined because of a pulled muscle.

GENE CONLEY

Played for the 1957 World Series champion Milwaukee Braves, and for the 1959, 1960 and 1961 National Basketball Association champion Boston Celtics.

GENE CONLEY

Pitcher who jumped the Boston Red Sox's team bus in midtown Manhattan on July 26, 1962, after absorbing a 13-3 loss to the New York Yankees. Gone from the club for four days, Conley tried to book a flight to Israel during his absence without leave—but he was foiled because he didn't have a passport. Teammate Pumpsie Green, an infielder, also left the bus (which was tied up in traffic), and he and Conley reportedly lived it up in New York that night. Green returned to the Red Sox in 48 hours.

CHUCK CONNORS

Better known as "The Rifleman" of television fame and as an actor in many other roles, Connors also was a major league baseball player in 1949 and 1951. After appearing in one game for the Brooklyn Dodgers in '49, Connors played 66 games for the Chicago Cubs in '51 and batted .239 in 201 at-bats. The first baseman hit two home runs for the Cubs, connecting off Dave Koslo of the New York Giants on July 18 and against Sal Maglie of the Giants on August 26.

COPACABANA

Observing Billy Martin's 29th birthday on May 15, 1957, six New York Yankees—Hank Bauer, Mickey Mantle, Whitey Ford, Yogi Berra, Johnny Kucks and Martin—partied at the Copacabana nightclub in New York beyond midnight. The revelry ended when Bauer was accused of striking a patron. Bauer was later cleared of the charges, but the Yankees fined all six players for their roles in the disturbance—and they traded Martin to Kansas City a month after the incident.

JIMMIE DYKES, JOE GORDON

Major league managers who in an unprecedented move exchanged jobs on August 3, 1960. The "trade" sent Dykes from sixth-place Detroit to fourth-place Cleveland and Gordon from the Indians to the Tigers. The possibility

The familiar face belongs to Dodger Chuck Connors, alias The Rifleman, prior to the start of his successful acting career.

A thoughtful Jimmie Dykes watches action during the 1960 Cleveland-Baltimore game that marked his managerial debut with the Indians. Only three days earlier, Dykes, manager of Detroit, and Joe Gordon, Cleveland manager, were "traded" for each other in an unprecedented move.

of such a swap was raised in trade talks earlier in the season when Detroit General Manager Bill DeWitt told Cleveland General Manager Frank Lane, "While we're talking about deals, let's talk about a big one. Let's talk about trading managers." DeWitt's remark seemed facetious; besides, Cleveland was playing well at the time and Lane wasn't inclined to make a change. When the season ended, the Indians and Tigers found themselves in the same spots in the American League standings as they were when the "trade" was made.

BOB FELLER

On Mother's Day, May 14, 1939, Feller's parents traveled from Van Meter, Iowa, to Chicago to see their son pitch for the Cleveland Indians against the White Sox. While Bob beat the White Sox, 9-4, it wasn't a great Mother's Day for Mrs. Feller. Sitting along the first-base line, Mrs. Feller was struck in the head in the third inning by a foul ball off the bat of Chicago third baseman Marv Owen. The ball broke her glasses, and Mrs. Feller suffered a cut above her right eye that required six stitches. After going into the stands to check on his mother, Feller returned to the mound and struck out Owen.

JIMMIE FOXX

The only major leaguer to win Most Valuable Player awards for two teams in the same league. Foxx was the American League's MVP as a member of the Philadelphia Athletics in 1932 and 1933, and he won the honor in 1938 while with the Boston Red Sox.

Game 7 of the 1934 World Series started getting out of hand when St. Louis' Joe Medwick slid hard into third baseman Marv Owen in the sixth inning, igniting the wrath of Detroit fans.

CHICK FULLIS

The man who replaced Joe Medwick for the St. Louis Cardinals in the bottom of the sixth inning of Game 7 of the 1934 World Series at Detroit after Medwick was pelted with fruit, vegetables, bottles and other debris. Medwick had slid hard into Detroit third baseman Marv Owen in the top of the sixth, and Tiger fans—unhappy about their club's 9-0 deficit—showed their displeasure with St. Louis' left fielder when he returned to his defensive position. To quell the disturbance over the Medwick-Owen incident, Commissioner Kenesaw Mountain Landis ordered Medwick out of the game (and the Cardinals sent in Fullis). St. Louis went on to wrap up the Series, winning, 11-0, behind a 17-hit attack and Dizzy Dean's six-hit pitching.

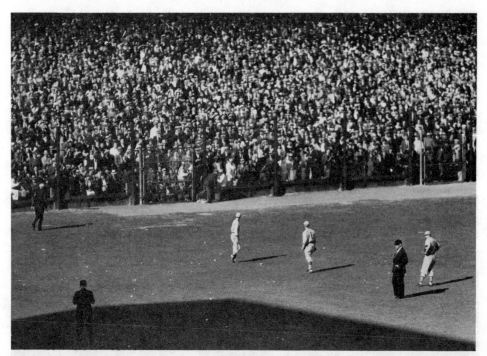

When Medwick took his position in left field (above), unhappy Detroit fans showered him with debris. Commissioner Kenesaw Mountain Landis conferred with Medwick and St. Louis Manager Frankie Frisch (below left) and eventually told Frisch to remove Medwick from the game.

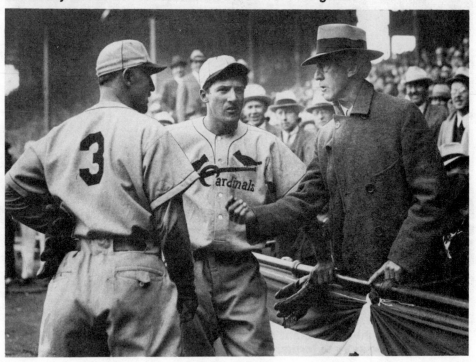

IN MEMORY OF
CAPT. EDWARD LESLIE GRANT
307TH INFANTRY · 77TH DIVISION
A.E.F.
SOLDIER · SCHOLAR · ATHLETE

KILLED IN ACTION
ARGONNE FOREST
OCTOBER 5·1918

PHILADELPHIA · NATIONALS
1907·1908·1909·1910
CINCINNATI REDS
1911·1912·1913
NEW YORK GIANTS
1913·1914·1915

ERECTED BY FRIENDS IN BASEBALL
JOURNALISM · AND THE SERVICE

The plaque on the monument that stood in center field at the old Polo Grounds told the story of former major leaguer Eddie Grant.

EDDIE GRANT MEMORIAL

The plaque in center field at the Polo Grounds that honored a former major league infielder who was killed in World War I. Grant, a Harvard graduate who played for Cleveland, the Philadelphia Phillies and Cincinnati before closing out his 10-year career in the majors with the Polo Grounds-based New York Giants, retired from baseball in 1916 and entered law practice. A year later, though, he enlisted in officers' training school. On October 5, 1918, a little more than a month before the end of the war, Grant was killed at age 35 in the Argonne Forest of France. On May 30, 1921, Grant's two sisters were at the Polo Grounds to help unveil the plaque.

PUMPSIE GREEN

The player who completed the integration of the pre-expansion era's 16 major league teams. The Boston Red Sox were the last club to use a black player, bringing up Green, an infielder, in 1959 (and Green made his debut July 21).

HANK GREENBERG, STAN MUSIAL

The only major leaguers to win Most Valuable Player awards at different positions. Greenberg was the American League's MVP as a first baseman for Detroit in 1935 and as an outfielder for the Tigers in 1940. Musial won the National League's MVP honor in 1943 and 1948 as an outfielder for St. Louis and in 1946 as a first baseman for the Cardinals.

BUMP HADLEY

New York Yankees hurler who on May 25, 1937, hit Detroit's Mickey Cochrane with a fifth-inning pitch that fractured Cochrane's skull and ended the playing career of the Tigers' 34-year-old player-manager. Ray Hayworth replaced his injured pilot, taking over as the Tigers' catcher against the Yankees.

BOB HAZLE

Called up from Class AAA Wichita (where he was batting only .279), Hazle earned the nickname "Hurricane" by hitting .403 in 41 games for Milwaukee in 1957 and helping the Braves to the National League pennant. The outfielder's only other big-league experience consisted of six games in 1955 and 63 games in 1958.

BOBBY HOFMAN

Utility player for the New York Giants whose ninth-inning line drive on the final day of the 1955 season brought Leo Durocher's managerial career with the Giants to a stunning finish. Durocher, having announced his resignation and acceptance of a television job, saw his club trailing Philadelphia, 3-1, entering the bottom of the ninth inning at the Polo Grounds. Two Giants reached base with no one out, and Hofman was the batter. Hofman lined a Jack Meyer pitch to shortstop Ted Kazanski for one out, and Kazanski's

Cal Hubbard, pictured (above) as the captain of the Green Bay Packers in 1933 and later (right) during his days as an American League umpire, has a special niche in sports. He's the only man ever to be elected to both the Baseball Hall of Fame and the Pro Football Hall of Fame.

throw to Bobby Morgan doubled off Joey Amalfitano at second. Morgan's throw to Marv Blaylock at first caught Whitey Lockman off the bag, completing a triple play for the Phillies.

CAL HUBBARD

The only man inducted into both the Baseball Hall of Fame in Cooperstown, N.Y., and the Pro Football Hall of Fame in Canton, Ohio. Hubbard was a standout lineman for nine seasons (1927-33, 1935-36) in the National Football League, an American League umpire for 16 years (1936-51) and then a supervisor of umpires.

VIC JANOWICZ

Football's only Heisman Trophy winner to play major league baseball. Janowicz, winner of the Heisman in 1950 as a halfback at Ohio State, was primarily a catcher-third baseman for Pittsburgh and played a total of 83 games for the Pirates in 1953 and 1954, hitting .214 overall with two home runs. Turning to the National Football League, Janowicz spent the 1954 and 1955 seasons with the Washington Redskins. In '55, he led the Redskins in rushing (397 yards) and scoring (88 points, on seven touchdowns, six field goals and 28 extra-point kicks).

NELLY KELLY

The name of the girl featured in the song, "Take Me Out to the Ball Game."

LERRIN LaGROW

Detroit pitcher at whom Oakland's Bert Campaneris hurled his bat in Game 2 of the 1972 American League Championship Series. Campaneris was 3-for-3 at the plate as he went to bat in the seventh inning, and the A's (up 1-0 in the series) led the game, 5-0. LaGrow's first pitch in the seventh struck Campaneris' left ankle. After falling to the ground, Campaneris got up and flung his bat toward the Tigers' pitcher. As the bat sailed over LaGrow's head, both benches emptied. Campaneris and LaGrow were ejected. The A's advanced to the World Series and Campaneris, suspended for the rest of the Championship Series, was permitted to play. However, Commissioner Bowie Kuhn suspended Campaneris for the first seven games of the 1973 season.

Dal Maxvill pinch-ran and went in to play shortstop for Oakland's Campaneris, and John Hiller replaced LaGrow on the mound for the Tigers.

NAP LAJOIE

The player who collected the most votes among those who did not make the Hall of Fame in 1936, the first year of balloting. Needing 75 percent of the 226 votes cast for election to the Hall, Lajoie garnered 64.6 percent (146 votes). He was elected to Cooperstown in 1937.

The harmonica-playing exploits of Yankee Phil Linz proved a hit with the fans, but the timing of the music puzzled Manager Yogi Berra (above).

PHIL LINZ

Reserve infielder for the New York Yankees whose harmonica playing on the team bus on August 20, 1964, angered Manager Yogi Berra. The Yankees had just lost their fourth straight game to the Chicago White Sox, falling 4½ games out of first place. Berra told Linz to quit playing the harmonica, but Linz played on—until the manager confronted him. Linz flipped the instrument toward Berra, who swatted it. Frank Crosetti, Yankee coach, called the incident the "first case of open defiance by a player" in his 33 years with the club. New York went on to win the '64 American League pennant.

DICK LITTLEFIELD

Pitcher who was the player the Brooklyn Dodgers acquired in exchange for Jackie Robinson in a December 13, 1956, trade with the New York Giants. (Robinson subsequently retired, voiding the deal.)

ROGER MARIS

The American League's Most Valuable Player in the season preceding Maris' 61-homer, MVP year of 1961 was . . . Maris. Obtained in December of 1959 from the Kansas City A's, Maris won A.L. MVP honors for the New York Yankees in 1960 by hitting 39 home runs, driving in 112 runs and batting .283. In fact, Maris had more overall MVP points (225 to 202) and first-place votes (8 to 7) in 1960 than he did in 1961.

CARLOS, LEE MAY

The only brothers to win The Sporting News' Rookie Player of the Year honor. Carlos, playing for the Chicago White Sox, captured the award in the American League in 1969; Lee, as a member of the Cincinnati Reds, won the National League honor in 1967.

DAVE MAY

The player the Atlanta Braves received from the Milwaukee Brewers for Hank Aaron on November 2, 1974. (In addition to May, an outfielder, the Brewers also sent minor league pitcher Roger Alexander to Atlanta in the trade.)

WILLIE MAYS

The major leaguer with the longest stretch, 11 years, between winning Most Valuable Player honors. Mays won the award with the New York Giants in 1954 and with the San Francisco Giants in 1965.

GIL McDOUGALD

New York Yankee player whose first-inning line drive on May 7, 1957, struck Cleveland pitcher Herb Score in the right eye. Score, a month away

Catcher Jim Hegan comforts Herb Score (above) after the Cleveland pitcher was struck by a line drive off the bat of Gil McDougald on May 7, 1957. Indians third baseman Al Smith heads for the mound to lend assistance. Teammates carry Score off the field (below) during the game at Cleveland's Municipal Stadium.

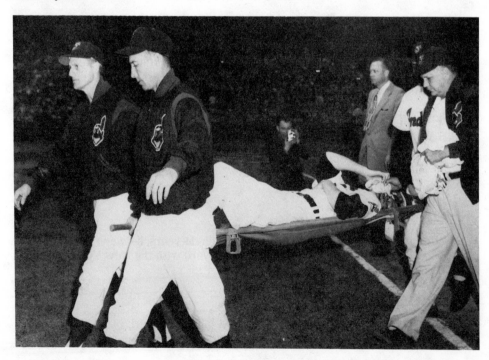

Almost 2½ months after being injured, Score (left) indicates he's all right during a chat with the Yankees' McDougald. Score never regained his pitching effectiveness, however.

from his 24th birthday, was relieved by Bob Lemon (who worked the final 8⅓ innings and beat the Yankees, 2-1).

Score, a standout pitcher for the Indians in 1955 (his rookie year) and 1956 (when he won 20 games), was nowhere as effective after the injury—although he blamed arm troubles, not the eye mishap, for his decline. Apparently headed for greatness, Score had led the American League in strikeouts in his first two seasons and posted a major league record of 38-20 through May 7, 1957. In 512⅔ career innings, he had struck out 547 batters, allowed only 338 hits and recorded a 2.63 earned-run average. After the eye injury, Score compiled a 17-26 record in a big-league career that ended in 1962 with the Chicago White Sox (to whom he was traded in 1960).

GIL McDOUGALD, MINNIE MINOSO

American League Rookie of the Year selections in 1951—the season in which Mickey Mantle broke into the majors with the New York Yankees. Minoso, an outfielder with the Chicago White Sox, won The Sporting News' rookie honor; McDougald, an infielder with the Yankees, took the Baseball Writers' Association award.

Like Mantle, Willie Mays of the New York Giants broke into the big leagues in '51. Mays, though, won both The Sporting News' honor and the writers' award as the top rookie in the National League.

MINNESOTA TWINS

The Twins-Senators games of August 27-28, 1963, were called off because of a civil-rights march on Washington, and an all-morning rain prevented batting practice before the August 29 doubleheader between the teams. So, without benefit of batting practice for about three days, the Twins went out and . . . hit eight home runs (tying a major league record) while winning the opener, 14-2. Minnesota then slugged four homers in the nightcap, beating Washington, 10-1.

RANDY MOFFITT

Owner of 37 lifetime pitching victories and 86 career saves in the major leagues through the 1982 season and brother of tennis star Billie Jean King.

DICK NEN

Dodger rookie (up from Class AAA Spokane) whose ninth-inning, game-tying home run in the finale of a three-game series at St. Louis on September 18, 1963, proved a key moment in that season's National League pennant race. The Cardinals, who entering the series had crept within one game of first-place Los Angeles by winning 19 of their previous 20 games, dropped the first two games at old Busch Stadium. With Bob Gibson pitching, though, St. Louis took a 5-1 lead into the eighth inning of the third game. However, the Dodgers rallied for three runs in the eighth; then, in the ninth, Nen homered off Ron Taylor in his second big-league at-bat to tie the score, 5-5 (Nen lined out as a pinch-hitter in the eighth, then took over at first base). Los Angeles went on to win, 6-5, in 13 innings, and Nen's homer seemingly demoralized the Cardinals. Starting the series with hopes of seizing the league lead or at least tying for first, the Cards instead fell four games back and finished six games behind.

Nen played only seven games of his 367-game major league career with Los Angeles and had only one hit as a Dodger—this home run.

DON NEWCOMBE

The winner of the major leagues' first Cy Young Award (an honor that had only one yearly recipient from its inception in 1956 through 1966). Newcombe was honored in '56 after posting a 27-7 record for Brooklyn, recording a 3.06 earned-run average for the Dodgers and pitching five shutouts.

For pitcher Randy Moffitt and tennis standout Billie Jean King, athletic talent was all in the family.

Jack Norworth had no connection with baseball other than the lyrics he wrote to 'Take Me Out to the Ball Game.'

HAL NEWHOUSER

The only pitcher in major league history to win two straight Most Valuable Player awards, earning the American League's MVP honor in 1944 and 1945 as a member of the Detroit Tigers. Newhouser compiled a 29-9 record in '44, registered a 2.22 earned-run average and threw six shutouts. In '45, he went 25-9, fashioned a 1.81 ERA and tossed eight shutouts.

JACK NORWORTH

In 1908, he wrote the lyrics to "Take Me Out to the Ball Game." Norworth didn't see his first big-league game, though, until more than 30 years after writing the lyrics.

GAYLORD, JIM PERRY

The only brothers to win the Cy Young Award. Gaylord, the only pitcher to win the award in both major leagues, was honored in 1972 with the Cleveland Indians of the American League and in 1978 with the San Diego Padres of the National League. Jim was a Cy Young Award recipient in 1970 for the A.L.'s Minnesota Twins.

FRANK ROBINSON

The only man to be named the Most Valuable Player in both major leagues. Playing for the Cincinnati Reds in 1961, Robinson was the MVP in the National League; as a member of the Baltimore Orioles in 1966, he was the American League's MVP.

BABE RUTH

Voted the greatest baseball player of all time by the Baseball Writers' Association of America in a poll taken during professional baseball's centennial year, 1969.

BOB SCHRODER

San Francisco player who pinch-hit (and struck out) for pitcher Juan Marichal on August 22, 1965, when Marichal was ejected in the third inning of a game against Los Angeles for hitting Dodger catcher John Roseboro on the head with his bat. Marichal was incensed because he thought Roseboro intentionally threw close to his head when returning a ball to Los Angeles pitcher Sandy Koufax.

Jeff Torborg replaced the injured Roseboro as the Dodgers' catcher, and Ron Herbel came on to pitch for the Giants in the fourth inning. Herbel worked 5⅓ innings and was a 4-3 winner.

BERT SHEPARD

Pitcher whose big-league career consisted of one appearance—and that came after amputation of his right leg below the knee (as a result of injuries

Despite amputation of his right leg below the knee, pitcher Bert Shepard still managed to make an appearance in the major leagues.

The Cubs won four pennants from 1906-1910, and the team's infield of (left to right) Harry Steinfeldt, Joe Tinker, Johnny Evers and Frank Chance contributed heavily.

suffered when his plane was shot down during World War II). Pitching on an artificial leg against the Boston Red Sox in the second game of an August 4, 1945, doubleheader at Washington's Griffith Stadium, Shepard worked $5\frac{1}{3}$ innings of relief for the Senators and allowed only three hits and one run. He walked one batter and struck out two as the Red Sox prevailed, 15-4.

CHARLEY SMITH

Infielder who was the player the New York Yankees obtained from St. Louis in the December 8, 1966, trade that sent Roger Maris to the Cardinals.

HARRY STEINFELDT

The Chicago Cubs' "forgotten" third baseman during the heyday of the club's Tinker-to-Evers-to-Chance infield combination. Obtained from Cincinnati before the 1906 National League season, Steinfeldt batted .327 for the '06 Cubs and helped the team to a major league-record 116 victories. During Steinfeldt's five years with the club (1906-1910), the Cubs won four pennants and two World Series titles.

When Joe Tinker, Johnny Evers and Frank Chance played their first game as a shortstop-second base-first base unit for the Cubs on September 13, 1902, Germany Schaefer was the third baseman. In the double-play combination's final appearance as a unit with Chicago on April 12, 1912, Ed Lennox was at third base.

MONTY STRATTON

Pitcher whose major league career ended when he was 26 years old after a hunting accident in November of 1938 forced the amputation of his right leg.

Monty Stratton (left) and Jimmy Stewart, the man who portrayed Stratton in a motion picture, take a timeout at the movie studio's practice field.

Stratton had led the Chicago White Sox in victories in 1937 and 1938, compiling 15-5 and 15-9 records. He later pitched in the minors, winning 18 games in 1946 for Sherman of the Class C East Texas League.

DR. DAVID F. TRACY

After compiling records of 59-95, 59-94 and 53-101 in 1947, 1948 and 1949, the St. Louis Browns hired Tracy, a New York psychologist and hypnotist, to help the team overcome its losers' complex in 1950. The Browns let Tracy go May 31 . . . when they were 8-25 and last in the American League.

TRADES

Major league deals involving two or more future baseball Hall of Famers:

1894—**Dan Brouthers,** Brooklyn Bridegrooms
Willie Keeler, Brooklyn Bridegrooms
for
Billy Shindle, Baltimore Orioles
George Treadway, Baltimore Orioles

Dr. David Tracy, a psychologist and hypnotist employed by the St. Louis Browns, peers at his "patients" (above) and huddles with Manager Zack Taylor (left). Tracy was dismissed six weeks into the 1950 season.

1900—Christy Mathewson, Cincinnati Reds
for
Amos Rusie, New York Giants

1916—Christy Mathewson, New York Giants
Edd Roush, New York Giants
Bill McKechnie, New York Giants
for
Buck Herzog, Cincinnati Reds
Red Killefer, Cincinnati Reds

1918—Burleigh Grimes, Pittsburgh Pirates
Chuck Ward, Pittsburgh Pirates
Al Mamaux, Pittsburgh Pirates
for
Casey Stengel, Brooklyn Dodgers
George Cutshaw, Brooklyn Dodgers

Christy Mathewson

1923—Dave Bancroft, New York Giants
Casey Stengel, New York Giants
Bill Cunningham, New York Giants
for
Joe Oeschger, Boston Braves
Billy Southworth, Boston Braves

1926—Frankie Frisch, New York Giants
Jimmy Ring, New York Giants
for
Rogers Hornsby, St. Louis Cardinals

Casey Stengel

1927—George Kelly, New York Giants
for
Edd Roush, Cincinnati Reds

1930—Goose Goslin, Washington Senators
for
Heinie Manush, St. Louis Browns
Alvin Crowder, St. Louis Browns

1931—Burleigh Grimes, St. Louis Cardinals
for
Hack Wilson, Chicago Cubs
Bud Teachout, Chicago Cubs

Frankie Frisch

Rogers Hornsby was involved in the 1926 trade that also included fellow Hall of Famer Frankie Frisch.

Owner Ted Turner (center) cheers on the Atlanta Braves during his one-game stint as manager in 1977. Coach Chris Cannizzaro (left) and catcher Vic Correll watch the action.

TED TURNER

Owner of the Atlanta Braves who during the 1977 season appointed himself as the club's manager—but he lasted only one day on the job. After the Braves had lost 16 straight games, Turner dispatched Manager Dave Bristol on a scouting mission to look at Atlanta's minor-league clubs. Turner, saying he wanted to know firsthand about managing and why the Braves were playing so badly, observed the goings-on and signed the lineup card at Pittsburgh on May 11. Actually, coach Vern Benson (with some advice from other coaches and Turner) managed the club; regardless, the Braves' streak reached 17 in a 2-1 loss. Turner was forced to step down as manager the next day when National League President Chub Feeney—with support from Commissioner Bowie Kuhn—turned down his on-field contract, saying it wasn't in the best interests of baseball. While Bristol was about to get his job back, Benson was in complete control as manager on May 12 when the Braves beat the Pirates, 6-1, and snapped their losing streak.

ALBERT VON TILZER

In 1908, he wrote the music to "Take Me Out to the Ball Game."

ARCH WARD

The sports editor of the Chicago Tribune who in 1933 came up with the idea of a major league All-Star Game.

CHARLIE WILLIAMS

Pitcher who was the player the San Francisco Giants received in the May 11, 1972, trade that sent Willie Mays to the New York Mets.

DEWEY WILLIAMS

Suspended for touching an umpire during the 1948 season, the Cincinnati Reds' reserve catcher served the suspension in uniform—but he never left the clubhouse. With Ray Mueller (another catcher) on the disabled list, Ray Lamanno was the Reds' only available catcher during Williams' forced layoff. Cincinnati received permission, though, to have Williams at the ready in the event Lamanno suffered an injury. An additional day would have been added to the suspension for each game in which Williams appeared, but his presence wasn't necessary.

TED WILLIAMS

Outfielder for the Boston Red Sox who won Triple Crowns in 1942 and 1947—but didn't win the American League's Most Valuable Player honor either season. Joe Gordon of the New York Yankees was the American League's MVP in '42, and Joe DiMaggio of the Yankees was the A.L.'s MVP in '47.

The End

Rest in peace Seattle Pilots, 1969-1969.